TWO ON THE AISLE

John Mason Brown

TWO ON THE AISLE

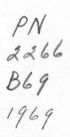

TEN YEARS OF THE AMERICAN THEATRE IN PERFORMANCE

KENNIKAT PRESS/PORT WASHINGTON, N. Y.

To

CATHERINE MEREDITH BROWN

By far the better half of
Two on the Aisle

"I am not one of those who, when they see the sun breaking from behind a cloud, stop to ask others whether it is the moon.

"My opinions have been sometimes called singular: they are merely sincere. I say what I think: I think what I feel. I cannot help receiving certain impressions from certain things; and I have sufficient courage to declare (somewhat abruptly) what they are. This is the only singularity I am conscious of."

WILLIAM HAZLITT

Contents

vii

Preface

MOST frequently the theatre which finds its way into books is not the theatre playgoers see or have ever seen. It is the theatre that lasts rather than the theatre of last night's performance. It is the theatre of tendencies, not of specific instances; the theatre of history safely made instead of history in the making. It is the product of sobering reconsiderations rather than of warm first impressions; of evaporated details, not of insistent particulars.

It can be bright, beckoning, and immensely satisfying, this theatre to which the book-makers invite their readers. Certainly at its best it is invaluable. But let none of us be deceived into thinking (even those of us who have written books on the theatre and who, God and our publishers being willing, hope to write more) that the theatre of the library often bears much resemblance to the theatre when it was still *in* the theatre and the book-writers, no less than their readers, were numbered among its audiences. By the time the theatre has found its way into books it has, as a rule, ceased to be the theatre this playhouse or that had to offer on this or that night, and has been swallowed up by that all-embracing, almost mystical continuity known as THE THEATRE. It has deserted the stage and usually been deserted by it.

13

Its plays have had their runs; its performers have closed their make-up boxes. No tickets are on sale; no spectators available. Its companies have been disbanded. The contributions of the director, the designer, the secondary players, and of the audience have become blurred or been forgotten. The printed text is all that is left of the acted play. The theatre's colors have faded, its lights dimmed. It is no longer a vessel inviting passengers to sail on what always promises to be the high seas. It is a ship which has sunk, or been beached, or which the years and the scholars have sent into drydock. Although it may loom large as a proud reminder of a proud past and of exciting voyages of discovery, this theatre of the book-makers is generally a phantom ship, uninhabited except by ghosts of greatness and not meant for habitation. It is a boat snatched out of its intended element. Even if it is still afloat and pushing forward, it is fated to be steered—contrary to all nautical practice—by pilots who have no other choice than to stand on a bridge, placed at the vessel's stern, with their glasses trained on the vanishing shore.

As a constant playgoer and occasional producer of volumes dealing with the stage, I have long since been aware of the differences which divorce the theatre we see in our playhouses from the theatre which usually survives in books. It is this awareness which has emboldened me to present the following somewhat startled pages in book form. To some theatregoers this volume's title may be warning enough. It is the heading I inherited for my column from such of my predecessors as John Anderson and Robert Littell when, in September, 1929, Julian Mason suffered me to become dramatic critic of the *New York Evening Post*.

Since that time, with summers out, when Broadway takes to the cowsheds where I refuse to follow it, this column has appeared almost daily in the *Post*. From it all the following "pieces" have been gathered. They were what those of us who write them refer to as our "stuff," but what the milder ones among those who may have read and disagreed with them would call our nonsense. With some editing, a sentence or two added here or dropped there, with some paragraphs omitted in which stale adjectives were tossed to all the members of a company, with two articles occasionally telescoped into one, with each section except one prefaced by a short introduction, but with no first-night expression of opinion changed since it first found its way from the newsstands to the ashcans, these "pieces" herewith follow. I have arranged them according to subjects rather than to dates, and collected them under general titles just as if, when they were dashed off, they were meant to fit into neatly ordered chapters. Do not be fooled by this. If these "pieces" confess their origins, I shall be unashamed and happy.

That there is a prejudice against reprints, and journalistic reprints in particular, I know full well because I happen to share it. It is a healthy prejudice anyone must feel who has a proper respect for books—as books. A book, written and conceived as such, is a balloon, flying in an atmosphere of its own making and at its author's altitude. It is a self-contained unit which, though it presumably opens up new vistas for us in this world on which we live, benefits by its arbitrary design. One thing is certain. Unlike journalism, which is also fated to fly at its author's altitude, a book is neither moored to the day's news nor supported by it. Presumably it justifies its existence by standing without alibis, by having been written (and rewritten) at one's leisure, by being the product of contemplation rather than of haste, and by representing its author's final word on any particular subject, said as well as that particular author has been able to say it at that particular period in his development.

Forgive this little tribute to books, which may seem doubly out of place in the preface to a book which I hasten to add is no book at all in the true sense of the word. But I, too, have railed in my time against scissors-and-paste jobs when they masquerade as what they are not, and gleefully look forward to damning them again whenever I encounter one of them in the future. I would be among the first to attack the present volume if, upon glancing through it, I discovered it pretended to be a book. I would like to make clear at the outset that what follows is not what would have followed if these pages had really been written as chapters. If they have any point, it is precisely that.

All of them found their way on to paper when their subjects had been freshly seen or were still seeable. All of them were written with Time as their enemy, or, as I prefer to think of it, as their ally, for Time has a way of equaling its unkindnesses only by its kindnesses. All of them have served as food for a newspaper column which, as anyone knows who has ever tried to feed one, is the hungriest animal known to the human zoo. All of them—the "follow-up pieces" dashed off by day, no less than the first-night reviews started as soon as I could rush home from the theatre, have been written to meet a deadline. In my first years on the *Post* that deadline was elastic and could on rare occasions be stretched to seven in the morning. Fortunately for me, during the past six years it has been advanced to 1:30 A. M. and is generally met on time, if not ahead of it.

I mention these personal and perhaps seemingly irrelevant details because they have a definite bearing on whatever unbookish, and hence theatrical, virtues I would like this volume to possess as a sample and reminder of what was characteristic of the American theatre when it was actually in performance on the stages of Manhattan during the last nine years. At least *Two on the Aisle* is about a theatre which was seen and judged in the theatre. Quite definitely it is about the theatre of the passing moment. But at any rate it can claim to be about that theatre before the moment was passed.

Although you will look in vain through these pages for flights of the higher criticism, I do promise you that in them you will find a reviewer's first impressions, and his reconsiderations, of plays and people, set down as honestly as he was able to record them when these impressions were still hot; when every detail cried for attention; when, for a blind moment at midnight, the whole pain and joy of life seem squeezed into the joyous pain of trying to re-create and rationalize and explain on paper the emotions experienced in the presence of the work of the men and women who combine to make our theatre what it is.

I know there are those who maintain there is nothing deader than a dead play unless it be a review of it. I know there are reviewers, whose work I envy, who cannot bring themselves to face again what they have dashed off under pressure. Although in going through the fading files of my stuff in the *Post* I have had countless occasion to realize the validity of both these points of view, I am far too stage-struck (which by no means keeps me from being painfully conscious of the defects in my reviewing) to agree wholly with either viewpoint. If I am willing to expose the readers of this volume to the risks of the first contention, I cheerfully expose myself to the dangers of the second. I have my reasons for so doing. As far as the theatre in performance is concerned, I happen to believe in the accuracy of first impressions, of judgments formed actually in a playhouse. For certainly, regardless of whatever else it may be, the theatre is first and foremost what it does to us as individuals when we are in it. That is the only theatre we ever know as playgoers. When we are members of an audience, and the houselights have dimmed, and the curtain has risen, that is the be-all and the end-all of everything which is done upon a stage.

I cannot bring myself to be ashamed of what I have written in these pages. Had I been ashamed of it, I would never have written it to start with. By this I do not mean to say I would not give my eye teeth for the chance to rewrite "piece" after "piece," to shake down one sentence after another, to have a fresh try at the whole blessed business. By this I do not mean to say that I am satisfied with the results. Or that I think what is said here is right because I said it. Or that I have not been sickened again and again by seeing how far what I have said is from what I wanted to say. But I do mean to say that I take pride in my profession, and have found much joy in it.

For nine years I have been on the *Post*. For nine years responding to what the theatre almost nightly offers has commanded my fullest energies, my whole time and thought, and the best of my perceptions (such as they may be). I have been haunted by the vision of what the theatre might be. I have been overjoyed on a few memorable evenings to find it realizing its splendid potentialities as I happen to see them. I have been maddened by sorry proofs of what it most frequently is, amused by its clowns, enchanted by its colors, gladdened by its music, delighted by its better performances, and fascinated even by some of its worst. All the while, too, I have been disheartened as a reviewer by the example which my confreres, past and present, have set me of what dramatic reviewing can and ought to be.

No book I could ever write could consume more hours, closer concentration, and greater enthusiasm, or represent more years of pleasant employment, than has the immediate setting down in terms of midnight adjectives of the impressions which follow. Although the theatre has sometimes tired me out, I must confess I have never tired of it. Caring for it so passionately, being more than content to serve it for so long as a night watchman, finding stimulation in so much of what it offers, and being willing to live abundantly in the midst of its palpable unrealities, may be a sign of lunacy or arrested development. I sometimes wonder, but I do not really care. I only know that, regardless of what you and I may think of the following pages, they were the best I was able to write when I wrote them, and that they were written by a man who had just been seeing the theatre when it was still in the theatre.

"It will be pardoned me if I speak a little of myself, when I am going to say so much about others," wrote Leigh Hunt, more than a hundred and thirty years ago, when he, with no rashness in his case, reprinted his reviews from the *News*. I must crave your pardon for having been so autobiographical in introducing the following pages. But a critic owes it to his readers to give them fair warning by saying something about himself, since the only truth he can hope to tell is the truth as he sees it. There is always a good deal of talk about what the critics are doing to the theatre. What is far more important, if I may say so, is what the theatre manages to do to its critics. This is the surest way of measuring not only the men who sit in judgment on it, but the theatre they review.

One more thing before I slip back into the darkened auditorium where I belong. Although I trust the following pages will revive for some readers (as rereading them has for me) many pleasures and irritations typical of the theatre of our day, no one is expected to agree with all or any of the verdicts herein delivered. Nowadays I do not always agree with them myself. Permit me to offer one illustration. I could provide innumerable others. In my first-night review (or should I say my first-day-and-night review) of *Mourn-*

ing Becomes Electra, when—as Brooks Atkinson would say—Mr. O'Neill stole my watch, I was so conquered by the excitement of that unforgettable evening that I wrote "(the play) remains to the end a *magnum opus* beside which *Strange Interlude* and most of the earlier, simpler plays sink into unimportance." With this opinion of *Strange Interlude* I heartily concur. But with the unspecified dismissal of the earlier and, of all things, "simpler" plays, I disagree. Nor would I at present think of praising the third part of *Mourning Becomes Electra,* or of passing over so lightly the Freudian pretentiousness in which much of it is bogged. That I did not feel these reservations when, under the spell of the Theatre Guild's production, I was responding for the first time to the tremendous impact of Mr. O'Neill's tragedy, is only a minor case in point of how different the theatre is in the theatre from the theatre which usually finds its way into books.

It is these very differences which have given me the courage to bring these day-to-day impressions together in more permanent form. I am fully conscious of how strange some of them may seem even now, and of how ridiculous many of them will prove should anyone stumble upon them a few years hence. I hope to live long enough to be able to smile at them myself, and laugh at what Time and the chilling years prove to be false in their estimates. But they are at least the candid reactions one inveterate playgoer had when he sat in the theatre of his day and that theatre could either be objected to or surrendered to in actual performance. That it was a vital, often exasperating, frequently stimulating, and occasionally magnificent theatre, I trust the following pages will indicate.

John Mason Brown

New York City
June, 1938

1. Shakespeare on the Contemporary Stage

KEEPING THE BARD ALIVE

FEW travelers to Stratford have failed to be astonished by the verses on Shakespeare's tomb which read, "Good frend, for Iesus sake forbeare To digg the dust encloased heare; Bleste be the man that spares thes stones, And curst be he that moves my bones." They are the worst "Fee-Fie-Foh-Fum" jingles ever to be ascribed to a major poet. The only good thing about them is that the theatre has always shown a scrupulous disregard for their instructions. Almost annually it has applied itself to the tantalizing, and not at all macabre, task of dusting and moving, and even shaking, the bones of Shakespeare's plays in one revival after another.

To this day his dramas remain the most tempting challenge known to the more ambitious actors, directors, and designers of our contemporary stage who are anxious to escape from the confinements of realism. They are tests of strength and ingenuity, of skill and imagination, of intelligence and pliability. The results may at times be disastrous, but they are always instructive. The glories of Shakespeare's verse make special demands on actors trained in subduing their voices to what is commonly the drab prose of daily speech. When the productions of his plays are in period dress, the costumes require a freedom, if not an expansiveness, of gesture few players are nowadays able to master.

The texts, even when they are done in modern dress, necessitate, by the very style of their writing, marked readjustments in their acting style. They cannot be squeezed into our representational theatre. They refuse to fit on to a stage which tries to hide the fact that its most realistic truths are made possible only by the skill with which it falsifies reality in order to create its illusion. Shakespeare's dramas are not sprung from a theatre which invites us to admire the skill with which it documents its perjuries. Unlike most contemporary scripts, his plays do not ask us to forget we are in a theatre. They urge us to remember we are there. They are the proud products of a presentational theatre, of a theatre which takes a full-blown pride in its medium as a medium. In the beauty of their every lovely line they boast their characters are not men and women as they are, but men and women as a poet has recreated them and given them the benefit of all that is magical in his tongue's utterance. Belonging frankly to this presentational theatre of the poet, they depend upon us as playgoers to grant them the imaginative collaboration from which their final puissance is derived. They invite us to revel in the realization that it is only by means of the glorious falsehoods of such a theatre that its golden truths can be achieved.

Needless to say, there are few contemporary actors who are technically equipped to shuttle back and forth from the demands of representational acting to meet the vastly different demands of presentational acting. Some of our best realists, as the following pages may make clear, have shown themselves to be goldfish on the carpet when they have attempted to play Shakespeare. Most usually our actors are the products (and, from the point of view of Shakespeare's scripts, the victims) of the realistic theatre at which they excel. It is not their fault if, overnight, they cannot readjust themselves to Shakespeare. Their failure, when they do fail in his plays, is attributable at least in part to the limited opportunities which have come their way. Since they have been trained to meet only the special requirements of realism, it is not surprising they are often unable to meet the no less special requirements of Shakespeare.

That there has been a shrinkage in acting since the days of Burbage, almost everyone will admit. That, from the point of view of modern audiences, Shakespeare has benefited by this shrinkage seems no less obvious. As playgoers we have been trained to realism even as our actors have been. The ranter, the seedy fellow who looked like a mildewed edition of Daniel Webster, the kind of player Percy Hammond once described as a Shakespearean oboe, has gone forever. So have the unrehearsed, raggle-taggle productions through which he used to chant. We may lack such single actors as our grandparents knew, but my firm conviction is that the best of our contemporary Shakespearean productions are better than the best they saw.

Our production standards are infinitely higher. We are as interested in the play as we are in the star. Our stage benefits not only by the miracle of lighting but can place at Shakespeare's disposal a hundred and one mechanical resources to keep his dramas moving as he wrote them and preserve his many-scened technique. The scene-designer and the director, who grabbed the spotlight in the first days of that visual impetus once identified as "The New Movement," no longer function as the exhibitionists they sometimes did. Like the actor-managers who preceded them, and from whose domination they rebelled, they, too, have been put in their proper places as contributors working towards a common aim We have our fine performers no less than our bad ones, and we realize a proof of their fineness is the generosity with which they cast their revivals.

The old orthodoxies have long since disappeared. One thing at least we have all come to know about Shakespeare on the contemporary stage, and that is there is no one way in which any of his plays must be done. His dramas are variables, capable of infinite and exciting theatrical restatements. Our single hope, as Arthur Hopkins once expressed it, is to have the radium of Shakespeare released from the vessel of tradition. We want his plays dusted and their bones shaken. We do not care how they come to life, so long as they live, and living do justice to the joys and sublimities of his texts. We want the theatre to protect him from his his weaknesses, redeem him from his epoch, and expose us to all that is timeless in his work. We refuse to have him left in his Stratford tomb, and the theatre refuses to leave him there. The real truth is he refuses to stay there himself.

MAURICE EVANS AS RICHARD II

IN THE world of the theatre, which is a world of constant coronations, Maurice Evans stands out as an actor whose sovereignty now seems to be as indisputable as it promises to be enduring. His Romeo, when he had succeeded the Kelvinator Montague of Basil Rathbone in Katharine Cornell's production of the tragedy, prepared the way. It was the first Italianate Romeo of our time; a lyric creation filled with the true ardor and the beauty of the text. His Dauphin in Miss Cornell's unforgettable revival of *Saint Joan* next demonstrated his range. It showed Mr. Evans was more than an unusually talented romantic. It made clear that a gift for the slyest of sly comedy was also at his command. Then came his characterization of the exiled Bonaparte in *St. Helena,* a play which deserved abundantly to succeed, and in which Mr. Evans gave a performance so remarkable in its illusion and its force that those of us who had already tossed our hats into the air because of him could scarcely wait for them to fall to earth again so that we could toss them even higher.

His Richard II makes further hat-tossings compulsory. It is one of the finest Shakespearean performances the modern theatre has seen. It is rich in sensitivity. It is possessed of those final qualities of illumination, divination and revelation which stamp the work only of such actors as can be truly said to function as interpretative artists. Mr. Evans does not spare us Richard's faults. Like Shakespeare he exposes them without mercy. But he, like Shakespeare, plants them so cunningly, that, manifest as they are, they add to, rather than subtract from, the sympathy one feels for this unstable monarch in the long hours of his grief.

He supplies his Richard with that "windy courage" to which, in Coleridge's phrase, he can lay claim. He introduces us to him as a king, who, according to the text's demands, is deceiving even in his hauteur. Yet already, if we watch Mr. Evans closely, he is preparing us for the tragic ending of this meteoric monarch. His regal mien is no more than a cloak for his irresolution. The arbitrary sentence he passes on Mowbray and Bolingbroke is a proof, not of his strength or his sense of justice, but of how ill-fitted he is to his high office.

Mr. Evans shows us the vanity, the weakness, the effeminacy, and the false pride of Shakespeare's ruler. He lets us feel in his treatment of the dying John of Gaunt the full cruelty of what is callow in his nature. From the very beginning, however, he establishes that other, and to a certain extent redeeming, Richard; that Richard who is proud of his title; who loves with his heart, if not with his will, the purple line he represents; and who in the frenzy of his rhetoric, though not in his actions, shows how great is his respect for the dignity of his office. His adoration of the throne and of what is mystical and, as he sees it, deserving of divine protection in his title are the skillfully established convictions of Mr. Evans's Richard. They breed pity from our contempt, and ultimately win our sympathy.

Mr. Evans is wise enough to follow the hints of the script and to turn the weakness of Shakespeare's introvert prince into his strongest claims as a tragic hero. He distinguishes clearly between the man as he is, and the man who in his mind's eye is haunted by a glorious vision of what his kingship ought to have been. In the great difference between the two of them, his Richard achieves his stature as a tragic figure.

No one could be more regal than is Mr. Evans when, after Richard's return from his disastrous expedition into Ireland, he speaks the majestic measures of—

I weep for joy
To stand upon my kingdom once again.
Dear earth, I do salute thee with my hand,
Though rebels wound thee with their horses' hoofs.

No one could be more full of the dread austerity of high office than he is, when from the parapets of Flint Castle he upbraids Bolingbroke's forces with—

We are amazed; and thus long have we stood
To watch the fearful bending of thy knee,
Because we thought ourself thy lawful king:
And if we be, how dare thy joints forget
To pay their awful duty to our presence?

*If we be not, show us the hand of God
That hath dismiss'd us from our stewardship.*

Throughout such moments of rhetorical self-realization,
even as through the earlier scenes of foppery and imperious
shallowness, Mr. Evans prepares us for the anguish of that
Richard who must later cry—

> *O that I were as great
> As is my grief, or lesser than my name!
> Or that I could forget what I have been,
> Or not remember what I must be now.*

Mr. Evans's Richard once again makes manifest his incredible ability for being different in each part he plays.
You will discover no traces of his Romeo, his Dauphin, or
his Bonaparte in his present luckless monarch. The only
way you will know it is Mr. Evans who is projecting the
character is that it is superlatively well played.

The production in which you will find him is uncommonly good in its ensemble effects, both as it is unobtru-
sively set and as it has been directed by Margaret Webster
from the "Old Vic's" prompt-book. You may wish Augustin
Duncan did more with his John of Gaunt, particularly with
the deathless splendors of his famous speech beginning
"This royal throne, this scepter'd isle." You may regret
William Post, Jr.'s Mowbray is not less vociferous than it
is and that hence he fails to give added force to his outbursts by not allowing them to be the "cold words" Shakespeare intended. But whatever minor faults you may come
upon here or there, I doubt if you can deny that this
Richard II is the kind of Shakespearean production of
which you may have dreamed but which you probably had
begun to believe was impossible on the modern stage.

Seeing it will, I think, convince you, as it convinced me, that in Maurice Evans the English-speaking theatre possesses by all odds its finest and most accomplished actor at the present time. He restores one's belief in acting, for he, more than any contemporary player, belongs to that Apostolic Succession of great actors which has stretched from Burbage's day right down to the day he is fast making his own. The one continuity relating his performances to each other is the continuity of excellence. Mr. Evans is not only a magnificent "character actor." He is the only player of our time able to raise "character acting" to the heights "straight acting" ordinarily enjoys. As Richard he may lose his kingly crown, but in doing so he gains another as an actor which is no less full of glory.

March 4, 1937

MISS CORNELL'S *ROMEO AND JULIET*

IT IS NOT often in our lifetimes that we are privileged to enjoy the pleasant sensation of feeling that the present and the future have met for a few triumphant hours. We know as we enjoy the passing moments of the present that most of them are destined to slip by unremembered. They have not the importance or the beauty or the intensity out of which the kind of abiding memories are made to which we return, boastfully or wistfully, when the present has been swallowed up into the past. Yet it was this very sensation—this uncommon sensation of having the present and the future meet by witnessing the kind of event to which we will be looking back with pride in the years to come—that forced its warming way, I suspect, into the consciousness of many of us last night as we sat spellbound at the Martin Beck in the presence of the acting wonders and the scenic splendors of Katharine Cornell's production of *Romeo and Juliet*.

The evening was an important one in Miss Cornell's career. It came to New York audiences as a testing-point in her development as an actress. It was the ordeal by means of which she was to demonstrate to a public that has long had cause to admire her in several good plays and many more trifling scripts whether or not she could meet the challenging demands of one of the greater classic roles. It was a nerve-wracking night, fated either to bring her disillusioning failure as a player or to crown her with a new significance in our theatre. To say she emerged triumphantly both as an actress and a manageress is but to state an agreeable truth. To add that beyond any shadow of doubt she is today "The First Lady" of our stage is but to state another and no less agreeable truth.

As a manageress she has given *Romeo and Juliet* one of the most beautiful, most spirited and best acted Shakespearean productions of our time. Her arrangement of the text (which is fuller than is customary and which includes not only the first prologue but also the final scenes of reconciliation after the death of the star-crossed lovers) is as generous to the various actors who appear in it as Shakespeare meant it to be. It moves forward breathlessly with an Elizabethan swiftness. As it does so, it is at all times enhanced by the vigor and pictorial effectiveness of Mr. McClintic's direction and the superlative loveliness of Mr. Mielziner's settings.

Mr. Mielziner's backgrounds never call undue attention to themselves or obstruct the drama's progress. They have been planned to shift with amazing rapidity. What they disclose—in the rapturous blue-greens surrounding the balcony, in the simple ballroom of the Capulets with its giant chandelier, in Friar Laurence's ceilingless cell, in the warmth and depth of Juliet's bedroom, and in the fearful blackness and ominous arches of the tomb scene—are settings which are not only the most richly imaginative of Mr. Mielziner's career, but backgrounds which are ideal in their helpfulness as well as their beauty.

In Mr. Mielziner's scenery and with Mr. McClintic's capable aid as a director Miss Cornell has produced a *Romeo and Juliet* including more good performances than any Shakespearean production we remember having seen. Miss Cornell is not one of those players who are fond of trying to seem better than they are by surrounding themselves with indifferent mummers. She does not have to stoop to such a device to hold her own. For *Romeo and Juliet* she has assembled the best actors she could find. She has brought together the kind of players one expects to find in an "all-star" revival. Luckily, none of her prominent performers indulges in those petty struggles for domination which are the bane of most "all-star" revivals. They act together in a remarkably co-operative spirit. They obviously respect each other. As a group their minds are set upon the play to which they are contributing their best abilities.

Miss Cornell's Juliet is luscious and charming. It finds her at her mellowest and most glamorous. It burns with the intensity Miss Cornell brings to all of her acting. It moves gracefully and lightly; is endlessly haunting in its pictorial qualities; and reveals a Miss Cornell who equals the beauty of the lyric lines she speaks with a new-found lyric beauty in her own voice. Only occasionally—and very occasionally at that—when she is called upon to utter such words as "prayer" or "fear" or "friar" does Miss Cornell mar her diction with a flattened "r." At all other times she adapts herself as tellingly to the new and special demands of Shakespearean verse as in the past she has fitted her speech to the dryer cadences of prose.

If she is a little shadowy in her first scenes, it is because the Juliet of the text is also shadowy in them. Even here she presents a glowing picture of youth, of girlish gayety, of daughterly acquiescence, and of unawakened ardor. Her Juliet begins to emerge in her first meeting with Romeo in the ballroom. Thereafter both she and Mr. Rathbone grant the moonlit enchantment of the balcony scene its full singing beauty.

If at moments Miss Cornell's earlier Juliet lacks a few of the tenderly smiling touches which Miss Marlowe and Miss Cowl brought to theirs; if it could underscore to humorous advantage the feigned horror of such lines as "swear not by the moon," or risk a little more impatience with the nurse, it must be quickly said it rises to true magnificence in its subsequent emotional scenes. It is at all times the work of an accomplished artist and an extraordinary actress. In the parting from Romeo, the meeting with Paris in Friar Laurence's cell, the phial scene and the tomb, it is an exciting realization of the many fine potentialities for tragedy which Miss Cornell has shown. To add that it is by all odds the most lovely and enchanting Juliet our present-day theatre has seen is only to toss it the kind of superlative it honestly deserves.

No less excellent than Miss Cornell's Juliet are the Nurse of Edith Evans and the Mercutio of Brian Aherne. Miss Evans's nurse, like Miss Cornell's Juliet, is in itself a lesson in acting. It dodges all the tiresome low-comedy tricks lesser players bring to the part. It has the completeness of a full-length portrait, and is spoken with great skill. It is the highly distinguished performance of a highly distinguished performer.

Although Mercutios always have a way of being so good that they put Romeos in the shade, Mr. Aherne's Mercutio is by all odds the best Mercutio we have seen. It has the brilliance of a diamond. Mr. Aherne races charmingly through the Queen Mab speech. He moves with amazing grace. He is full of "roguery"; turns easily from bubbling fantasy, set forth with much mock unction, to easy conversational tones, and is deeply affecting in the death scene.

Basil Rathbone as Romeo is handsome; wears his costume well; enunciates clearly; and handles the verse with fluency. But though he has his moments of excellence, he is throughout much colder than one might wish. He indulges in pauses which are not helpful, and speaks more slowly than is good for the production.

Among the others who must be mentioned with gratitude are Charles Waldron because of his admirable performance of Friar Laurence; Moroni Olsen because of his clear-cut Capulet; John Emery because of his extremely good Benvolio, and Orson Welles because of his passable Tybalt. Once again the playgoers of this town stand in Miss Cornell's debt. The exciting truth is they have never stood more deeply in her debt than they do today.

December 21, 1934

MISS CORNELL'S JULIET REVISITED

THE well-known tragedy of most actresses who are sufficiently experienced to do justice to Juliet is that for five long acts they are haunted by a merciless text which insists the total number of their years is no more than fourteen. Fortunately for all of us, including Shakespeare, Miss Cornell does not convince us against our wills that it must be Lady Capulet rather than her moonstruck daughter who is answering to the call of Cupid. She is not one of those Juliets who carry their own balconies.

Obviously Miss Cornell is more than fourteen. Yet just as obviously she manages to be youth incarnate. The script and her performance are not in conflict. Without being the age of Shakespeare's Juliet, she suggests the illusion of that luckless maiden's years. To the creation of this illusion she brings not only her own extraordinary personal glamour but all the technical richness her career has yielded her.

Of all the Juliets we have seen, Miss Cornell's is the only one which satisfactorily embodies the descriptions of Juliet's movements as given in the script. Her "fair daughter of rich Capulet" may be adult in form but she is young in motion and in heart. She literally runs, as Mr. Lockridge phrased it, with her arms outstretched to love. As she glides, free-limbed and lovely, with enchanting and seemingly unconscious grace, across the stage, one feels instinctively the young girl Shakespeare saw in his poet's mind has come to life.

"O, she is lame!" is Juliet's own complaint when she waits impatiently in the orchard for the tidings from Romeo her old nurse has been sent to fetch.

> . . . *love's heralds should be thoughts,*
> *Which ten times faster glide than the sun's beams,*
> *Driving back shadows over louring hills:*
> *Therefore do nimble-pinion'd doves draw love,*
> *And therefore hath the wind-swift Cupid wings. . . .*
> *. . . yet she is not come.*
> *Had she affections and warm youthful blood,*
> *She would be as swift in motion as a ball.*

Later, when Juliet enters Friar Laurence's cell for her secret marriage to Romeo, Shakespeare is no less specific in characterizing her actions. "Here comes the lady," says the Friar.

> *. . . O, so light a foot*
> *Will ne'er wear out the everlasting flint.*
> *A lover may bestride the gossamer*
> *That idles in the wanton summer air,*
> *And yet not fall; so light is vanity.*

Miss Cornell's Juliet is Shakespeare's Juliet in all of these respects. She does seem to move with the rapidity of thought. She is carried on the wings of a "wind-swift Cupid." She is possessed of such affections and of such warm, youthful blood that she is "swift in motion as a ball." She treads the earth with feet that will "ne'er wear out the everlasting flint." She is a lover who could bestride, without falling, "the gossamer that idles in the wanton summer air."

Her actions are not the only virtues of Miss Cornell's performance. Her Juliet is innocent and unawakened yet hotly eager for love. Later she is vibrant with the all-consuming passion which seizes upon her. Girlish as she is, her heart and mind are mature enough to do justice to the poetic beauty and the human anguish Shakespeare wrote into the character of his fourteen-year-old maiden. Miss Cornell's voice, which in her prose parts of the past has always been a haunting instrument, now not only adjusts itself to the entirely different demands of verse but is more than equal to its new-found opportunities.

January 4, 1935

MISS BANKHEAD TRIES CLEOPATRA

TALLULAH BANKHEAD barged down the Nile last night as Cleopatra—and sank. With her sank one of the

loveliest, most subtle, and most stirring of all Shakespeare's
major tragedies. As every reader knows who has responded
to the pulse-beat of its verse, this drama of two lovers who
considered the world well lost, when lost for love, is a
magical script. It is a vigorous creation, world-wandering
in its scenes and reckless in its splendid energy. Young love
of the Romeo and Juliet kind is not its concern. Its story is
no teary tale of youthful misfortune. It is an adult tragedy,
as glorious in its midsummer maturity as is the sad saga of
Verona's warring houses in its shimmering springlike qualities. Its final deaths are not brought about by tardy mes-
sengers and slow-footed friars. They are due to inner defects
which eat like cancers into the careers of a grown man and
a grown woman who are greatly placed and who have had
the benefit of a longer exposure.

This man and the woman he loves are not in love with
love. They are oppressively in love with one another. They
are weakened, almost sickened, by an affection they cannot control. Each is an addict to the drug of the other.
Passion hovers like a thick cloud of incense over the text
which lives because of their sacrifices and their deaths.
These lovers are not trapped by coincidence in a tomb.
They find their honor and themselves in the exultation of
their dying. By so doing they lift the humor, the pathos, the
sensuality, the verbal perfume, and the ubiquitous narrative of a passion-tossed tale into one of the supremest tragic
flights of Shakespeare's genius.

At least they do so in the play as Shakespeare wrote it.
But *Antony and Cleopatra* as seen at the Mansfield is not
entirely Shakespeare's drama. That is one of its first, and
most conspicuous, of its many conspicuous defects. Professor William Strunk, Jr., has put in his appearance. He
has bobbed up as Shakespeare's helpmate and mentor. If he
is unable, or unwilling, to play Beaumont to his Fletcher,

he does not hesitate to serve William in a bold editorial capacity. Scissors and blue pencil in hand, he has attacked the Bard, apparently under the impression that he knows Shakespeare's business better than Shakespeare did himself.

Shakespeare almost invariably needs editing. But we had thought the modern theatre had outgrown its Colley Cibbers, its Drydens, and its Tates. 'Way back in 1681 when Tate was kind enough to improve on *King Lear*, he confessed in his preface he had found the play "a heap of jewels unstrung and unpolish'd; yet so dazzling that I soon perceiv'd I had seiz'd upon a treasure."

Tate's benevolence is almost worthy of Professor Strunk. He does not hesitate to cut the tragedy as vitally as if it were Mardian. Nor does he stop there. He begins it in Rome instead of Alexandria. He donates to a first-act messenger Enobarbus's famous description of the barge. He reduces Enobarbus to an insignificant part, instead of leaving him as the conscience of the play, or, if you prefer, the Mr. Dooley and the Will Rogers. He attempts to house a notoriously roving script in the prison of a few sets. He places Actium in Egypt as far as we could tell. He leaves Charmian alive in his re-ordered last scene and dispenses with the snake-bringing clown. Furthermore, he shows his misunderstanding of the tragedy's meaning by denying to Octavius Caesar the chance of hearing of Antony's death and speaking the magnificent speech which begins, "The breaking of so great a thing should make A greater crack."

Don't think Professor Strunk's improvements on *Antony and Cleopatra,* which are focused chiefly on the story's pulp-magazine features, are the only things wrong with the production at the Mansfield. From beginning to end it is a terribly stuffy and mummified affair. The script is botched to start with and what is left of it is even more botched in the reading.

Although there is no one on the stage who can do justice to Shakespearean verse, the production is as heavily set by Jo Mielziner as if it were to be acted by some pre-Benson mummers who had played with Irving and Tree and were well up on the worst features of their scenic traditions. The text's free, burning spirit is no better captured in Reginald Bach's dull direction than it is in Mr. Mielziner's cumbersome and unimaginative settings. Then there are the actors. We must admit we never saw Miss Marlowe as Cleopatra. We admire her too much to regret having missed her. Nor did we see Miss Cowl. But for many years now we have been haunted by the vision of the queen and woman Shakespeare drew. His Cleopatra is not Miss Bankhead's.

Miss Bankhead can be a brilliant performer. She has many exciting gifts and often projects her glowing personality. But as the Serpent of the Nile she proves to be no more dangerous than a garter snake. As the tremulous, mercurial, arrogant, pleading, heartsick heroine of the tragedy, she seems nearer to a midway than to Alexandria. She is beautiful. Yet her Cleopatra has no authority. Although she has a few, scattered moments of pathos toward the end, her performance is apparently designed without any dominating idea or any real comprehension of the character. She strikes some Egyptian poses. She screams termagant-wise when angry. But she cannot keep pace with Cleopatra's changing moods, or suggest her flaming tragedy. The truth is Miss Bankhead is never regal and seldom appears to have peeked with one eye closed into the complex and fascinating heart of Egypt's monarch.

As Shakespeare wrote his play, and as history also dictates, Antony and Cleopatra are as necessary to one another "as the bow is to the arrow." If Miss Bankhead fails as Cleopatra, Conway Tearle fails even more distressingly as Antony. The Antony we see in our mind's eye, the Antony Shakespeare drew and his Cleopatra dreamed of, is not Mr. Tearle's mouthing and tired Marcus Antonius. He is the Antony Mr. Shaw had his middle-aged Julius Caesar describe when he promised his kittenish Cleopatra that from Rome he would send her "a man, Roman from head to heel and Roman of the noblest; not old and ripe for the knife; not lean in the arms and cold in the heart; not hiding a bald head under his conqueror's laurels; not stooped with the weight of the world on his shoulders; but brisk and fresh, strong and young, hoping in the morning, fighting in the day, and reveling in the evening."

Although John Emery is a pictorial Octavius, his Caesar is little more than that. As a picture it is moreover better as a silent than a talkie. Thomas Chalmers is disappointing in the strangely reduced role of Enobarbus. And the others, even more than the principals, are all so negative that it is impossible to realize the play being performed is *Antony and Cleopatra*. No one would ever guess at the Mansfield that what is being so badly done and spoken there is one of the drama's greatest and most inflammable glories.

November 11, 1937

CAESAR WITH AND WITHOUT TOGAS

AS DONE AT THE MERCURY

THIS IS no funeral oration such as Miss Bankhead and Mr. Tearle forced me to deliver yesterday when they interred *Antony and Cleopatra*. I come to praise *Caesar* at the Mercury, not to bury it. Of all the many new plays and productions the season has so far revealed, this modern-dress version of the mob mischief and demagoguery which can follow the assassination of a dictator is by all odds the most exciting, the most imaginative, the most topical, the most awesome, and the most absorbing. The touch of genius is upon it. It liberates Shakespeare from the strait-jacket of tradition. Gone are the togas and all the schoolroom recollections of a plaster Julius. Blown away is the dust of antiquity. Banished are the costumed Equity members, so ill at ease in a painted forum, spouting speeches which have tortured the memory of each member of the audience.

Because of Orson Welles's inspiration and the sheer brilliance of his staging, Shakespeare ceases at the Mercury to be the darling of the College Board Examiners. Unfettered and with all the vigor that was his when he spoke to the groundlings of his own day, he becomes the contemporary of us who are Undergroundlings. What he wrote with Plutarch in his mind, we sit before with today's headlines screaming in our eyes.

New York has already enjoyed its successful Shakespearean revivals in modern dress. There was *Hamlet*. There was *The Taming of the Shrew*. Then, under this same Mr. Welles's direction, Harlem flirted with a tantalizing, if unrealized, idea in its Voodoo *Macbeth*. But these productions, vivifying as they have proven, have at their best been no more than quickening experiences *in* the theatre. The astonishing, all-impressive virtue of Mr. Welles's *Julius Caesar* is that, magnificent as it is as theatre, it is far larger than its medium. Something deathless and dangerous in the world sweeps past you down the darkened aisles at the Mercury and takes possession of the proud, gaunt stage. It is something fearful and turbulent which distends the drama to include the life of nations as well as of men. It is an ageless warning, made in such arresting terms that it not only gives a new vitality to an ancient story but unrolls in your mind's eye a map of the modern world splotched increasingly, as we know it to be, with sickening colors.

Mr. Welles does not dress his conspirators and his Storm Troopers in Black Shirts or in Brown. He does not have to. The antique Rome, which we had thought was securely Roman in Shakespeare's tragedy, he shows us to be a dateless state of mind. Of all of the conspirators at work in the text, Mr. Welles is the most artful. He is not content to leave Shakespeare a great dramatist. He also turns him into a great anticipator. At his disposal Mr. Welles places a Time-Machine which carries him away from the past at which he had aimed and down through the centuries to the present. To an extent no other director in our day and country has equaled, Mr. Welles proves in his production that Shakespeare was indeed not of an age but for all time. After this surly modern Caesar, dressed in a green uniform and scowling behind the mask-like face of a contemporary dictator, has fallen at the Mercury and new mischief is afoot, we cannot but shudder before the prophet's wisdom of those lines which read:

> *How many ages hence*
> *Shall this our lofty scene be acted over*
> *In states unborn and accents yet unknown!*

To fit the play into modern dress and give it its fullest implication, Mr. Welles has not hesitated to take his liberties with the script. Unlike Professor Strunk, however, who attempted to improve upon *Antony and Cleopatra*, he has not stabbed it through the heart. He has only chopped away at its body. You may miss a few fingers, even an arm and leg in the *Julius Caesar* you thought you knew. But the heart of the drama beats more vigorously in this production than it has in years. If the play ceases to be Shakespeare's tragedy, it does manage to become ours. That is the whole point and glory of Mr. Welles's unorthodox, but welcome, restatement of it.

He places it upon a bare stage, the brick walls of which are crimson and naked. A few steps and a platform and an abyss beyond, from which the actors can emerge, are the setting. A few steps—and the miracle of spotlights which stab the darkness with as sinister an effect as the daggers of the assassins which penetrate Caesar's body. That is all. And it is all that is needed. In its streamline simplicity this setting achieves the glorious, unimpeded freedom of an Elizabethan stage. Yet no backgrounds of the winter have been as eloquent or contributive as is this frankly presentational set. It is a setting spacious enough for both the winds and victims of demagoguery to sweep across it like a hurricane. And sweep across they do, in precisely this fashion.

Mr. Welles's direction is as heightening as is his use of an almost empty stage. His groupings are of that fluid, stressful, virtuoso sort one usually has to journey to Russia to see. He proves himself a brilliant innovator in his deployment of his principals and his movement of his crowds. His direction, which is constantly creative, is never more so than in its first revelation of Caesar hearing the warning of the soothsayer, or in the fine scene in which Cinna, the poet, is engulfed by a sinister crowd of ruffians. Even when one misses Shakespeare's lines, Mr. Welles keeps drumming the meaning of his play into our minds by the scuffling of his mobs when they prowl in the shadows, or the herd-like thunder of their feet when they run as one threatening body. It is a memorable device. Like the setting in which it is used, it is pure theatre; vibrant, unashamed, and enormously effective.

The theatrical virtues of this modern dress *Julius Caesar* do not stop with its excitements as a stunt in showmanship. They extend to the performances. As Brutus Mr. Welles shows once again how uncommon is his gift for speaking great words simply. His tones are conversational. His manner is quiet; far too quiet to meet the traditional needs of the part. But it is a quiet with a reason. The deliberation of Mr. Welles's speech is the mark of the honesty which flames within him. His reticent Brutus is at once a foil to the staginess of the production as a whole and to the oratory of Caesar and Antony. He is a perplexed liberal, this Brutus; an idealist who is swept by bad events into actions which have no less dangerous consequences for the state. Like many another contemporary liberal he is a Caspar Milquetoast, so filled with the virtues of Sir Roger de Coverley that he can do nothing.

George Coulouris is an admirable Antony. So fresh is his characterization, so intelligent his performance, that even "Friends, Romans, Countrymen" sounds on his tongue as if it were a rabble-rousing harangue he is uttering for the first time. If only he began it with *"My* friends, Romans, countrymen," you could swear last night's radio had brought it to you freshly heated from a famous fireside. Joseph Holland's Caesar is an imperious dictator who could be found frowning at you in this week's newsreels. He is excellently conceived and excellently projected. Some mention, however inadequate, must also be made of Martin Gabel's capable Cassius, of John Hoysradt's Decius Brutus, of the conspirators whose black hats are pluck'd about their ears, and Norman Lloyd's humorous yet deeply affecting Cinna.

It would be easy to find faults here and there; to wonder about the wisdom of some of the textual changes even in terms of the present production's aims; to complain that the whole tragedy does not fit with equal ease into its modern treatment; and to wish this or that scene had been played a little differently. But such fault-findings strike me in the case of this *Julius Caesar* as being as picayune as they are ungrateful. What Mr. Welles and his associates at the Mercury have achieved is a triumph that is exceptional from almost every point of view.

November 12, 1937

AS UNDONE BY MR. LEIBER

AMONG the most difficult of Shakespeare's plays to produce in the modern theatre is *Julius Caesar*. Its scenes in the senate and the forum, its howling mobs and marching armies, its brave parade of great names and its outbursts of purple rhetoric known to every schoolboy, present grave problems to contemporary actors and directors. They call for a virtuosity few moderns are equipped to give. They require breadth, intelligence, spirit. They demand a style which would carry conviction in the market places. They necessitate a senatorial windiness of actors who must project characters in the midst of their harangues. They need settings large enough to hold the big words spoken in them, and direction which can catch the sweep of great and populous events.

All of which is to suggest, in as polite and friendly a manner as possible, that the Chicago Civic Shakespeare Society's recently reorganized, and supposedly augmented, company is in no way equal to the task it has dared to undertake in producing *Julius Caesar*. Some of its leading players—Fritz Leiber, Tyrone Power, Helen Menken, William Faversham, Viola Roache and Pedro De Cordoba—have big names either in or out of New York. Most of them speak clearly and possess those thunderous, throaty, oceanic voices which are supposed to be Shakespearean.

But their talents—at least as shown in *Julius Caesar*—are surprisingly small. Mr. Power's Brutus seems no more than a resounding set of vocal cords wrapped up in a toga. Mr. De Cordoba's Cassius is an uncrafty but sonorous splutterer who never appears to think, or plot, or plan. Neither one of them brings anything but Shakespeare's words to the organization of the conspiracy or the famous quarrel scene. They are not characters; they are plain reciters.

Mr. Jenks's Caesar is a pompous attitudinizer who requires three acts to die. Mr. Leiber's Antony is better than the performances of most of his newly acquired confreres, but it is none the less appallingly inadequate. His accent has thickened; his delivery of the funeral oration has neither irony nor real eloquence, nor any of the mob-catching qualities in which the text abounds. His readings lack the manifestations of the conscious planning which should obviously lie behind them. Miss Menken's Calpurnia echoes the reverberate thunder of the company as a whole. Only Miss Roache's Portia is characterized and played with simplicity and conviction. The settings, which are a series of muddy colored draperies, do not aid the production. Neither does the uninventive direction. Here is as ham a production of *Julius Caesar* as you are likely to see. It is well-intentioned, but enough to drive anyone away from the play in a "flood of mutiny." It is tank-town Shakespeare, if anything ever was.

November 18, 1931

WALTER HUSTON AND THE OTHELLO
OF TRADITION

AMONG the major tragic parts in Shakespeare, Lear and Othello must surely be the most difficult from the actor's point of view. Yet colossal as are the challenges of Lear, my suspicion is Othello presents the crueler hazards. "The greatness of Lear," said Charles Lamb when he advanced the paradox that the plays of Shakespeare are less calculated for performance on the stage than those of almost any other dramatist, "is not in corporal dimension, but in intellectual; the explosions of his passion are terrible as a volcano—they are storms turning up and disclosing to the bottom that sea, his mind, with all its vast riches. It is his mind which is laid bare. . . . On the stage we see nothing but corporal infirmities and weakness, the impotence of rage; while we read it, we see not Lear, but we are Lear,—we are in his mind, we are sustained by a grandeur which baffles the malice of daughters and storms."

Although as a rule Lamb's contention seems to me to be as insupportable as it is brilliantly advanced, I must admit every attempt at a stage presentation of *Othello* I have seen has sent me back to his essay feeling in the case of *Othello*, as in the case of *Lear*, that the perversely literary Elia had stumbled upon a truth which is truer than a paradox has any right to be. I realize, of course, there have been several Othellos (yes, and two or three Lears) in the past who have been so magnificent that they reduced Lamb's argument to an ingenious absurdity. I am willing to believe Colley Cibber when he says that Betterton, whose voice was of a kind which gave "more Spirit to Terror than to the softer Passions," excelled even himself as the Moor. I trust Hazlitt when he hails Edmund Kean's Othello as "his best character and the highest effort of genius on the stage," and adds that in parts of it he thinks Kean "rises as high as human genius can go." I do not doubt the critic of the *New York Mirror* who on July 1, 1825, reported that as "a true and vivid picture of conflicting passions," the Moor of Edwin Forrest (who was not yet twenty-three) "is superior to any in this country except Kean's." I in no way question Henry James when, admiring the tiger-like Othello of Salvini as the most complete picture of passion given on the stage in his day, he goes on to say "it has from the first the quality that thrills and excites, and this deepens with great strides to the magnificent climax. The last two acts constitute the finest piece of tragic acting that I know."

My only question is: Where are the Moors of yesteryear? Five Othellos I have seen in this country—Mr. Mantell's, Mr. Leiber's, Mr. Hampden's, Mr. Merivale's and now Mr. Huston's—and two or three abroad. But not one of them has projected for me in the theatre the Othello of the text. Mr. Hampden's was by far the most satisfactory, even though it ended up by seeming no more than a benevolent member of Tuskegee's English department. It did possess, however, the nobility which is required in the earlier scenes, and which is often lacking. Yet none of these players has been able to make the tragedy exciting by so rising to the passion of its title part that one is willing to overlook the flimsiness of the plotting.

If *Othello* is to be realized on the stage, if the play is to hold a persuasion behind the footlights equal to the fascination it affords in the library, it needs not only an uncommonly fine actor to play the Moor (which Mr. Huston unquestionably is in realistic modern scripts) but a performer who is a great Shakespearean actor (which Mr.

Huston unquestionably is not and has had no occasion
to be).

"Good will and personal candor are not potent enough
to transform a modern actor into a hero of Elizabethan
drama," observed Mr. Atkinson in his review of this revival of *Othello*. To prove his point, Mr. Atkinson compared Brian Aherne's excellent Iago (which is the outstanding feature of the present production) with Mr.
Huston's colorless, though dark-faced, Othello. Mr. Aherne,
observed the sage of the *Times*, is a romantic actor who,
though he might be "distressingly self-conscious" in *Dodsworth*, is first-rate at handling the verse and the villainies
of the swaggering Iago. Mr. Huston was a splendid Dodsworth. But the very qualities which fitted him perfectly to
the needs of Mr. Lewis's hero are the ones which render his
Moor ineffectual.

Of the two parts, Iago is the more grateful and the easier.
Stage history boasts more successful "Ancients" than it
does Othellos. Iago, wrote Shaw in his days as a critic, is
"within the compass of any clever actor of normal endowments." This can be taken as a Shavian exaggeration.
But there is some truth in it, even though that truth in no
way detracts from the fine skill shown by Mr. Aherne. I
have seen too many bad Iagos not to prize such a performance as his. Mr. Shaw was on firmer ground when, after
citing Othello's speech

> *Like to the Pontic sea*
> *Whose icy current and compulsive course*
> *Ne'er feels retiring ebb, but keeps due on*
> *To the Propontic and the Hellespont,*

he added "if Othello cannot turn his voice into a thunder
and surge of passion, he will achieve nothing but a ludi-

crously misplaced bit of geography. . . . The actor cannot help himself by studying his part acutely, for there is nothing to study in it. Tested by the brain, it is ridiculous; tested by the ear, it is sublime. He must have the orchestral quality in him, and as that is a matter largely of physical endowment, it follows that only an actor of certain physical endowments can play Othello."

Mr. Huston has a body fit for Othello, but he lacks the gestures, the voice and the special training the part demands. In his body that heart of the Moor, which pounds so furiously when once jealousy has accelerated it, does not beat. This is a fatal defect. For the Moor's heart is the heart of the play.

Mr. Huston's Othello suffers from all the failings which, in the best analysis of Othello as an acting part that I have ever seen, George Henry Lewes long ago observed in Fechter's performance. I wish Mr. Huston would either read or reread Lewes's essay in *Actors and Acting*. He would profit by it. So would the play as Mr. Huston acts it. His Moor is far too tame for comfort, illusion or sense. He commits the sin of making Charles Lamb seem right on the question of Shakespeare in the theatre.

January 9, 1937

JOHN GIELGUD'S HAMLET

NOT SINCE John Barrymore made Elsinore his own, has a Hamlet of the interest of John Gielgud's been seen—and heard—in New York. If to some of us the Mr. Barrymore who was remains even now the Hamlet we shall continue to see in our mind's eye as the perfect embodiment of the Prince, it will be Mr. Gielgud's voice in the future we shall hear lending its color to many of the nobler speeches. Such a voice, such diction, and such a gift for maintaining the melody of Shakespeare's verse even while keeping it edged from speech to speech with dramatic significance, is a new experience to those of us who since the twilight days of Forbes-Robertson have seen a small army of actors try their wings, and sometimes our patience, as Hamlet.

Mr. Gielgud is young enough to be the part and old enough in Shakespearean experience to play it exceptionally. The verse offers him no difficulties. He is its master and gives abundant proof of his mastery. He is no mere reciter, but an illuminator of what he has to say. He turns the searchlight of his thinking and his feeling on sentence after sentence which gains a new force and meaning because of what he finds in it to reveal.

He is an actor who, though he lacks Mr. Barrymore's natural endowment as far as looks are concerned, is nonetheless possessed of a sensitive, clear-cut face. It is so molded that it can amplify every passing thought which takes possession of his mind. It equals his voice in flexibility.

Without tearing a passion to tatters or sawing the air too much, Mr. Gielgud can suggest the whirlwind of the frenzy which has overtaken him. He has an exciting personality. He moves with grace and is not afraid of taking full advantage of the many steps which Jo Mielziner has placed at his disposal for some of the full stage scenes in Mr. McClintic's visually arresting production at the Empire.

If, in spite of the frequent brilliance, occasional superiorities and steady interest of Mr. Gielgud's Hamlet, his Prince still plays second-best to Mr. Barrymore's, one reason is that Mr. Gielgud's Hamlet lacks the consistency Mr. Barrymore brought to the part. Many of the details of his Hamlet are fine. Some are magnificent. But they are not assembled into a characterization which is large enough to connect and explain them all. Their validity is for the scene in which they occur, rather than for the total impression.

Mr. Gielgud's Hamlet is frequently more mercurial than is good for it. He changes it to fit new speeches, and in the process often seems to be presenting us new Hamlets to whom he has not hitherto introduced us. The Mr. Gielgud, for example, who reads the speech to the players benevolently, with a professional's interest in its admonitions and no remembrance of the scheme to trap the King which underlies that interest, is an entirely different person from the Mr. Gielgud who delivers with tremendous austerity the seldom heard "How all occasions do inform against me" soliloquy.

Then the Mr. Gielgud who solemnly speaks his first bitter aside about "A little more than kin, and less than kind," wakes up slowly to the wit which he must later show in his encounters with Polonius, Ophelia, Rosencrantz and Guildenstern, the First Grave Digger and Osric. It takes almost two acts for Mr. Gielgud's Hamlet to become aware of the sharpness of his tongue. Mr. Barrymore's was caustic from the first. Furthermore, the Mr. Gielgud who swears his love for Ophelia at the grave gives no indication of having really loved her before that time, as Mr. Barrymore did in the unforgettable intensity of his "Get thee to a nunnery" scene.

Yet because of the excellence of its details and the thrilling revelation of some of its single readings, Mr. Gielgud's Hamlet is a performance which deserves the loud cheers that greeted it last night when the final curtain had fallen. Mr. Gielgud is strangely disappointing in the Closet scene, when he dispenses with the traditional properties for the "Look here, upon this picture, and on this"; and is weakest throughout in his irony. He is at his best—and a fiery and exciting best it is—in the play-within-a-play, in his first encounter with the Ghost, and in the blood-stained last scene. Again and again during the course of the evening he delivers his individual speeches with such beauty and intelligence, such insight and tension, that one gladly overlooks the lapses in his interpretation.

Mr. McClintic has brought to the patterning of his production the same sweep which made his direction of Miss Cornell's *Romeo and Juliet* notable. His staging is vivifying, pictorial and inventive, especially in the uses to which it puts the levels and steps of Mr. Mielziner's unit setting for the inner stage. But the performances of the well-known players Mr. McClintic has gathered about Mr. Gielgud are of varying merits.

Although completely negative until the mad scene, Lillian Gish's Ophelia then turns into the most effective, if untraditional, Ophelia we have yet witnessed. Judith Anderson's Queen is stately and captures the eye, but leaves much to be desired in the Closet scene. Malcolm Keen's Claudius is, especially at the beginning, a welcome relief from the red-bearded, ranting Claudiuses usually on hand. John Emery's Laertes has real verve and distinction. And Arthur Byron's Polonius is handsome enough, but a Polonius who is as slow to suggest his humorous garrulity as Mr. Gielgud is to suggest Hamlet's wit.

The Ghost, who is always a problem to a generation whose belief in the supernatural stops with ghost-writers, is now almost as adventurously dealt with as he was when Robert Edmond Jones turned him into Tinkerbell by suggesting him with a shaft of light. There are two or three Ghosts lurking around the stage of the Empire these nights, one of whom remains unseen and speaks the Ghost's speeches through an amplifier, which makes him seem just a little ahead of his times in Elsinore.

Mr. Mielziner's settings, like the Vandyke costumes in

which he has dressed most of the characters, are interesting. But, next to Mr. Shakespeare's play, the most interesting feature of the evening is, as goes without saying, Mr. Gielgud. Although one may quarrel with this or that feature of his Hamlet, Mr. Gielgud is unquestionably a rare actor, possessed of the stuffs from which rare actors have always been made. He is decidedly worth seeing—and seeing again and again.

October 9, 1936

HAMLET AS LESLIE HOWARD

ALTHOUGH there are now two productions of *Hamlet* in town, there remains only one Hamlet—the Prince John Gielgud is playing at the Empire. Leslie Howard's revival at the Imperial has a costly look. The ancient Denmark in which it is set is majestically suggested. It is placed for the most part by Stewart Chaney in a great hall of the palace which, though it is used as freely as if it were a combination dining room and living room, is none the less impressive. Its scenes move swiftly in the conventional order. There are many buglers, banner carriers and supernumeraries. Several of the secondary characters are well played. Quite a number of the episodes are visually interesting. But if ever the Prince of Denmark met with a tragedy, he meets with one at the Imperial. The old saying about *Hamlet* with Hamlet left out has at last become a reality.

This *Hamlet* does not find Mr. Howard playing Hamlet. It merely finds him being Mr. Howard, which is quite a different thing. He has memorized Hamlet's lines. But Mr. Howard speaks them as some talented high-school boy might speak them. Although he knows the words, he does not even attempt to suggest what they are saying.

Does this Hamlet feign madness? Does he surrender to the "antic disposition"? Has he a deep and probing mind? Is his a tortured spirit? Has he a sardonic wit? Is he plotting to avenge his father's murder? What is his attitude toward the Ghost? Does he love his mother? Has he any interest in the play-within-the-play? Is he a fellow who is tormented by the fate which has overtaken him? Does he jest with Polonius and mock Rosencrantz and Guildenstern? Has he a poet's soul and a thinker's passion? Do the problems of life and death agitate his mind?

These are only a few of the questions to which every Hamlet must find his own answer but which Mr. Howard leaves completely unanswered. He does not interpret Hamlet; he merely repeats his lines. He walks through Elsinore as if he were walking down Bond Street. His spirit is still in "slacks" even if his body is not. He is handsome, and one would say, to look at him, a thinker. Yet he plays Hamlet as if he were acting *The Petrified Forest* in ancient dress. He is whimsical where he should be tragic; quizzical where he ought to be ironic; mute where he needs to be eloquent. His clothes, though becoming, appear to embarrass him, because they are not what he is accustomed to. They make him seem awkward in many of his movements and call for gestures he is unable to supply.

It is not that Mr. Howard understates the part. It is merely that he does not state it at all. He never reaches for its meanings, is never troubled by its dilemmas, and seems unaware of its possibilities. His Hamlet is empty; hopelessly empty. His thoughts do not find expression in his face, his body or his voice. He speaks clearly, but what he speaks are words, words, words. He is such a suave fellow throughout that it is impossible to understand what the King and

Polonius are talking about when they refer to his madness. If he is feigning madness, then O. Z. Whitehead, who plays the Second Gravedigger, is pretending to be Mussolini.

There is no method in Mr. Howard's madness, or apparent purpose in his playing. He dodges not only the intellectual content and the poetic beauty of the verse but also its theatrical implication. His byplay is as uninventive as his readings are innocent of dramatic significance. All of the qualities of understatement which rightly enough have endeared him as an actor in modern scripts are exposed not as virtues but as limitations in his performance of the Prince. Although his Hamlet is perhaps better than was his Romeo on the screen, it is doubtful if any distinguished player has ever attempted the part and acted it throughout with less distinction.

Mr. Howard's production makes it difficult to follow the text with interest. A drama, rich in excitements, becomes so tame at the Imperial that one's mind wanders away from it again and again. The tension, the revelation and the vocal beauties which make Mr. Gielgud's performance irresistible at the Empire are missing in Mr. Howard's costly labor of love at the Imperial.

Mr. Howard's supporting cast is uneven, as is the way of supporting casts in *Hamlet*. Wilfrid Walter is an admirable Claudius, Mary Servoss an unsatisfactory Gertrude, and Aubrey Mather has his moments as Polonius. John Barclay speaks the Ghost's lines with dignity, Clifford Evans is an excellent Laertes, Joseph Holland a fair Horatio, Stanley Lathbury an amusing First Gravedigger, and Pamela Stanley a colorful Ophelia until she fails, and fails completely, in the mad scene where most Ophelias triumph.

November 11, 1936

RAYMOND MASSEY'S DANE

IF THE EYES were everything and the ears and memory nothing, Norman Bel Geddes's production of *Hamlet* would be an extremely satisfying one. Its visual excitements are varied and many and of a sweeping virtuoso sort our theatre seldom sees. It is a constant, often magnificent, pageant of colors and lights, and of groupings which are extraordinarily effective. It sweeps forward without any of the customary waits, moving with a pictorial fluidity that is breath-taking. But in spite of the high tension of at least three of its major scenes, and the liberating novelty of some of its effects, it remains a *Hamlet* which is as much smothered by its production as it is aided by it.

With the best of good intentions Mr. Geddes has elbowed Hamlet out of Denmark and taken possession of Elsinore himself. Both as a designer and a director he plays the conquering part of that Fortinbras he has excluded from the text. Dispensing with scenery as it is ordinarily understood, Mr. Geddes has reared at the Broadhurst the kind of "sculptured stage," or if you will "architectural setting," for which he has shown such a fondness in *Lysistrata*, *Arabesque*, and other productions in the past. It is a huge affair of steps, levels and platforms which admits allegiance to neither time nor place.

Being a Geddes setting for a Geddes production of a Shakespearean play that Mr. Geddes has adapted and lighted, these formal indications of background do not content themselves with staying behind the footlights. They spill over into the auditorium and send a jagged apron well out into the first two or three rows of valuable orchestra seats.

Though their rugged outlines are in themselves lacking in beauty and though one misses a final, integrating sense of design in the uncertain relationship that exists between these platforms and steps and the gray pylons and flats which back them, Mr. Geddes's architectural abstractions have their decided advantages. They expedite the action, and, because of the magic of his lighting, they suggest the changes in locale demanded by the text with a remarkable ease and speed.

On such a permanent setting, Mr. Geddes, the director, works with an unusually keen eye for groupings and visual effects. For the play within the play, the return of Laertes and the final duel, he arranges his stage and moves his crowds so that they aid greatly in intensifying the action. Nor is he less mindful of the pictorial effects of his actors in many of the less populous scenes. The meetings with the Ghost; the liberties taken with "To be or not to be" (Claudius and Polonius are hidden at one side of the stage behind a platform, and Ophelia at the other, while all of them listen to Hamlet as he begins his soliloquy offstage and finishes it under the glare of a spotlight in the center); and the very obvious trickeries with shadows during the King's praying and Hamlet's interruption, all indicate a stage-designer working as a director. Mr. Geddes's direction is, in other words, more a part of this scenery than of the play.

As an adaptor Mr. Geddes is as visual as he is in his settings or his production. He cuts unsparingly and surprisingly. He omits Fortinbras (which is just as well). He slices familiar speeches in two. He discards Osric. He overlooks the trip to England. He does not prepare for the poisoned foils. He blue-pencils at least one of the most time-honored wheezes of the grave-diggers, and in general boils the play down to its melodramatic bone by stressing its action and minimizing both its poetry and its subtlety.

The most striking of Mr. Geddes's innovations lies in his having a Ghost who is as silent as Harpo Marx while Hamlet is speaking his lines for him. Whereas this device is startlingly right in the Queen's Closet, whereas it is at all times more fortunate than the violet ray version of the elder Hamlet Mr. Jones used in the John Barrymore production, it is none the less employed with a strange lack of logic. The first encounters of Hamlet with his father's shade obviously lose much when Hamlet is so occupied with speaking for the Ghost that he has no time in which to react to his words. So, too, does the swearing scene. Why the Ghost should be seen at all, when he is supposed to be purely subjective, is a question hard to answer.

If Mr. Geddes's actors were better; if his Polonius, his Claudius, and his Hamlet were worthy of their backgrounds, their costumes, and their groupings, then this new *Hamlet* might be as exciting to hear as it is to look at. But they are not. The best performances of the evening are given by Colin Keith-Johnston, who is an ideal Laertes, and Celia Johnson, whose Ophelia has a touching pathos when its mad scenes are reached.

John Daly Murphy is the worst of all possible Poloniuses. Looking like Shylock, and utterly lacking any sense of enjoying his own garrulity, he muffs almost every scene and line that falls his way. Mary Servoss begins extremely well as Gertrude, but when the later and severer tests must be met she does not rise to them. David Horne's Claudius is almost as negative as the Ghost. Nor is it aided by the tin crown which rests uneasily on his forehead during the whole of the evening. Leon Quartermaine, though he is not an unusual Horatio, has at least the voice, the diction and the dignity that are necessary.

Even in this day of designers and directors, *Hamlet* still

has a stubborn way of depending upon the man who plays Hamlet for its success and meaning. Nor is Mr. Geddes's production at all times aided by Raymond Massey's performance of the title part. Mr. Massey has fine, simple moments. He frequently strikes attitudes that are visually right, for he postures well even though he moves badly. He fences with fire, upbraids his mother with spirit, and wanders effectively in and out of the spotlight's rays.

Beside many of the old-timers he may seem naturalness itself. But he is still very far from being the Hamlet of the lines he is speaking; or the Hamlet John Barrymore once ignited with the fire of genius. Nor does the astonishing way in which he gains right effects here and wrong effects there help matters. Mr. Massey's acting is so uneven that he is only every other inch a Hamlet. His Dane is anything but an intellectual prince faced with the tragedy of reaching a decision and forced into action against his will. He is a Grand Guignol creation. He pouts rather than ponders; is surly instead of ironic; and is not so much melancholy as morbid.

Neither Mr. Massey's face nor his voice is happily suited to the part. His words flow from his mouth clearly enough and are well articulated in the quieter passages. But in his more excited outbursts, there seems to be no control behind his speech. He merely explodes, emitting torrents of sentences with such speed and indistinctness that they become meaningless. The voice with which he speaks them has no real melody to it. It is thin and commonplace, and fails to preserve the music of the verse.

Mr. Massey is at his best in his soliloquies, with his mother, at the play, and during the duel; and at his most unfortunate in his scenes with the players, with Rosencrantz and Guildenstern, and with Polonius. With the aid of Mr. Geddes's shadowy settings he lends a *Cabinet of*

Dr. Caligari quality to the play which is as strange as it is out of place.

November 6, 1931

THE LUNTS' *TAMING OF THE SHREW*

THE LUNTS have treated Shakespeare as if he were our contemporary or we his. Had they been Billy Rose, and he one of the authors of *Jumbo*, they could not have used his script as a more serviceable scenario for a circus.

They have subjected an old farce to the most respectful kind of disrespect. They have freed it of its dust, taken advantage of its every unimagined playing possibility, and staged and acted it with such skill and unction that it still succeeds in romping its way through scene after scene as one of the major laugh-getters of our time.

Their Shakespeare is not the cadaver who was recently buried under all the ineptitudes of Mr. Merivale's and Miss Cooper's *Othello*. He is very much alive. He is a master showman, a shrewd librettist, a laughing fellow who in his mirthful mood has room for midgets and for tumblers, for charming songs and man-made horses. He is not only the gayest but the giddiest Shakespeare who has had a farce-comedy produced in our time. If we remember Sothern's Petruchio as one of his glibber performances, and look back to the modern-dress revival of *The Taming of the Shrew* as a high point in Shakespearean resuscitation, let it be quickly said that Mr. Lunt's wife-tamer thinks of more comic opportunities than Mr. Sothern's ever dared to dream of. In comparison to this present offering, the modern-dress performance seems as stodgy as Gladstone.

This first completed essay of the Guild's into Shakespearean production makes one wish that, in spite of picketing playwrights, Shakespeare and the Guild would meet more often. It is an irreverent show. It cuts the text freely and adds to it things which dull scholars have never been able to find in it. But it has the high virtue (of which Shakespeare would have been the first to approve both as a playwright and a manager) of doing what it needs to do when it needs to do it, and of more than getting away with it.

This new *Shrew* is a *Shrew* with Christopher Sly liberally thrown in. The program says the prompt book serving as the guide "incorporates some small part of the long-neglected Christopher Sly dialogue to be found in *A Pleasant, Conceited Historie,* called *The Taming of the Shrew,* an earlier play which William Shakespeare must have read." Whether Shakespeare ever read this earlier play or whether after reading it, he rewrote it to meet his needs, is beside the point today. My suspicion is that, if he had watched Richard Whorf's excellent performance of Christopher Sly last night, or listened to his frequent comic interruptions, or witnessed any of the helpful audacities in the present text and staging, he would have joined the rest of us in welcoming each and every one of the hilarious innovations which vitalize his script.

The entertaining production at the Guild Theatre is by far the most spirited and convulsing the comedy has seen in our time. It gains at every turn—indeed at every turn of almost every phrase—by the sparkling imagination not only of its playing but also of Harry Wagstaff Gribble's direction. It literally pounces upon old lines to win new and unexpected laughs. It ferrets out from the text a hundred and one novel excuses for side-splitting, unconven-

tional business. Not only this, but it moves forward before Carolyn Hancock's gayly decorative settings in the
admirable costumes of Claggett Wilson to the jaunty and
enchanting notes of Frank Tours's music.

Every feature of the evening glows with a quickening
sense of sport for sport's sweet sake. It gives the happy
impression of being as much of a lark for those who are
on the stage as it is for those who face it. This is a blissful
state of things which leaves little or nothing to be desired.

Add to the excellence of Mr. Whorf's red-nosed and
drunken Sly, Bretaigne Windust's Tranio, which has great
style and assurance; Sydney Greenstreet's rotund and ever-
comic Baptista; and George Graham's droll Gremio—not
to overlook the capering steeds supported by four male
legs, and the versatile midgets—and you may get some
idea of the spirit and the dash and the informed capability
of the evening as a whole. Miss Fontanne's Katherine is a
minx of boiling tempers and formidable rages who bristles
with animation. Vocally Miss Fontanne lacks the range
to turn from the scoldings of the earlier scenes, and the
hungry wheedlings of the middle ones, to the lyric beauty
of her final speech on a woman's duty to her husband (a
speech by the way which Miss Marlowe read magnificently
even though she missed most of the shrewish aspects of
the Shrew). But Miss Fontanne's Katherine has energy
and fire, and more than serves its laughing purpose. Mr.
Lunt's Petruchio takes its place among his most distinguished performances. It misses no chances. It finds him
reading Shakespeare with surprising ease. It is richly humorous, has tremendous drive, benefits by an unfailing
invention, and is a memorable achievement in acting.

The production as a whole is so gay and so right that,
unlike most Shakespearean revivals, it does not force the

Bard to turn in his grave but permits him to leave it. The season is not apt to produce a more enjoyable offering.

October 1, 1935

ARCHNESS IN ARDEN

THE FOREST of Arden is unquestionably too full of dinga-dongas and hey, nonny nonnys for strap-hangers to tarry therein in complete comfort. Its gayety is too sylvan for city folk to stomach without the first-aid of a bicarbonate of tolerance which we do not like to take in Shakespeare's presence. Its clowns are of a different age. The cruel dust of time has settled heavily upon them. Its jollity is too much like May Day at a girls' school not to try occasionally the patience of those whose feet are unaccustomed to dancing on the green. Its story-telling is too rash, too unadvised, too sudden for those who, since Franklin's day, have been taught that the lightning can serve a scientific purpose. Its last-act marriages are far too numerous to win the belief even of readers who have been hearing of the mass-marriages blessed by Il Duce and Der Fuehrer. These are the liabilities of *As You Like It*. They are self-evident, particularly in the theatre. And they are serious. Still there are assets, glorious assets, many of which were made the most of in the spirited revival the play was given by the Surry Players at the Ritz on Saturday night.

It is not fair to blame these well-intentioned, often capable, actors for the faults of Shakespeare's most cheerful comedy. It is only fair to judge them on the basis of how they have sought to overcome them. Or on how they have managed to preserve the script's shimmering, though by no means overwhelming, virtues. The mere fact that the faults are self-evident is apt to force a director into stressing them by trying too assiduously to hide them. Samuel Rosen is a director who shows creditable invention. He has a hundred welcome devices for underscoring the pleasant qualities of the fooling. From time to time he captures the joyous attributes of the make-believe in a stylization which is as jubilant as it is projective. But his job is not an easy one.

His stylization often gets the better of him. So does the play. Then he makes what is perhaps the most natural of mistakes under the circumstances. He begins to overdo. He tries to keep the text fresh and green by dropping so much soda in the pot that the poor comedy frequently struggles to the surface only to explode pathetically. Mr. Rosen is a great one for running exits, phony caperings, uncalled for whistlings, duplicated (hence supposedly laughable) byplay, heavy tumblings, and overstressed business. The feebler the moment in the play, the harder Mr. Rosen works. When Shakespeare co-operates—as he often does—Mr. Rosen relaxes. So do his actors. So does his audience. Furthermore, it then begins to enjoy itself. For Mr. Rosen has some admirable actors at his disposal. If the College Board Examiners will forgive me for saying so, Mr. Shakespeare has given them many lovely lines to speak and some scenes to act that are utterly irresistible.

One thing is certain about the performance at the Ritz. It is rare to find so many players assembled on one stage who are able to face Shakespearean verse without fear and do its sense such constant justice. Katherine Emery is a radiant Rosalind. Her voice is huskier than one might wish, and she suffers occasionally from Mr. Rosen's well-meant archness. Still she is vital and gay, young and charming. Although Shepherd Strudwick is an unusually solemn Orlando—indeed a budding Hamlet who has gone on a hike with Ernest Thompson Seton—he is likable. He looks well, handles the Ganymede scenes delicately, and reads with remarkable clarity. Frederick Tozere is less despondent than Jaques usually is. Quite rightly he has found his own kind of melancholy. It is on the whole an effective kind, especially in his reading of the "Seven Ages of Man." As Celia, Anne Revere suffers—as good actresses can—under the handicap of playing a part which she understands intellectually but is not able to do satisfactorily. Although most of the secondary characters are far better played than is customary in a Shakespearean revival, it is a pity that some of the low comedy scenes should seem to have taken *Tobacco Road* as their model.

November 1, 1937

2. Old Wine in New Bottles

PLAYS WHICH REFUSE TO STAY IN THE LIBRARY

THERE ARE plays, long since first performed, which refuse to stay on the library shelves. The anthologies cannot hold them. They burst out of the history books. The classrooms are prisons from which they effect frequent and successful breaks.

By no means are they all great plays, these dramas which prove Time a slow-witted jailer. But, like the great plays and the lesser ones William Shakespeare fathered, a lust for life is in their blood-streams. Trash or tragedy sublime they may be, classic or claptrap, yet the will to live is strong within them. Unlike many of their noblest kinsmen, those masterpieces once belonging to the theatre but long since forced to eke out a new existence as dramatic literature, these dramas are not willing to live for a scholar's interest or at a reader's whim.

With an irreverent gesture at Brattle Street's Homer, they mock him for ever counseling us to let the dead Past bury its dead. They insist upon returning to the freedom and fullness of the boards they knew. The years may have treated them roughly. They may even have sentenced them. But these plays refuse to die, or if they do die, they die slowly. Within the prison-house of Time, they prove restless and unruly inmates. Until their heartbeats have lapsed into the faintest murmurs, they spend their days in the dark of the libraries, signaling to those who stand outside in the present, beckoning to them, imploring them to effect their release.

Nor do their appeals fall on deaf ears. If they speak the language of the theatre people to whom they have turned for help, they will get out. Make no mistake about it, they tempt their rescuers with fat bribes. It is not necessarily because they were good plays that the keys are slipped to them. It is because, good, bad, or indifferent, they can still be played. It is because good actors know no peace until they have played in them. It is because they contain good parts crying to be acted. It is because they still have something to say to playgoers, either in the mightiest and hence most timeless terms of man's observation of man, or else in the tawdriest and most dated terms of greasepaint. It is because they present directors and designers with irresistible challenges. It is because they offer audiences no less attractive challenges, providing them, if they have ever read these scripts or seen them performed, with pleasures unlike those they can hope to derive from any new play, witnessed for the first time.

To know how well an actor is acting, we must really know what he is acting. A special virtue of revivals is that they invite us to face them with this knowledge. We come to them, as we cannot come to what is truly a first-night, with definite expectations of our own. We are aware of what the play has already said to us. Its author's words have spoken directly to us in the original without the aid or hindrance of that special form of translation every produced play must undergo. Or our memories of other performers in these selfsame parts accompany us down the aisle. Our attention is permitted to shift from the first impact of a dramatist's story-telling to a detailed consideration of how he has told that story, and how in its present version (for each new production of a play comes close to amounting to that) he has been assisted or thwarted by those who have been bold enough to try to retell it for him. We know what is coming, and watch for it. These familiar moments become the actor's "points." We no longer depend on our first impressions of what is being done to inform us of the merits or the defects of the manner of its being done. We experience a new interest in how it will be done. For once we are in a position to judge actors as interpreters, because for once we are aware of what it is they are interpreting.

There are those who feel that every season during which many revivals are made is bound to be a season during which few new plays of excellence have been written. To be alive the theatre's first concern must always be capturing the image of its own shifting present. Yet surely there is room enough for old plays as well as new.

Miss Le Gallienne's Civic Repertory sought valiantly to function as a circulating library for theatrical classics. In its haphazard fashion and doubtless without meaning to do so, Broadway performs a like function. It is no repertory theatre—except from the point of view of its patrons. It ignores the best interests of its actors by treating them as if they were so many "accommodators" to be called in for this or that emergency. But of its patrons it takes commendable care. On almost any night, when a season is in full swing, it sets before them a repertory of amazing diversity.

It is a good, if unconscious, service Broadway performs by remembering the old even when the new is naturally its major preoccupation. It allows actors to vary their style to meet the demands of period plays and test their talents on the stage's sturdiest fustian no less than on its most imperishable writing. It dares directors and designers to make those restatements which must ever be made when the theatre's past is to be acceptably readjusted to its present.

For audiences these revivals throw open the doors to the foibles as well as the grandeur of yesterday. They permit playgoers to flavor the thinking and the planning of what was, and to note the different tastes which in different epochs have mothered different conventions. Sitting before these dramas from the past, spectators are forced to observe, often against their will, that plays do not number the span of their lives by mortal calendars. The truly great ones can outlast Methuselah. But the others, the ones that were right enough for their own day and only that, can age more swiftly than fashions. When restored to the footlights' glare. they can wither almost as rapidly as fruits, once plucked, spoil in the noonday sun. Ten years is a short interval in our lives. To a play ten years can do the damage of a century. No wonder one speaks of the run of a play. No wonder a prison pallor can settle so quickly on the faces of the weaker ones when they have been confined, even for a short time, in the darkness of a library.

ELECTRA WITH BLANCHE YURKA

MISS YURKA'S Electra is no princess born of a great household. She is a fury at the palace gates; a brooding creature of the heath who has little or no connection with Clytemnestra and Aegisthus. Her yellow hair is a disheveled mop. Her clothes are the meanest of raiments. In costume, make-up, and posture she is a detailed picture of human woe and female wretchedness. She does not belong to that world of awesome beings who move with buskined tread through the realms of Greek tragedy. She is observed and created in the terms of present-day realism. Unlike Margaret Anglin's, Miss Yurka's is a peasant Electra. She never stands erect. When she does lift herself from the floor it is only to move about with shoulders crouched.

Miss Yurka makes her descendant of Pelops' mighty line a sullen scullery maid; a drudge of the Cinderella kind who deserves happiness and a glass cothurnus at the final curtain. To show the indignities to which this princess has been subjected by her mother and her step-father, she blackens her hands and arms with a stuff so palpably smudged and catching that one's attention wanders inescapably from Sophocles's fearful story of revenge to such irrelevant considerations as the laundry list and Ivory Soap every time Miss Yurka puts her hands on the white arms or white garments of her fellow players, or runs them through her own yellow hair.

Vocally Miss Yurka is wise enough to begin, as many Electras do not, so that she has something left to give when she reaches her later climaxes. But she does not pitch her Electra in the great tradition. She refuses to have anything to do with the heroic manner. Emerging from the little dog's house at one side of the stage, where apparently she lives, she keeps her Electra on all fours so much of the time that one is forced to confuse her with the all-mothering Nana in *Peter Pan*. Miss Yurka's Electra is earthbound, even when the best interest of a scene, if not its sense, demands she should spring to her feet.

The blood of Ibsen's Gina courses through her veins, modernizing her, humbling her, and, of course, reducing the scale of the whole tragedy in which she is involved. Miss Yurka has moments that are right; indeed startlingly effective. Her handling of the urn scene is moving. Her Electra is strong with her own strength and frequently interesting to watch. But she lacks grandeur and style. Miss Yurka takes her tragedy sitting down, or sprawling at full length. By doing so she not only makes Electra unnecessarily monotonous, but robs her of much of the tragic dignity which might otherwise be hers.

At least Bergson would say so. And he would have his reasons for so doing. When some years ago he wrote his *Laughter—An Essay on the Meaning of the Comic,* he discussed among many other things the relation of posture to the tragic and the comic. Any incident is comic, argued he, which calls our attention to the physical in a person, when it is the moral side that is concerned. The public speaker who sneezes at the pathetic moment of his speech, the fat man whose excessive stoutness is laughable, and the bashful man are people who, according to Bergson, are embarrassed by their bodies. "This is why," he claims, "the tragic poet is so careful to avoid anything calculated to attract attention to the material side of his heroes. No sooner does anxiety about the body manifest itself than the intrusion of a comic element is to be feared. On this account, the hero in a tragedy does not eat or drink or warm himself. He does not even sit down any more than can be helped.

"To sit down in the middle of a fine speech would imply that you remembered you had a body. Napoleon, who was a psychologist when he wished to be so, had noticed that the transition from tragedy to comedy is effected simply by sitting down.

"In the *Journal inedit* of Baron Gourgaud—when speaking of an interview with the Queen of Prussia after the battle of Jena—Napoleon expresses himself in the following terms: 'She received me in tragic fashion like Chimene.

"Justice! Sire, Justice! Magdeburg!" Thus she continued in a way most embarrassing to me. Finally, to make her change her style, I requested her to take a seat. This is the best method for cutting short a tragic scene, for as soon as you are seated it all becomes comedy.' "

Whether one goes the whole way with Napoleon and Bergson or not, Miss Yurka's Electra does lose much by its constant closeness to the floor. It does not become comic, to be sure, but it ceases to be heroic. Its whole conflict is reduced in scale, because as Bergson would point out, it creates the image of "the body taking precedence over the soul."

January 9 and 18, 1932

RUTH GORDON IN *THE COUNTRY WIFE*

"MISS PEGGY (or Mrs. Margery Pinchwife)," said Hazlitt, "is a character that will last forever, I should hope; and even when the original is no more, if that should ever be, while self-will, curiosity, art, and ignorance are to be found in the same person, it will be just as good and as intelligible as ever in the description, because it is built on first principles and brought out in the fullest and the broadest manner." It is precisely as such a mixture of "self-will, curiosity, art, and ignorance" that Ruth Gordon plays this deceiving minx in Mr. Miller's revival of *The Country Wife*. Miss Gordon has not only captured the full flavor of a bawdy text and brought out its minutest innuendo; she has also caught in smiling terms the basic truth of the ardent, mocking, contradictory little creature Wycherley drew as his heroine.

Being a woman fresh from the country and ignorant of

city ways, the whole point of Miss Peggy is that she is free of those airs and graces which distinguish the ladies of the town. She does not belong to that fashionable coterie which inspired the artifices of Restoration Comedy. She is at once a novice, an intruder and a contrast. The simplicity of Miss Gordon's playing, with its wide-smiling, wide-eyed innocence of manner and its unmistakable animality of spirits, serves as a perfect foil to the fanflutterings and the handkerchief-twirlings of her fellow actors who are busily projecting the faithless wives, the rakish gallants, and the foppish wags of Charles II's London.

In such a town, Miss Gordon's Peggy is as out of place as an apple in Cartier's window. This is exactly as it should be. She is, however, an apple in which a worm has turned. Her manners may be country manners, yet her goal is the very same goal at which the most sophisticated of the town ladies aim. Miss Gordon's performance of this pert deceiver is one of the best performances of her career. It finds her escaping from the "church mouse" gamin she has been repeating for many seasons now, to achieve a characterization as novel as it is right.

In only one scene, at least on the opening night, did she overstep the mark. This was when, seduced by the deserved laughter which had greeted her every appearance, she began to play the letter-scene in a broader fashion than Hazlitt ever had in mind when he used the word "broadest" to describe the manner in which Wycherley had brought out Mrs. Pinchwife's attributes. Miss Gordon suddenly began to forget her country honesty, and to overact as mercilessly as if she were the heroine of a spoof revival in Hoboken. By so doing, she temporarily hushed the gayety of those who admired her most. Fortunately her absence from grace was only momentary, and soon again she was playing with that dazzling mixture of expertness and charm which make her Mrs. Pinchwife a true delight.

As for Mr. Wycherley's comedy, it is interesting to see how, in spite of the beauty of Mr. Messel's costumes and settings, and the style of Mr. Miller's actors, one nowadays revolts from its incessant harping on one theme long before the evening is over. It is not a question of prudishness but of fatigue. Lustily as you may laugh at first, you end up wanting something pure and wholesome just by way of change. Much to your surprise you begin to long for ham and eggs, Ella Wheeler Wilcox, or a glimpse of Mrs. Roosevelt photographed in her Girl Scout uniform. You resent the idea of Wycherley's naughtiness growing tiresome. You want it to remain breath-taking. But it slows up, as slow up it must, by chugging along so stubbornly on one, and only one, comic cylinder.

December 7, 1936

MISS GISH IN *CAMILLE*

WHEN EVA Le GALLIENNE added *Camille* to her repertory down on Fourteenth Street, her Marguerite Gautier was not played for the traditional points. It dodged the pyrotechnics in which the part abounds. If anything, it was underdone. Mr. Nathan even insisted it was the first Camille he had ever seen die of catarrh.

I mention Miss Le Gallienne because last night another *Camille* was shown to this town. This time it is Lillian Gish who has essayed the part. The production in which she finds herself is the Robert Edmond Jones revival of the younger Dumas's tattered script which Delos Chappell offered to the theatregoers of Colorado with many flourishes and much success during the past summer.

If, to some of us, Miss Le Gallienne's Marguerite seemed subdued to a Chekovian key, permit me to assure you her interpretation is noisily virtuoso compared to Miss Gish's. Miss Gish's *Dame aux Camélias* is quietness itself. It is the ultimate in negation. What Matilda Heron, or Clara Morris, or the "Divine Sarah" would have thought if they had dropped into the Morosco last evening, I cannot pretend to imagine. My suspicion is they would not have recognized the tawdry script in which they were accustomed to shake the rafters. Had they seen the raging waters of the Atlantic suddenly turned into a phosphorescent mill pond, I doubt if they would have been more surprised.

On one score, at least, they might have felt the pangs of envy. With memories of their own autumnal sturdiness still rankling in their hearts, they would have been forced to listen to a frail and luminous woman, who, in the words of the program, seemed young enough to die, even as Marguerite's prototype had died, at the age of twenty-four. If they laid claim to any sort of generosity, they would have found other qualities to admire—even in the midst of their horrified amazement. Miss Gish last night threw overboard every tradition of the part she was playing, by consistently refusing to meet the falsities of the text in the spirit of their writing. She treated the bogus old script as if it were real. She folded it around her shoulders as if it were not a moth-eaten mantle. She spoke its artificial lines with as much simple conviction as if she were trying to please the curator of the Agassiz Museum by bending over his famous "Glass Flowers" to inhale their fragrance.

Technically Miss Gish is about as wrong for Marguerite

Gautier as an actress could be; that is, if you judge her by
the time-honored "acting points" her speeches invite and
suggest. But, by being wrong, her acting (or, if you will,
her lack of acting) often has a radiant rightness about it
that is strangely satisfying. By defying the conventions, it
lends an unexpected freshness to the text. If you can
imagine a Mother Superior playing Thaïs, Ophelia cast
as Cleopatra, or a gazelle pulling an old-fashioned fire
engine through the streets, you may have some notion of
what *Camille* is like in Miss Gish's tranquil hands. But
you have to see her performance to sense the unexpected
beauty she manages to lend the text at many moments.

As she demonstrated in her lustrous performance in
Uncle Vanya, and as she has proved innumerable times
on the silent screen when she used to dart from tree to
tree defending her honor, Miss Gish is the most ethereal
of our actresses. Her voice is flatter at times than one
might wish. Her acting has occasionally a tired, listless,
passive quality which can be as disconcerting as it is in-
appropriate. But there is an effulgence about her person
which cannot be denied. She has a miraculous way of
lighting up the darkness, of filling a stage with an un-
earthly brightness, and giving an unconscious splendor to
portions of even so ramshackle a script as this long-lived
sample of the younger Dumas's juvenilia.

Last night, Miss Gish's light did not fail her. Wrong as
her performance may have been according to tradition,
it was the only living thing in a dead script. Her frail
innocence was a new explanation of Marguerite's professional success, and a fairly convincing one at that. Though
Miss Gish failed to rise to her acting opportunities by not
seeming to act at all, her negative Marguerite was not
without its gleaming moments. At such times it illumined
Dumas's empty script like a candle, a very bright candle,

flaming in a hollow pumpkin. Even the sins of her *Camille* had a radiance about them which made them shine like good deeds in a naughty world.

November 2, 1932

JED HARRIS'S *A DOLL'S HOUSE*

ALTHOUGH to contemporary audiences *A Doll's House* is bound to seem not only a slightly musty but decidedly illogical play, it remains a drama which has not lost its special interest for students of the theatre. They know its importance as a prophecy of the realistic Ibsen who was to be, and of the modern theatre which was to come in his wake. They also remember its significance as a picture— once sensational—of the so-called New Woman. Rightly enough, they have been taught to believe that when Ibsen had Nora walk out of Helmer's home, her closing of the door was a shot heard 'round the world. But Time and Papa Ibsen, the realist, are not always on the best of terms. In spite of the old-fashioned neatness of his planning, in spite of the individual complexity of his characters, both specialists and general playgoers are forced to admit their interest in *A Doll's House* is nowadays more academic than human.

It is all very well for the scholars to become excited because here is a script in which, halfway through the third act, you suddenly have a candid camera picture of Ibsen shedding the snake-skin of Scribe, and emerging as the Ibsen of the later sociological dramas. But from the average theatregoer's point of view, *A Doll's House* has paid the price of the victories it helped to make possible. One sits before it today with emotions which are as different

and as cooled from those it first evoked as are the feelings
one at present experiences when looking at a cartoon by
Raemaekers from the feelings aroused by the same cartoon
during the World War.

Men and women who now see *A Doll's House* find it
hard to believe in the relationship between Nora and
Helmer. What's it all about?, they ask themselves in this
day of joint bank accounts. If Nora has forged her dying
father's signature in order to save her sick husband's life,
why should she hesitate to tell him what she has done
when he is well? Why should they not solve their joint
problem jointly? What's all the worrying for? And what
right has she got to walk out on her children anyway?
Granting that the Ibsen forum at the end of the last
act is fun of its kind, and exciting as a proof of Ibsen's
invasion of his subject, wouldn't the discussion have been
made unnecessary if someone had just said the right thing
at the right moment during all the tarantella monkeyshines and labored Scribean ingenuities of the previous
acts? Such persistent, and nowadays quite logical, questions do not aid Ibsen in establishing either the interest
or the credibility of this drama which was written (as he
noted in Rome in 1878) to show, "There are two kinds of
spiritual laws, two kinds of conscience, one in men and a
quite different one in women."

Nor is the revival at the Morosco as helpful throughout as
it might be. Thornton Wilder's acting version saves Ibsen
from many of William Archer's antimacassar phrases. It
has the virtue of lightening and colloquializing the English
for a new generation, and of dispensing with some of the
unnecessary soliloquies. But it also suffers from the fault
of trying to spare Ibsen the embarrassment of a few of
his carefully chosen Scribean devices. It loses several characterizing values in the attempt. Mr. Wilder, for example,

cuts the "larks," "squirrels," "little birds," and most of the other painful pet names which Helmer squanders on Nora. But he fails to put anything in their place. Furthermore, by apparently trying at moments to modernize Ibsen's technique, he only calls attention the more unmistakably to the play's vintaged plot. The more old-fashioned the dramaturgy, the more valid would its ideas remain. Mr. Wilder seems at times to be making the mistake of trying to snatch grandmother's diamond out of the gold setting for which it was designed and put it in something resembling platinum.

Although Mr. Harris's direction is competent, it occasionally fails to reveal the full values of the script. Ruth Gordon brings certain qualities to Nora that are peculiarly right. But she never meets the most difficult problem of the part, which is preparing for the liberated and miraculously adult woman who must ultimately emerge. She is at her best in her childlike moments of gayety and pathos, and even carries off the tarantella hokum with undeniable dash. Yet she is a monotonous actress. One tires of her tricks, her mannerisms. Her Nora is as chirrupy as a sparrow, and, sparrow-wise, refuses to change its tune. Miss Gordon muffs the second-act scene with Dr. Rank, and is completely disappointing in the all-important third-act discussion. She never becomes the New Woman; she just remains Miss Gordon. With her *A Doll's House* makes the fatal mistake of seeming to begin and end in Schwarz's toy shop.

Dennis King's Helmer is unnecessarily cold and inaccessible in its earlier scenes. Yet Mr. King's is a performance which increases in excellence until it suddenly surrenders to dramatics in the third-act forum, of all places. Although Paul Lukas's Dr. Rank appears to enjoy far better health than the text suggests, it is at once skillful and ingratiating. Margaret Waller's Christina is satisfying throughout, but Sam Jaffe's Krogstad is overfriendly and vaguely drawn. Donald Oenslager's setting has the merit of being as helpful to the action and as felicitous in its details as it is unobtrusive.

December 28, 1937

MISS LE GALLIENNE'S HEDDA

NO DRAMA the modern theatre has produced is more amazingly constructed than is this study of General Gabler's enigmatic daughter. It is a triumph of preparation, of shrewd planning, and of both characterizing and story-telling details which slip as neatly into place as do the most intricate parts of a well-cut jig-saw puzzle. Yet in spite of its technical perfection *Hedda Gabler* has its compelling human values. Its people possess a fascination of which time has not robbed them and a complexity which is tantalizing. They are not ordinary characters who reveal all that they have to reveal about themselves at one hearing. They do not play themselves. They are deeper than that. They present grave challenges to their performers because they need to be interpreted; because an actor's thinking must be added to Ibsen's thinking before any one of these men and women can be adequately projected.

For that very reason *Hedda Gabler* continues to appeal to actors as well as to audiences. It can live a magnificent life in the theatre for which it is so magnificently devised. But just as surely as *Hamlet* depends for its complete realization upon the actor who interprets the prince, just so surely does *Hedda Gabler* depend upon the actress who interprets General Gabler's daughter. In either case the play —as a play—holds compensations of its own which no performances, however bad, can completely obscure. But in *Hedda,* as in *Hamlet,* the real excitement of the text can be no more than guessed at if the player who undertakes the title role fails to rise in terms of creative acting to the opportunities in which the script abounds.

The trouble with Miss Le Gallienne's Hedda at the Broadhurst is—as it was when she first attempted the part down on Fourteenth Street—that Miss Le Gallienne's preoccupation appears to be the words Hedda speaks rather than what lies behind these words. Her Hedda is not a subtle woman; she is merely a despicable one. Miss Le Gallienne succeeds admirably in making her hateful, but she never explains why her Hedda (being as obviously hateful as she is) could fascinate Tesman or Thea, or Judge Brack or Eilert Lövborg. She denies Hedda the icy coquetry which is implied in the text. She is irritable rather than malevolent, antagonistic rather than seductive. If she thinks ahead in terms of evil, she does not make her thinking plain. Her plans are not hidden. Those who are caught in her web are not caught without fair warning. She rejoices in the most defiant and conspicuous sort of laughter to advertise her coldness, her heartless impulses and her villainy. By all odds the best performance of the evening is Hugh Buckler's suave, intelligent and excellently characterized Judge Brack. It is the outstanding and one highly professional feature of a production as makeshift as are the familiar velvet hangings in which it is housed and the strangely nondescript clothes in which it is costumed.

December 4, 1934

L'AIGLON AND MISS LE GALLIENNE

THE "Divine Sarah" was fifty-six when first she donned the uniform of the luckless little Duke of Reichstadt. Anatole France, Paul Hervieu, Jules Lemaître, Halévy and Sardou were among the notables who had gathered in the playhouse which still bears her name to see her make her debut as "The Eaglet." In those far-off days of 1900, when the Dreyfus case was raging like a plague in France, Bernhardt faced an audience composed of antagonistic Nationalists and Dreyfusards who were eager to find in Rostand's fervid hymn to the glories of a long-dead Emperor an excuse for venting their own partisan feelings.

But Sarah conquered. Daring to play a frail boy of twenty, she made those playgoers forget not only politics and her age, but respond rapturously to all that was magnificent in her acting of "The Eaglet" and exciting in the steadfast claptrap of Rostand's script. "I never witnessed a more authentic triumph on the stage," wrote Maurice Baring, who was present on that memorable night. "I never saw before or since an audience which was prepared to be hostile so suddenly and completely vanquished . . . all agreed [Sarah] had excelled herself . . . [The play's] cunningly administered thrills . . . were deliriously received by a quivering audience. . . . It was one of the greatest feats that have ever been achieved in the history of the stage."

I refer to Bernhardt's debut in *L'Aiglon* because all subsequent productions of the play have been as haunted by imaginings of what she must have been like in it as was the pathetic Duke of Reichstadt by his great father's

memory. I refer to it, too, because the kind of excitement
Sarah created in her audiences is precisely the kind of
excitement Rostand's script was devised to arouse. It is
essentially an actor's play—a thing of big, old-fashioned
scenes which hit shamelessly below the belt, of canvas and
of greasepaint, of Sardoodledum set to song, of melodious
verses and creaking melodramatics, of tall rhetoric and
full-blown romanticism, of easy pathos and somewhat
tarnished grandeur. Although it may pretend to be a
grenadier's march in honor of the great Napoleon that is
taking place in the paneled rooms at Schoenbrunn or upon
the vast star-lit field of Wagram, it is actually being performed in the sawdust of a circus ring.

No wonder it has tempted several players since Bernhardt first appeared in it. Or that it still fascinates readers
who peruse its rodomontade either as Rostand wrote it
or as Louis N. Parker (or better still, Basil Davenport)
has rendered it into English. It seems—it ought to be—it
was—a veritable field day for a virtuoso performer and
a theatrical picnic for those plentiful admirers of the dead
Napoleon to whom his bees stand only for such romantic
honey. But judging from the reports of what happened
when Maude Adams played it in New York thirty-four
years ago, or when Michael Strange and Alexander Kirkland attempted it here and in Washington only a few
seasons back—yes, and judging, too, from what happened
in Miss Le Gallienne's often spirited performance of it
at the Broadhurst on Saturday night, there is even less
cause for wonder that, without Bernhardt and in the
presence of a modern audience, *L'Aiglon* cannot but resemble a great display of fireworks which have been set
off on a rather rainy night.

Neither time nor Clemence Dane has been kind to its
tricks: time because of the changes in taste it has brought

about, and Miss Dane because in all the quieter scenes she has pruned Rostand's speeches of the rhetoric and the poetry which are essential to the action they were designed to heighten. Miss Dane has turned some of the great harangues into the same sort of feeble jingles she recently wrote for her own *Come of Age*. In her hands the pulsing Alexandrines of the original have dwindled into couplets which sound suspiciously like

> *Father's feeling awfully blue,*
> *He's lost the battle of Waterloo.*

But in spite of both time and Miss Dane (the melancholy Dane of this production) and due largely to Miss Le Gallienne in her better moments and Mrs. Bernstein's pleasant costumes and settings, a few of the "big scenes" in *L'Aiglon* still remain effective at the Broadhurst.

Miss Le Gallienne has the physique to be visually convincing as "The Eaglet." She wears her white uniform and her purple greatcoat well. She bows in a courtly manner, affects a mannish stride, gestures gracefully, and endows Rostand's weakling with much charm. If her performance begins tamely and continues unevenly, it does have its satisfactory stretches. And in the last scene of all, it does find her at her topnotch best, playing so simply, so earnestly and with such beauty that she manages to make the proud hokum of the little Duke's death immensely touching.

If she is not able to give life to the history lesson, if the blow she administers to one of Marie-Louise's suitors at the ball is slightly ridiculous, if she fails (and fails sadly, I'm afraid) to meet the terrific demands of the Wagram scene, she is pleasant when she tries to wheedle the Emperor Franz into sending her back to Paris. She is admirable in the Mirror scene. She speaks many of her speeches well, and is excellent (as had been noted) in the Death-bed scene. What one misses in Miss Le Gallienne's performance is the kind of glowing and triumphant the-atricality which Bernhardt's Duke of Reichstadt must have possessed and without which neither the part nor the play can quite get along. Miss Le Gallienne sets off a number of firecrackers before the evening is over (which are not without interest in their way) but she illumines the part with no sky-rockets. And sky-rockets are the very things of which *L'Aiglon* stands in need—glorious, blind-ing sky-rockets beside which the constellations seem as pale as fireflies.

November 5, 1934

THE CHERRY ORCHARD WITH NAZIMOVA

UNLIKE most pieces written for the theatre, but like all of Chekov's longer plays, *The Cherry Orchard* can be witnessed again and again with ever deepening pleasure. It does not exhaust itself with one seeing or with ten. Familiarity with it breeds admiration rather than con-tempt. The vast majority of modern plays, as everyone must know who has tried to sit them out a second time, do not wear well. Although they may be amusing enough in the manner of casual neighbors at a dinner table, they refuse to become friends. Their patter may be lively. They may have an interesting story or two to tell. But they seldom get beyond the point, if indeed they get that far, of being able to make a good first impression.

The Cherry Orchard is different—wonderfully different.

Its interest is not dependent upon its novelty. No matter how often you may have listened to its speeches, it never gives the impression of repeating itself. It does not go stale when once the secret of its plot (if such it can be called) has been discovered. Nor do its lines run dry after a single hearing. Like Chekov's other actively inactive plays, it seems to have a rich and complete life of its own.

The reason for this is, I suspect, that in *The Cherry Orchard* as in his other long plays, Chekov used the theatre as no other modern dramatist has used it. Turning his back on all the regulation hocus-pocus of the nineteenth-century stage—the well-made plots, the grease-paint situations, the big scenes and bigger curtain lines—he dared to realize each man is his own acutest problem. He refused to make his characters so many yes-men to his situations. He knew men and women far too well and loved them far too deeply to iron out their complexities and turn them into the shadowless heroes and heroines, villains and villainesses in which most plays abound.

Furthermore, he had an obvious respect for his chosen medium which many dramatists do not seem to share. Instead of writing down to the level of what audiences are supposed to want and be able to understand, instead of simplifying everything so that it could fit comfortably into the conventional needs of an unreal world, he gave so much of his poignant best to the stage that he made this unreal world seem as real as reality itself.

His method was anything but realistic. No people, even on the estates of Czarist Russia, have talked as Chekov's characters do when, one by one and without listening to each other, they suddenly erupt into autobiography. His method is an incomparably happy one for realism. It gives more than the illusion of truth. It is the quintessence of truth. It boasts the virtue of being selective, even while the men and women who speak it seem to be spilling out their very souls. What Chekov had to say is not easily stated. It was as complex as the characters through whom he said it. That, of course, is why *The Cherry Orchard* lives anew each time it is seen. One forgets, when one sits before it, that it is a play one is seeing, that Chekov ever had to use paper to write it and wield a pen. In Gerhardi's phrase, the medium seems accidental.

When Miss Le Gallienne first presented *The Cherry Orchard* back in 1928 her production was an uncommonly good one. It was thoughtful and loving and managed to reveal to a surprising degree the poignant depths of the script without actually plumbing them itself. It had its ragged moments. Many of its secondary actors were obviously feeling their way through parts which seemed to lie beyond their gifts. But it was so earnestly Chekovian, in the best sense of the word, that one could not but be grateful for it. It was not Chekov *à la* Moscow Art Theatre. It was Grade C milk as far as the Stanislavsky production was concerned. Yet it was Chekov none the less, and, what was much more important, Chekov in English. It was self-respecting even if it was uninspired; excitingly indicative even if it was incomplete.

Then, as is now the case and as must always be the case as far as *The Cherry Orchard* is concerned, the production centered upon the actress to whom the all-important part of Madame Ranevsky was entrusted. The manner in which this irresponsible woman is played is bound to be the keystone of the whole tragi-comedy. Miss Le Gallienne was as lucky five years ago as she is at the present time to have Alla Nazimova, herself a Russian, for the role.

Madame Nazimova, as everyone must know who has followed her career from the time of her Ibsen revivals at the Plymouth through some of her unfortunately bizarre performances on the screen down to her notable work in such varied dramas as *The Cherry Orchard, Katerina, A Month in the Country* and *Mourning Becomes Electra,* is the possessor of one of the rarest talents on our stage. Her veins are charged with that special sort of electricity which is known as theatricality. She has the virtue of being different, of having a face which is truly an actor's mask and of handling her body so that each and every movement she makes is charged with pictorial effectiveness. Her exoticism, as it has been tamed since her days in Hollywood, is now the servant rather than the master of the script to which she brings it.

Miss Le Gallienne's company has followed Madame Nazimova's lead. Her actors have bettered with the years. Although Leona Roberts is tempted to overplay the governess sadly, although several of the smaller parts remain no more than rough sketches of what they should and ought to be, those members of the original cast who find themselves once again in roles with which they are familiar have grown. The production is not yet Chekov *à la* Stanislavsky. Nor will it ever be. But as a production it has advanced to Grade B Chekov, which is something. Miss Le Gallienne as a director must, of course, be thanked for this. It is easy to see she has refused to let the performance harden in a mold. She has kept it pliant, given it the benefit of her ever-increasing skill as a director and granted it the warmth which comes from her informed enthusiasm for Chekov.

Just as Miss Le Gallienne must be thanked, so must Chekov himself. In many ways the actors who find themselves playing even the smallest of his parts must count themselves among the luckiest of actors. His people, I imagine, are not the sort of characters which leave their interpreters alone. Instead of being bloodless indications who rely for life upon the personalities of those who play them, they invite actors to lose themselves in them. They cannot be mastered at one rehearsal or at two, in one year or in three. They have secrets they reveal only to those who have the courage, the intellect, the gifts and the persistence to ferret them out. Always they leave room for growth. No wonder the members of the Moscow Art Theatre could act his plays with pleasure for twenty years on end, or that Chekov occupied a place in the contemporary theatre no other dramatist has filled.

March 18 and 20, 1933

THE SEA GULL WITH THE LUNTS

ALTHOUGH Treplev is thinking in terms of dramatic abstractions when he condemns realism in *The Sea Gull*, there can be no denying Chekov managed to turn realism itself into a new form of expression when he wrote his play. *The Three Sisters* and, even more particularly, *The Cherry Orchard* lay ahead, as final proofs of how superb was his genius for the stage. Yet already in *The Sea Gull* he had shown a magnificent mastery of an idiom which was fated to be his, and his alone.

He had abandoned the pretty moral, so dear to many dramatists both before and since his time. He had discarded plotting as plotting is ordinarily understood. With the eyes of a physician he had looked into the hearts of his characters—into their pasts, their presents, their futures. Then he had summoned these frustrated, tortured, antagonistic people into his play, and turned the theatre into their souls' confessional.

He had not, as Treplev dreamed of doing, avoided the commonplace phrases. He had only refused to use the *clichés* of the stage. The commonplace phrases of daily life were treasures which he seized upon in *The Sea Gull*. He did not record them as our dictaphonic dramatists have done. He rearranged them into patterns of his own. He employed them to create that extraordinary illusion of reality which is so successfully achieved in all his long plays that no one is made aware of the unreality of the means by which these overpoweringly real effects are reached.

His concern was what lay beneath the surface rather than upon it. This was enough to set him apart from the majority of modern dramatists. It explains, as last night once again made clear, the constantly enriching fascination of his plays. Speaking with what has been happily described as "the voice of twilight Russia," he gave expression to the hopes, the silliness, the vanity, the pathos, and the meanness of his country bourgeois. His genius was to let them seem to speak for themselves; to turn them into geysers of autobiography. Yet always he spoke for them as a superlative artist, transforming their prattle into significant revelation; putting inconsequentials to a large purpose; deriving plot from the mere friction of character upon character; and not only evoking a mood of rare luminosity but sustaining it with unerring surety.

Although he was to write dramas possessed of greater amplitude, *The Sea Gull* still stands out as a play of incredible fullness and depth. If it lacks the design of *The Cherry Orchard,* if it proves more elusive than *The Three Sisters* or *Uncle Vanya,* it is none the less to be treasured as a masterpiece.

It is an impossible play to synopsize. Its Chekovian

virtue is that it is far larger than anything that happens in it. It is not merely about an older actress who is jealous of her playwright son. Nor does it limit itself to telling how a famous novelist, who is the actress's lover, destroys a young country girl who cares for the nearby lake as if she were one of the sea gulls which hover over it.

Its people are its story. What they do matters not half so much as what they think and feel and suffer and say. They are unhurried by any plot. They pause to ventilate their souls. They have plenty of time in which to talk as Trigorin does about the horror of being a famous novelist in one of the modern theatre's most probing scenes. Or they talk as Sorin does about what he had hoped for in vain from life. Or like Nina they tell us of their plans for tomorrow. But always their talk is action. It may speak despairingly for a vanished Russia. But always it speaks for more than that Russia. For what it lays bare are some of the eternal truths of human hope and suffering and character everywhere.

Then, too, Chekov of course never forgets his actors. By his amazing honesty in exposing his men and women, he manages to create in *The Sea Gull*, as in all his other long plays, a whole stageful of unparalleled acting parts. He challenges the truest talents of his actors and of his producers. And the Theatre Guild, in this its first production of a Chekov script, has on the whole met these challenges extremely well.

Stark Young's text is a decided improvement on its predecessors in English. Robert Milton's direction is fluid and clarifying. And the settings of Robert Edmond Jones (which in this case are better than his costumes) contribute to the mood by their grace and beauty.

The company at the Shubert is for the most part ex-

tremely good. Sydney Greenstreet's Sorin is an admirable
portrait, excellently conceived and vividly drawn. As the
frustrated Masha, Margaret Webster shows her uncommon skill as a performer. Richard Whorf, always an expert,
captures the full anguish of Treplev. Uta Hagen's Nina
is a lovely and sensitive characterization. And John Barclay
is highly satisfactory as the doctor.

Although *The Sea Gull* is not intended to be a starring
vehicle, it is perhaps natural enough to have playgoers
mistake it for one just now inasmuch as the Lunts are appearing in it. Mr. Lunt does his best, and a very fine best
it is, to discourage such an attitude. His Trigorin fits
easily into the ensemble. He is quiet, unassuming, and
co-operative. His second-act scene, in which he discourses
on the trials of literary fame, is charmingly played. His
whole performance is acted not only from within the
character he is creating but well within the demands of
the ensemble.

Miss Fontanne is not so successful in meeting either
need. Her red-wigged Irina does not seem to have been
approached from within. She is a totally external creation; a noisy, blatant, road-company Queen Bess. Rightly
enough Miss Fontanne sees Irina as the essentially unpleasant woman Chekov drew. But there is no subtlety about
her Irina. She refuses to let us discover her faults for
ourselves. She wears them with as much concealment as a
sandwich man carries his ads. Accordingly she never explains the fascination Irina has for Treplev and Trigorin
and the entire household. Miss Fontanne forces us to
wonder how, if her Irina cannot give a better performance
in masking her faults in her daily life, she could ever be
the great actress she is supposed to be on the stage.

March 29, 1938

ABIE'S IRISH ROSE RETURNS

ANNE NICHOLS'S little comedy—you doubtless can recall its name—was given its 2,533d performance in New York last night. Although more than fifteen years have passed since it first opened, and ten years have slipped by since it first closed, *Abie's Irish Rose* remains more or less the same. It is no better than it ever was. I doubt if it is very much worse. It has, of course, no more to do with criticism than have the Gumps or the Katzenjammer Kids. Not that this has ever depressed Miss Nichols or that it will depress her now. Her play is more of an institution than a play. You and I may think it very poorly run as such, and grumble at the fare. But who are we to presume to complain when so many millions have found pleasure in it, and when there were even those who laughed happily at it, after all these years of freedom, at the Little last night?

The secret of the success of *Abie's Irish Rose* has, I suspect, always been contained in its title. Win the Abies and the Irish Roses of this world at one and the same time, and you have captured the largest audience our theatre knows. Both of these races relish fun at their own expense. Both of them are proud enough to be proud of their foibles even when they are smiling at them. Both of them laugh easily, enjoy verbal onslaughts, and dote upon comic exaggerations.

Miss Nichols has been thoughtful enough to take all of these characteristics of her Montagues and Capulets into consideration in writing her story of the Murphy girl who pretends to be a Murphesky so that she can marry into the house of Levy. No one can say that vaudeville is dead

in this country while *Abie's Irish Rose* continues to be
played. It is the most slapdash conglomeration of Irish-
Jewish jokes imaginable. They were stale jokes when Miss
Nichols first persuaded countless thousands they were new
by crossing them in her own fashion. And time has not
made them any fresher.

The trouble is that when once you get on to the blend
(which you are sure to have done as long ago as you may
have first heard of the play's title), Miss Nichols's comedy
has said the major part of its say. From then on, Miss
Nichols merely continues to repeat herself, stating and
restating the same joke again and again throughout a very
dull evening. It is a joke which, when you have heard it
rephrased for the thousandth time, finally wears down
your resistance so that you laugh, in spite of yourself, at
the last act when the irate Jewish and Irish grandfathers
continue their feud on Christmas Eve.

Let no one tell you *Abie's Irish Rose* is a well-written
play *because* it ran for years and years and made millions
of dollars.. It is a burlesque show without strip-tease
artists; a funny paper that can be listened to instead of
having to be read; a series of Steig drawings for *Romeo
and Juliet*, with some caricatures of John McCormack
thrown in for good measure. Blame its success—for it was
a success, you know—upon its sure-fire ingredients rather
than upon any skill that was shown in preparing them.

Miss Nichols has Bertha Walden, who is playing Mrs.
Isaac Cohen, say, with typical Nichols humor, as she goes
into Rosemary's kitchen in the last act: "Believe me I
have never looked on a ham in my life." I think it only
fair to state at this point that Miss Nichols forces Miss
Walden to indulge in a slight inaccuracy. I don't know
about Miss Walden, but it seems to me that, unless eyes
deceived me, I saw several hams on the stage of the Little

last night. Perhaps I am wrong. No doubt some of the acting which bothered me so much was just as hammy as it needed to be for Miss Nichols's completely hammy play.

May 13, 1937

3. From England and Ireland

ENGLISH AND AMERICAN TASTES

WHEN in college I studied geology, I encountered for
the first time a fascinating theory known as "Continental
Creep." As I remember it, it sought to explain why the
three huge bodies of land south of the Equator have
gradually slipped to the eastward of their northern breth-
ren. It was a good theory as far as it went. But, inasmuch
as it devoted itself to continents, and to southern continents at that, it completely overlooked the movements
of two countries—and, even more particularly, two cities
—separated by the North Atlantic.

It is the theatre which during the past decade has been
running a night school for the geologists, the theatres of
London and New York. If the geologists have been attending, they must have learned much to their surprise
that, although no maps show it and no steamship companies admit it, the North Atlantic is much wider than
it was ten years ago. The Ireland of Sean O'Casey's *Juno
and the Paycock* and *The Plough and the Stars*, of Len-
nox Robinson's *The Far-Off Hills*, and Paul Vincent Carroll's *Shadow and Substance* is as near to us as it was
when Synge, Yeats, and Lady Gregory first brought it to
these shores. But England has been creeping away from

us so steadily, and we from it, that the wonder is it should have been audiences, rather than the rockmen and the navigators, who were the first to notice it.

Stranger still, not all of England has moved. Neither has all of the United States. England's theatrical past, near and distant, has long since taken out its naturalization papers here. Mr. Shaw remains a part of us, a skyscraper on the horizons of both American and English thinking. Mr. Coward is as much at home, and as welcome, by the Hudson as by the Thames. John van Druten's *There's Always Juliet* has proved that comedies can still be written which suffer no sea change, and which reduce the widening Atlantic to the convivial dimensions of a swimming pool. Mr. Maugham, in and often out of revival, is as close to us as he ever was. There are many other English plays, such as *Journey's End, The Barretts of Wimpole Street,* and *Victoria Regina* which America has taken to its heart of recent years. English actors (except for some of the too-too sick-making "Green Carnation Boys" who insist upon Winnie-the-Poohing all over the place) continue to be prized. Edna Best, Herbert Marshall, and Leslie Howard have been rightly admired for the matchless polish with which they play drawing-room comedy. And, though England may have defaulted on its war debts, Philip Merivale, John Gielgud, and Maurice Evans have made us cheerfully admit we are indebted to England for some of the outstanding acting memories of our time.

Even so, the North Atlantic has widened, and whole shires of the English theatre have slipped farther away from us than countless states of the American theatre have ever been from England's ken. Although as playgoers we may not have heard about Cornwallis and Yorktown until

just about the time of Charles Frohman's death, our
colonial days are not only over but forgotten. As far as
our culture and our entertainment are concerned, we no
longer have any umbilical connections with the Mother
Country. If she frowns on what we think is funny, as
mothers will, and does not bother to understand us, we
are just as apt to yawn over her old wives' tales and be
out of touch with her.

The fact that London has applauded a play does not
mean, as it once did, that New York is therefore anxious
to receive it. On the contrary, such news as often as not
fills Americans with advance doubts. If the English are
bothered by our slang, we are no less bothered by theirs.
We writhe as we listen to their "old beans," their "Ma-
ters," their "mumsies," and all that sort of thing. They
sit straightfaced before our lunacies, wondering what point
can give wisdom to our wisecracks. They find us curious;
we find them strange, if for no other reason than their
lack of curiosity.

They like leisurely murder plays of a psychopathic
nature. We feel these melodramas are too niggardly with
their cadavers; that they do not have enough corpses to
go around. The English, as DeQuinceyans whose respect
for "Murder as a Fine Art" is second only to their fondness for tea-between-the-acts, find most of our thrillers
just so much child's play, filled with oubliettes and un-
explained and inexplicable clutching hands, and depending for their excitement on itinerant bedding.

They will put up with talk, where we demand action.
They are loyal to age, where we, in our exuberant fickle-
ness, like youth and change. They keep hoping for American dramas which reveal us as the foolish savages they
secretly trust we are. We continue to hope for English

plays which will set Englishmen before us who are in some way different from the stolidly arrogant sons and daughters of John Bull we have always known. They laugh at our sentimentality; we roar at theirs.

They howl with glee for more than a year at *George and Margaret,* and will have none of *You Can't Take It With You,* dismissing it as "a madhouse of irrelevant bad manners unseasoned by wit." America gives as generously of its affection and its praise to the New York company and the two road companies of *You Can't Take It With You* as it does of its ducats, and then turns a cold shoulder on *George and Margaret.*

The English sit like undertakers in the presence of some of our best-loved comedians; we sit as if we were confronted with a Martian when we are asked to laugh at their beloved George Robey. We send them serious plays at which they laugh; they send us comedies we can only take seriously. Theirs is a different sweet-tooth from ours. From the advent of A. A. Milne's more cloying patisseries right down to the arrival of such a smudge of molasses as *The Two Bouquets,* they have from time to time sent us whimsies, so self-conscious and iron-willed in their cuteness, that, Boy Scouts though we may have been, we have had no other choice than to react to them by wanting to grab a piece of chalk and run for the alley fence, or by yearning to read *Ulysses* out loud to Bishop Manning.

Then, of course, there is that good old question of tempo, and of our jangled nerves, and of the totally different speed at which we and the English live away from our playhouses. Naturally our theatrical expectancies are differently conditioned by such dissimilarities. J. B. Priestley once insisted tempo was an overstressed difference between us. But neither his arguments nor his plays (at least as they have been received here) have proved his point. To our more impatient spirits, most English dramas, both as written and produced, appear to move more slowly than do the elevators in New York's Public Library.

For better or for worse, the curse of Babel has fallen upon us and our English cousins. Although John Palmer once maintained that curse only fell among men when they learned to laugh, no one can prove it did not originally descend when the first man found he could not muster tears over what was causing his friend to shed them.

It seems unlikely nowadays that even a shotgun wedding could unite the editors of *Punch* and *The New Yorker*. In thinking of the contemporary English and American theatre, let us not forget about the stranger who dropped into a church and listened to a sermon, delivered with such eloquence, that it had reduced the entire congregation to tears. "What's the matter?," finally asked a parishioner who could no longer endure to see the stranger sitting dry-eyed before his preacher's oratory. "Why don't you cry?" "Why should *I* cry?" demanded the stranger. "*I'm* not a member of the parish."

England and America are no longer members of the same parish. At least not all of the time. They belong to parishes separated by an ever-widening sea. A play must be built to more than a Queen's taste, or a President's for that matter, if it is to span the Atlantic today.

I mention these retroactive differences between the English and American theatre in no spirit of unpleasantness. They must find their way into any candid picture of the theatre of this decade, since during that time they have emerged as one of its most pronounced and tantalizing features. I feel compelled to note them at this point, if for no other reason than that they were not observable in the work of most of the Englishmen discussed hereafter.

TIME AND MR. SHAW

TO MOST of us who have been born into a Shavian world, the idea of Mr. Shaw's getting old is insupportable. We were fated to arrive when he was already on the stage, and had made the scene his. It had been his for so many triumphant and diverting years, and it seemed so right that it should be his, that some of us have taken it for granted that Time, like smug Victorianism or a hundred other foes which he has vanquished, would never stand a chance against him. Having seduced the world, as surely as ever Cleopatra turned Antony into her slave, by his wit, his bravery, his energy, his mind, his plays, his prefaces, his pamphleteering, his speeches, his pranks, his smiling Puritanism, his unfailing originality and the daring of his clean spirit, we felt certain age could not wither him, nor custom stale his infinite variety.

We knew his hair had silvered and that, as Mr. Ervine put it, that once-flaming beard of his had changed in *Too True to Be Good* from a "red badge of courage" into a "white flag of truce." We were well aware the satanic Shaw of his early and middle years had made such devil's disciples of us all that to the world at large—as is ever the ironic fate of successful rebels—he had become the sainted G. B. S. of the post-war period. America was eager to canonize him at last, if only he had made such canonization possible, when he delivered his unfortunate speech at the Metropolitan. But his white hair did not seem to us to symbolize a victory for Time. It was only his prophet's right; the traditional makeup of a wise man; the proof of wisdom, not of age; the color of sainthood, not of winter. Winter and Mr. Shaw had nothing in common. As soon expect to find ice halting Niagara's flow as to discover snow settling on his springtime energy. The whiter his hair became the greater was the contrast between it and the youth of the mind and body and spirit of the man on whom it grew. That was but one of his jokes. And one of his victories, too.

To most of us—particularly to those of us who struggle ineptly to have our petty say by the torturing process of putting one word next to another—Mr. Shaw has seemed far more than a mere mortal. Yes, and more, too, than even one of his own supermen. We have come to take him for granted in the world in which we live, but in that world we have never ceased to regard him with the amazement that is the due of all natural wonders. Old Faithful does not ask you to agree with it, but while it raises its splendors skyward you have no other choice than to marvel at it. It performs because it must perform, because there is no stopping it, because God and Nature have ordained it. And so it has been with Mr. Shaw. Great as he has been as an author, the customary displays of authorship have never been able to harness his spirit. He has been greater than any of his plays. His books have been such inevitable releases for his energy that the labors of authorship have never shown in his writings. He has written because he could not help but write; been witty because he had no other choice than to be witty, and eloquent because eloquence has been the effortless language of his spirit.

It is for these very reasons that those of us who love him and who have hitherto felt no more ashamed in confessing this love for him than we would have been if w had proclaimed our love for the mountains or the sea, are saddened by such a cruel proof of time's inexorability as *The Simpleton of the Unexpected Isles*. This latest—and, we almost hope, the last—of his plays does not disclose a Mr. Shaw who has clay feet. It only reveals one whose feet are mortal and upon whom the inescapable snow of an old man's winter seems to have settled. Natural as this is; bearable as it would be in the case of other men; in the case of Mr. Shaw it proves truly disturbing. For most of us have refused to believe that mere mortality and G. B. S. admitted even a bowing acquaintance.

February 23, 1935

MISS CORNELL'S *SAINT JOAN*

OF ALL Shaw's plays, *Saint Joan* seems to have upon it the most enduring marks of greatness. In it he stumbled upon a subject larger than himself and by surrendering to it succeeded in making it as large as any noble statement of it needs must be. His play is final proof of Joan's sorcery. It shows that the simple Maid of Orleans, who was accused of witchcraft in her day, was still able to cast her spell on Mr. Shaw even when she had been so long dead she could with safety be admitted to the company of saints.

Her conquest of Mr. Shaw must be counted among her major victories. She can be credited with having changed his spirit as a dramatist just as surely as once upon a time her prayers were credited with having changed the wind upon the Loire. Certainly the Mr. Shaw of *Saint Joan* is not the ordinary Mr. Shaw. In it he has listened not only to her voice but to the bell-like voices of the saints she claimed to have heard. She turned him into a poet who does not have to write in verse to achieve poetry. Most of all she brought him a discipline as a playwright he has never shown before or since.

In *Saint Joan* his subject comes first and Mr. Shaw afterwards. He steps aside to give Joan the stage. He illustrates the quickening qualities of her miracles and her faith. He makes clear the problems which she, like anyone with advanced ideas, presented to her age. He shows how in word and deed she incurred the quite understandable disfavor of the Church and her secular contemporaries. He characterizes the men who followed her into battle, who deserted her when her prison doors stayed closed, or who gave her a far fairer trial than the melodramatists are willing to admit. And he points the final irony of her canonization in a world not yet ready to receive its saints which would doubtless burn her all over again were she ever to revisit it. In setting forth these things Mr. Shaw keeps himself out of the picture. He does not turn monologist or go off on tangents, regardless of how tempting or diverting they may prove. He gets off his occasional gibes at the English, but he refuses to cut capers for their own sakes, or to turn clown. Neither does he grow pompous in the manner of so many historical dramatists when they attempt to recreate the language of another day. His speech is easy, effortless, colloquial, witty and very much alive. Yet at all times it is relevant, even when it becomes more copious than may be comfortable or necessary. Again and again it rises to passages unforgettable in their eloquence.

In *Saint Joan* Mr. Shaw shows himself to be a dramatist who has abandoned his slouchy Norfolk jacket and donned the same kind of shining armor the Maid of Orleans was wont to wear. The result is a play that—in spite of its unsparing length—is a masterpiece possessed of moral grandeur. Above it hovers a light similar to the one Joan saw dancing above Robert de Baudricourt's head. It is the most stirring expression the modern theatre has produced of the hungry rationalities of the spirit which transcend the limited rationalities of the mind. If, by Mr. Shaw's definition, a miracle is an act which creates faith, *Saint Joan* is indeed a dramatic miracle of good humor and fairness, of tension and eloquence, of fervor and reason which confirms one's faith in the theatre. Even its epilogue, which was widely condemned when the Guild first produced the play back in 1923, now seems to be a further demonstration of Shaw's wisdom. In spite of its talkiness and the abrupt change in mood it represents after the glories of the Inquisition scene, it succeeds, as Shaw meant it should, in granting a sad point and a great glory to this story of the Maid.

The production Miss Cornell has given *Saint Joan* at the Martin Beck is a memorable one. It has been beautifully set and costumed by Jo Mielziner in a series of quickly changing backgrounds enclosed in three Gothic arches. The brilliant colors of the costumes stand out dramatically from the darkly suggested depths of Rheims Cathedral, the threatening shadows of the Inquisition Court, the gray-browns of the scene by the Loire and the tapestry-like qualities of the interiors. Only when Cauchon and Warwick are crowded together at the front of the stage for their first meeting does Mr. Mielziner's scenic scheme fail to be highly helpful and imaginative. Mr. McClintic's direction is fluid, sensitive and evocative. It is possessed of the same kind of energy and the same kind of pictorial qualities which characterized his *Romeo and Juliet*. It is not his fault if Mr. Shaw is not given to using the blue pencil as much as he should.

With typical generosity Miss Cornell has surrounded

herself with an extraordinary cast. Maurice Evans, recently Miss Cornell's Romeo, makes clear his astonishing versatility by giving a richly comic and perfectly characterized performance as the weakling Dauphin. Brian Aherne is admirable as the suavely domineering and sarcastic Warwick. Kent Smith is no less capable as the dashing Bastard of Orleans. Charles Waldron is not only pictorially stunning but enormously effective in the scarlet robes of the Archbishop of Rheims.

In spite of the fact that it leaves something to be desired and is sometimes given to overplaying, Eduardo Ciannelli's Cauchon is telling in its coldly sinister way. John Cromwell, who has a voice of uncommon beauty and uses it well, is touchingly simple and compassionate as Brother Martin. After beginning indifferently, George Coulouris succeeds in communicating the anguish of the gruff English priest who repents his share in the trial after having seen Joan burned. The truth is that, with the exception of Irving Morrow's pointlessly noisy performance as De Courcelles, there is no one in the cast of *Saint Joan* who is not satisfactory—and usually far more than that—in meeting the demands of the text. Although Arthur Byron was obviously nervous last night, he managed to deliver the Inquisitor's long speech impressively and well. What he stood in need of was more of that fateful serenity and commanding dignity which belong to the Inquisitor and which will doubtless come to Mr. Byron when he is less ill-at-ease.

Miss Cornell's Joan glows with all the radiant qualities of the text. To the Maid she brings the same shimmering sense of innocence and youth she brought to her Juliet. Only this time it is a peasant girl, ruddy and healthy, she creates; a peasant girl whose ears, one is willing to believe, hear divine voices and whose eyes see beyond the stars.

There is a definite growth in Miss Cornell's Joan from the moment of her first entrance as a smiling rustic to the final plea which she speaks in a suit of golden armor for a world that will be ready for its saints. At first sight she belongs so naturally to the soil that one can understand all the more poignantly the dithyramb to the freedom of the countryside with which she turns relapsed heretic at the trial. Yet even at the outset there is an illumination about her which must belong to the saints. It is a quality born of the spirit which almost shines through the flesh.

Miss Cornell's Joan is neither bumptious nor sanctimonious. She is the mixture of modesty and assurance Mr. Shaw describes. Her modesty is her own; her assurance heaven-sent. Miss Cornell takes as readily to armor as the real Joan did. She looks extremely well in her boyish costumes, handles her slim body gracefully and completely creates the difficult illusion of the warrior Maid. At times she pitches her voice a little higher than she might. At other times, as when she comes to the dithyramb to the countryside at the trial, she plunges somewhat breathlessly into speeches that would benefit by a more lyric treatment. But her Joan comes as a triumph for her not only as a manager but also as an actress. It is one of the finest things she has done.

March 10, 1936

GORDON CRAIG

THERE can be no denying Mr. Craig has both a mind and a style very much his own. His mind is not noted for its logic. It cannot start at A and travel to Z in a straight line. Its path is lost before it gets to B, for his mental

processes are as directionless as the most meandering of
Boston's thoroughfares. When he thinks, he does, however, think like an artist. It is here Mr. Craig's great value
has lain.

It is not only by the visionary beauty of his many
haunting designs that he has—in years now passed—
helped to rechange the modern theatre's course and become its prophet and its high-priest, to the immense irritation of such a practical man of blueprints and specifica-
tions as the Guild's Mr. Simonson. It is also by means of
those other hazy sketches of his—those essays, editorials
and books which have poured forth from his pen—that he
has won his importance. His writings, like his drawings,
have been designs; not for one production, but for the
theatre as it might be; for the ideal theatre, in which
base commerce would play no part, in which the superman would reign supreme, in which, as goes without saying, Mr. Craig would be the only superman worthy of the
job.

Although the style in which Mr. Craig has stated his
many theories is different from the style which indi-
vidualizes his drawings, it is no less distinctive. It can be
as irritating as it is satisfying, as shrill as it is musical, as
colloquial as it is eloquent, and as pettish as it is prophetic.
If its attributes are contradictory it is because the mind for
which they speak is no less so. Mr. Craig's is a mind—
hence a style—abounding in so many inconsistencies that, in
terms of the parlor game, one is forced to wonder if he
were not sprung from such uncongenial "spiritual parents"
as William Blake and Mother Goose, or Savonarola and
Gene Stratton Porter, or William Jennings Bryan and
Christina Rossetti, or Inigo Jones and Aimee Semple
McPherson.

As surely as the mystic, the poet, the soothsayer, the

spellbinder and the preacher are all present in Mr. Craig's makeup, just so surely is the Boy Scout Master also very much on hand. In between his most evocative paragraphs he has always had a way of going suddenly Baden-Powell, and of talking about doing "a good turn every day," and of urging his followers to make fires by rubbing sticks together.

The amazing thing about Mr. Craig is that often he himself does succeed in rubbing the dry sticks of his sentences together so that sparks seem to fly up afterwards from them. It is because of these sparks of his, and the widespread light they have cast, that the modern theatre stands deeply in his debt. They force us to forgive him his silliness and his petulance, his windy tosh and his impracticality, and to respect him for his passionate idealism and the hot dream of beauty which has haunted his days and nights. They even make us willing to put up with what is unhousebroken in his ego, and to admit with admiration that the personal pronoun with which he loves to dot his sentences is in the truest sense of the word a "Seeing 'I.' "

September 9, 1935

SOMERSET MAUGHAM AND NOEL COWARD COMPARED

WHEN *Easy Virtue, Hay Fever,* and *Bitter Sweet* first appeared together in book form, Somerset Maugham wrote a graceful introduction, saluting Noel Coward as the representative of the younger generation of British dramatists and playfully pretending Mr. Coward had forced him to take his place upon the shelf. As a recent reader of Mr. Maugham's *The Summing Up*, I could not help going back to the shelf upon which I had put Mr. Coward's *Present Indicative* for safekeeping, and getting it down to see what it is that these two books, written by men who have brought talents of unusual brilliance to the service of the English stage, have to say about their authors. I don't mean directly in terms of the events which have charted their lives. I mean indirectly in the quality of thought, the habits of mind, the personal interests and characteristics, and the experiences upon which they can draw and which are bound to color and explain not only their work but the expectations we have the right to bring to it.

Both *Present Indicative* and *The Summing Up* are rewarding books, possessed of uncommon honesty. Both Mr. Coward and Mr. Maugham are capable of surveying with dispassion their limitations as men and writers. They can appraise their achievements with a similar detachment. Both of them are professionals, fascinated by the technical problems of their crafts. If they share an equal contempt for critics, it is because they know more about their jobs and themselves than any critics have ever been able to tell them. Both of them have been accused of superficiality. Both of them have tried their hands at melodrama with varying results. Both of them have succeeded in producing comedies which, however different they may have been (and the differences are considerable), have been witty and sophisticated and rewarded with much appreciative laughter. Both of them are endowed with a versatility too well known to require further comment.

The parallels do not stop here. There are many duplications in the lives and reactions of the two men. Both Mr.

Coward and Mr. Maugham have had their health threatened by tuberculosis. Both of them are high-strung, nervous people who have had to guard their writing energies against the constant social demands which have been made upon them because of the entertaining nature of their gifts. Both of them have won luxurious lives for themselves. Both of them have, in a sense, been victimized by their own success. Both of them have realized the dangers with which it has confronted them. Both of them have sought "to escape from it all," and have found on tramp steamers and in travel, and especially in journeys to the East, the rest, the consolation, and experiences with which to renew their writing energies and add to their works. They have also faced other problems in common.

There are countless passages in *Present Indicative* and *The Summing Up* which could be interchanged without anyone's being the wiser, so similar are they in thought, feeling, and expression. Mr. Maugham, for example, expresses his dislike of sight-seeing by saying, "So much enthusiasm has been expended on the great sights of the world that I can summon up very little when I am confronted with them." Mr. Coward explains his irritation in the presence of the world's noblest antiquities by remarking, "Perhaps the sheen on them of so many hundreds of years' intensive appreciation makes them smug."

It is Mr. Coward who writes, "It occurred to me that I had been living in a crowd for too long; not only a crowd of friends, enemies, and acquaintances, but a crowd of events: events that had followed each other so swiftly that the value of them, their cause and effects, their significance, had escaped me. . . . Success had to be dealt with. . . . I remember leaving the sea and the sky and the stars in charge of my problems and going below to my cabin chuckling a little at my incorrigible superficiality."

These words might almost have been written by Mr. Maugham. It is he after all who confesses at one point, "I was tired. I was tired not only of people and thoughts that had so long occupied me; I was tired of the people I lived with and the life I was leading. I felt that I had got all that I was capable of getting out of the world in which I was moving; my success as a playwright and the luxurious existence it had brought me; the social round, the grand dinners at the houses of the great. . . . It was stifling me and I hankered after a different mode of existence and new experiences. . . . I was tired of the man I was, and it seemed to me that by a long journey to some distant country I might renew myself."

Although they share many other passages of startling similarity, no two books could really be more different than are *Present Indicative* and *The Summing Up*. Their intentions are unalike. Their subjects are different. They speak for different men. They ventilate totally different minds. Mr. Coward was gayly writing his memoirs. He was setting down, with his special skill, the outward record of a remarkably successful life. He was telling us with charming candor the story of a boy-actor who grew up to be a whole theatre in himself. He was describing his friends, his triumphs, his worries, and his failures. He was also taking us behind the scenes in his own mind, for so theatrically-minded is Mr. Coward, and so perfect an expression is he of all that is glittering, accomplished, and facile in the greasepaint world, that even when he lets us look into his innermost being, it is impossible not to feel he has taken us with him on a delightful tour backstage. When Mr. Coward described Constance Collier's table at the Fifty-Fifty Club as "an island of theatre washed only occasionally by wavelets from the outer sea," he was writing the most accurate summary which will probably ever be written of his own amazing and immensely interesting career.

Although both Mr. Coward and Mr. Maugham have succeeded in the theatre, their attitude toward it is not the same. Mr. Coward loves it. It is his whole life. He is not made fretful by the limitations of the medium. He delights in accepting the stage's every challenge and meets them well. He does not feel his mind is confined by considering the needs of actors and directors. Most usually he is his own hero and his own director. Although he has graduated from acting into writing, he still uses his make-up box for an inkwell. He has the actor's appreciation of applause. A large and friendly audience is not something he despises.

This is not Mr. Maugham's approach. His is a lonely spirit where Mr. Coward's is essentially gregarious. First and foremost he is a writing man with a notebook in his hands. People to him are not people but characters for him to observe with the clinical dispassion he mastered during his early days in medicine. He confesses he sympathizes with Goethe's admission that he composed verses in the arms of his beloved while, with singing fingers, he softly tapped the beat of the hexameters on her shapely back. London's Ivy Restaurant is not the capital of his intellectual empire. Actors stand in the way of what he is trying to say. He dislikes directors. He hates making concessions to an audience. The lonely reader rather than the gathered crowd is what interests him as a writer. The theatre brought him financial comfort, but he can feel no spiritual comfort in a playhouse where so many people are assembled to hear him say what he believes, for the delectation of Demos, must always be his second-best.

Mr. Maugham lives on his curiosity where Mr. Coward lives on his nerves. On the basis of *Present Indicative* it

would seem Mr. Coward had read practically nothing. To
be sure he does admit that as a boy he devoured week by
week such gems as *Chums, The Boy's Own Paper,* and *The
Magnet.* Then there are passing references later on to Guy
Boothby, E. Phillips Oppenheim, William Le Queux, Stanley Weyman, the early novels of Edgar Wallace, and
Marie Antoinette's secret memoirs. Of course, Shaw, Jones,
and Pinero are dramatists he knows well. But most of his
reading seems to have been theatre-gained; derived from
scripts in which he had himself played.

Mr. Maugham, on the other hand, appears to have
read everything. His mind is constantly refreshed by the
works of the greatest writers and thinkers. Meredith,
Hardy, Jeremy Taylor, Dryden, Swift, Dante, Sir Thomas
Browne, Shakespeare, Pater, DeQuincey, Lamb, Gibbon,
Matthew Arnold, Hazlitt, Rousseau, Dr. Johnson, Pliny,
Aristotle, Goethe, Stendhal, Balzac, Hume, Kant, Spinoza
—these are the names which tumble without pedantry
from his pen. They are a definite part of his living and his
thinking. Their thoughts flow into his mind as Mr. Lorentz
tells us the Judith, the Grand, the Osage, and the Platte
combine to make the Mississippi. No wonder *The Summing Up* is not an ordinary volume of reminiscences. It is
written brilliantly but seriously as the last will and testament of the principles evolved and the problems solved
by a master builder, not as testament of fortunate and
gilded youth. It is not a book of memoirs, but the
autobiography of an ever-informed, ever-sensitive, ever-
hungry mind. It is not an invitation to the delightful
world of the backstage, but a no less tempting invitation
into the clinical laboratory of the most adroit technician
among contemporary writers.

April 11, 1938

FAREWELL TO *DESIGN FOR LIVING*

WHEN *Design for Living* concludes its prosperous run at the Ethel Barrymore tonight, the fast dwindling season will have lost its brightest ornament. No other comedy of the year has rivaled this one in the fleetness of its fooling, the ebullience of its spirits, the polish of its dialogue or the amazing expertness of its trickery. Nor has any comedy within recent memory had the advantage of three performances equaling in their brilliance those given by Mr. Lunt, Miss Fontanne and Mr. Coward. Above everything else, Mr. Coward's play is an entertainment, shrewdly devised for the delight of those who act in it and those who see it. In spite of the more serious things it may start to say, it is essentially a *pièce de théâtre;* a pleasure of the passing moment; a diversion which makes the moments pass so gayly one forgets about time. Its topsy-turvy tale of tangled lives, of love among the artists, and affections rotated like crops, is something to be seen rather than read. So inescapably bound up with the merits of its performance is it that it refuses to suggest in print the full joys it holds upon the stage.

In many ways *Design for Living* is a strange play. It is really three plays rolled into one. At least, it is one play in which three things only remotely connected with one another are simultaneously expressed. First and foremost, it is an uncannily adroit theatre comedy, sustained and made uproarious by that genius for delicious nonsense which Mr. Coward must count among the happiest of his many happy gifts. Then it is, or rather it sets out to be, a serious, though giddy, study of the intricate emotional relationship existing between two men and one woman, all of whom are deeply fond of one another. Lastly it is a highly personal script in which the Mr. Coward who is the modern theatre's most successful "Wonder Boy" bitterly takes stock of the spoils which belong to the victor.

After seeing it a second time and enjoying it even more fully than I did at first, I am more convinced than ever that as far as the Leo-Otto-Gilda story is concerned, *Design for Living* is not the play Mr. Coward started to write. What that play was I cannot pretend to know. But I am inclined to suspect the heavy seriousness which characterizes almost the whole of the first act must have been used originally to point to a conclusion vastly different from the present one, which is really no conclusion at all. Just why Otto and Leo, who obviously are no longer in love with Gilda, should return to take her away from Ernest or how the three of them can ever be expected to solve their problems by setting out in life on a bicycle built for three are questions to which Mr. Coward fails to give answers. The result is that, when all is said and done, his play, in its present writing, seems to be no more than a gorgeous bit of fooling which is really about nothing at all. It is such gorgeous fooling, however, and is written (when it once gets going) with such an unflagging instinct for the ridiculous and such a complete mastery of phrase that nothing else appears to matter. Its nonsense, which is self-sustaining, becomes an end in itself.

As the weeks have slipped by, Mr. Lunt, Miss Fontanne and Mr. Coward have thrown themselves more and more into the parts they play. Their performances have the same all-conquering surety which made them so memorable on the first night. But they have now found time to add amusingly to their "business," to put in little songs and snatches which were not there before and in general to heighten the contagious absurdity of the more hilarious stretches in the text. Broadway will be the loser in more ways than one when the final curtain drops at the Ethel Barrymore tonight. For such a play, such performances— and such audiences—would be welcome in any season. In this pinched year of grace they seem little less than miraculous.

May 20, 1933

HELEN HAYES AND *VICTORIA REGINA*

ONE of the best-known and most poignant episodes in Mr. Coward's *Cavalcade* was the scene in which the various members of the Marryot family crowded onto the balconies of their London home to watch with their backs to the audience the passage of Queen Victoria's funeral procession. "Five kings riding behind her," was the mother's comment as the music of the "Dead March" began to fade into the distance. To which her little son added, in one of Mr. Coward's inspired moments and a moment which humanized regal grandeur and made Victoria's greatness all the greater by reducing it to simple terms, "Mum, she must have been a very little lady."

Helen Hayes, who plays the Queen in Mr. Housman's *Victoria Regina,* is a very little lady. But like the imperious woman she impersonates, she is a highly successful empress. It is not the first time in Miss Hayes's career she had been called upon to ascend a pasteboard throne. When the Guild Theatre was opened it was she who, in the flapper period of her development, deliberately brought a touch of F. Scott Fitzgerald to her interpretation of Cleopatra in Mr. Shaw's *Caesar and Cleopatra.* It was she, too,

who only two seasons back was giving a performance of
unforgettable loveliness as the luckless woman who was
the heroine of Mr. Anderson's romantic *Mary of Scotland.*

Miss Hayes succeeds with Victoria, as she succeeded
with Mary, in being a queen without ever forgetting she is
a woman. She does not resort to any of the "Lady-Come-
To-See" tricks by means of which most stage queens be-
tray that at heart they are commoners' children whose no-
tions of royalty are as naïve as Daisy Ashford's. Miss
Hayes has the good sense and the artistic perception to
realize what makes a queen a queen is not the costume she
wears when she rides through the streets in a gold coach
to open Parliament, but the blood coursing through her
veins and the spirit born of it.

Her Mary needed no coronets and ermine to proclaim
her station. The first costume in which Miss Hayes dressed
her was a regality of spirit which seemed entirely natural.
She clothes her Victoria in a similar garment. At the
Broadhurst, however, Miss Hayes finds herself playing a
different kind of queen from any she has hitherto attempted. Caesar's Cleopatra and Bothwell's Mary have
little in common with the "Vicky" Albert was forced to
share with England. In the dramas in which they appeared
these women remained more or less one age from curtain
rise to curtain fall. The pageant of their much shorter
lives was not unfolded during the course of a single evening as is the pageant of Victoria's reign during Mr. Housman's conversational biography.

Obviously Mr. Miller has had to leave out a good deal
of Mr. Housman's script. A playwright with the theatre,
rather than a publisher, in mind would have planned his
text so that these omissions would not have to be so numerous or so necessary. He would have heightened his material. He would have given it a more emotional as well

as a briefer statement that was no less historical in its choice of incidents. He would, too, have constructed his play so that it gathered momentum as it went its way and topped it with a much more definite climax. Although *Victoria Regina* occupies nearly two and one-half hours of playing time, Mr. Miller has been able to get only twelve of Mr. Housman's thirty episodes onto his stage. Mr. Miller cannot be blamed if the result—jewel-like as it is —resembles at times a necklace which has been badly restrung and from which several important stones are missing. What is left of Mr. Housman's play may not be exciting, but it is pleasant. Mr. Housman is steeped in the period. He has a nice command of straightforward speech which, though it is not intensified enough to rank as dialogue, is none the less revelatory and entertaining as conversation.

Mr. Housman is neither over-reverent nor too malicious. He has sharp eyes for human values. His episodic trick may be, and unquestionably is, easy. But his historical imagination is vivid and warming, particularly in such episodes as the charming one in which the young Victoria comes in to watch Albert shave; or in the scene in which Albert returns from a night spent at Windsor to prove the wisdom of his disobedience to the Queen by his findings there; or in Victoria's proposal to Albert and her management of his brother, Ernst; or in the episode in which the royal couple face a public drive knowing full well that a madman plans to shoot at "Vicky."

It is these likable qualities in Mr. Housman's writing of which Mr. Miller's admirable production takes full and fortunate advantage. One is conscious of the lacks in the play as a play but still capable of enjoying the evening. Such taste as Mr. Whistler has shown in visualizing the cluttered paintings, the knickknacks, the gilded cupids and yet the spacious opulence of Victorian palaces without ever making his settings overfussy is rare and at all times praiseworthy. Mr. Whistler has a sense of the theatre Mr. Housman lacks but which comes valiantly to Mr. Housman's aid.

Mr. Housman confronts Miss Hayes with a plentiful number of challenges. She is asked to change before our eyes from the young girl who was awakened early one morning in 1837 to be told that she was queen, to the old lady who in 1897 was wheeled onto the balcony at Buckingham Palace to receive the cheers of her subjects at the time of her Diamond Jubilee. To span the long years separating these two events is no easy assignment, particularly as in her performance Miss Hayes is forced to suggest many of the traits of Victoria which are clearly indicated in the printed text but which for practical playing purposes have had to be dropped from the acting version. *Time* magazine, in its excellent story on the Washington opening of *Victoria Regina*, suggests that Miss Hayes's queen "can be considered as a sort of retrospective exhibition of some of the memorable parts she has played during the past seventeen years."

It mentions Miss Hayes's dreamchild in *Dear Brutus* in connection with her young Victoria; compares her scene with Lord Melbourne to her *Bab* period; notes a resemblance between her more intimate conversations with Albert and certain of her tender moments in the cinema version of *A Farewell to Arms;* likens her tragic power at the time of Albert's fatal chill to her leave-taking from Bothwell in *Mary of Scotland,* and sees a certain similarity between Miss Hayes's fat-faced Widow of Windsor in the last two episodes and her withered disguise for the closing shots of *The Sin of Madelon Claudet*. This is not to suggest Miss Hayes repeats herself in *Victoria Regina*. She does not. What she does in the course of the single evening to which she lends the continuity of her own fascinating personality is to demonstrate how wide is her range and how charming, intelligent and gifted she is as a performer.

It is not her fault if the acted text does not let us see more of Victoria, the egotist; Victoria, the willful; Victoria, the mother; Victoria, the ever-industrious monarch; Victoria, the ruler who rose to greatness; Victoria, the woman whose taste in art and literature was strangely mediocre; Victoria, the wife who gradually shared her power with an Albert who knew how to manage her; or Victoria, the widow who applied herself conscientiously to knowing what her ministers were up to and having an active hand in the government of a great empire. The fault is entirely Mr. Housman's for not having constructed his play with a shrewder understanding of the stage. Even so, Miss Hayes manages to create an extraordinary characterization of the Queen. In only one respect does her performance differ from the Victoria one imagines. That is when, in the last two rather feeble episodes, she fails vocally to live up to her astonishingly effective makeup as the aged monarch, and denies her the forbidding dignity which must have been hers.

Vincent Price is no less good and no less authoritative as Albert than Miss Hayes is as Victoria. Newcomer though he is, Mr. Price has astonishing ease, genuine presence, and an ingratiating manner. He has a rich singing, as well as an effective speaking voice, and shows in this first real opportunity which has come to him exceptional promise as an actor.

January 2, 1936

INA CLAIRE IN *ONCE IS ENOUGH*

ALTHOUGH no Time-Machine is visible in the Duke of Hampshire's country house in *Once Is Enough,* it soon becomes clear that Frederick Lonsdale is following Maxwell Anderson's example and employing one. The major difference seems to be that where Mr. Anderson relies upon his to carry his characters back to the "good old days" at the turn of the century, Mr. Lonsdale's is used to take playgoers on a pleasant excursion into their own not-so-distant theatregoing past. Mr. Anderson's Time-Machine is the brain-child of the inventor who is his hero. Mr. Lonsdale's is the product of his own familiar comic invention. Mr. Anderson's is seen; Mr. Lonsdale's is heard. Where Mr. Anderson in his second act deliberately whisks his moderns back to their younger days, Mr. Lonsdale (perhaps unconsciously) transports his audiences for each of his three acts to the kind of carriage-trade comedy they used to know and relish before the Big Bad Wolf of the Depression introduced them to the new values of a vastly altered universe.

Mr. Lonsdale does not concern either himself or his audiences with a choir rehearsal and a church picnic. As an Englishman, writing in the best white-tied tradition of the British drama, his scepter'd isle is the realm of the well-subsidized week-end. His earth of majesty is a drawing room. His fortress built against Nature for his own laughing purposes is an English country estate. His demi-paradise is that other Eden known to England before the problems which have confronted Anthony. His play is a teeming womb of well-dressed men and women, fear'd by their breed and famous by their birth, who are unrenowned for their deeds even as far from home as the next house.

His characters with the exception of a few untitled guests and the stately footman are all Lords and Ladies, whose one job in life seems to be visiting Their Graces, the Duke and Duchess of Hampshire. They belong to that artificial flock which Charles Lamb served as an inspired shepherd. They have got out of Christendom into the land of Cuckoldry, the Utopia of infidelity, where intrigue is duty, and bad manners perfect freedom. Mr. Lonsdale takes us slumming through a world in which, Joshua-wise, he has commanded the sun to stand still. If there is brightness in this universe he supplies it only by the glitter of his triviality and the flickering candles of his wit. It is not to present-day England he takes us but to an island in the Dead Sea, unventilated by thought, conscience, human awareness, and curiosity.

The inhabitants of this island have apparently never read a book, much less glanced at a newspaper or listened to a radio. They are Georgians who prattle as unconcernedly as if they were Edwardians. They treat the Empire as if it were the Albany Night Boat flying under the Union Jack. To them it is merely a series of conveniently distant places to which erring husbands can run off with their best friends' erring wives. Mr. Lonsdale's people feed only on Her Grace's food, and the epigrams Mr. Lonsdale tosses at them from time to time. Their chief worry as they sprawl on this sofa or on that, sipping port, suffering from cirrhosis, and prattling about the secrets of each other's alcoves, is whether or not Her Grace will be smart enough to prevent His Grace from running off to South Africa with a woman and creating a little disgrace.

It would be inaccurate to describe Mr. Lonsdale's new comedy as being new. He has written it before and given it a brighter statement. So have countless other dramatists before and since Oscar Wilde. Yet I must admit I had an agreeable time at *Once Is Enough*. It did not annoy me to discover Mr. Lonsdale has remained unaltered in a changed world. As a matter of fact his polite refusal to admit any changes whatsoever struck me as being a gesture of considerable boldness. I found myself as interested in listening to his vanished point of view as I would have been had I had a chance to meet that lonely mountaineer in Kentucky who, fifty years after Appomattox, had to be told the Civil War was over. Mr. Lonsdale's play had for me at once the interest of a museum piece and of a place I had known and enjoyed a good many years back. It took me on something of a sentimental journey. I discovered I was laughing with it as well as at it. As a study in realism it can, of course, be taken no more seriously than the entrance of the Peers in *Iolanthe,* which at moments it suggests. Yet surely there is room even in this altered world for genteel comedy. No less surely those who say that the comedy of manners does not aspire high artistically do not know what they are talking about. Theatregoing would be a pretty tedious and unsatisfactory business if all our dramatists were like the Messrs. Blitzstein and Odets, interesting as they are in their own way.

What redeems *Once Is Enough,* and fills the evening with radiance and charm, is Ina Claire's playing of Her Grace. Miss Claire is completely at home in such a comedy as this new-old one by Mr. Lonsdale. She is brilliant even when Mr. Lonsdale fails her. If any comedienne in our democratic theatre is entitled to be saluted as Her Grace, Miss Claire is that player. Whatever may be old-fashioned and outmoded in Mr. Lonsdale's thinking and his writing becomes fascinating and contemporary in her performance. Once again Miss Claire proves herself to be an ever alert

foe of dullness, and the best friend of High Comedy known
to our stage.

March 7, 1938

MR. ELIOT'S *MURDER IN THE CATHEDRAL*

IT IS not until it reaches its final act that T. S. Eliot's
Murder in the Cathedral comes into full and glowing life
theatrically. Before then, interesting as it is by flashes as
a statement of Thomas à Becket's preparation for his martyrdom, and visually arresting at all times as the production is which Halsted Welles has directed and Tom A.
Cracraft has set at the Manhattan, Mr. Eliot's liturgical
drama resists the medium for which it was fashioned with
that sullen stubbornness which is the mark of plays written
by poets who do not happen to be dramatists.

Then suddenly the academic ice thaws in which Mr. Eliot's finer phrases have been imprisoned. His play sweeps
forward torrentially to its murderous climax, the communi-
cative buffoonery of its ironic epilogue and the miraculously regained ecstasy of its overlong, but none the less
beautiful, concluding chants to the glories of faith and
martyrdom.

The Mr. Eliot who fails in the first part of his narrative
to take his audience into his confidence; the Mr. Eliot who
is more reticent about his central character's worldly and
spiritual life than any dramatist has the right to be who
hopes to gain the interest and understanding of playgoers;
the Mr. Eliot who has chosen to make complicated thoughts
more complicated than they can stand to be in choral lamen-
tations which are difficult to follow; the Mr. Eliot whose

Becket listens to the voices of several tempters whose invitations are murkily presented; the Mr. Eliot whose poetry has wavered between austere beauty, sudden spurts of doggerel and dramatic wastelands of obscurity; the Mr. Eliot who has halted his tragedy to have his Becket step into the pulpit to deliver a sermon which, though it could well serve many present-day ministers as a model, certainly makes no concessions to the theatre's needs—abruptly and without warning turns into a dramatist, almost in spite of himself, in the hugely impressive final portion of his *Murder in the Cathedral.*

A static drama is here metamorphosed into an active one. The dark shadows of a Gothic cathedral are pierced by the brilliant illumination of the stage. A script which has been relaxed and almost oppressively dull becomes taut, nervous, vibrant and exciting. Suspense stalks furiously abroad. The worldly dilemmas and the recently found spirituality of Cheapside's Tom Becket cease to be abstractions hazily expressed. They change into concrete interests of such dynamic and immediate concern that the long gulf of time which separates us from Canterbury's martyr is bridged. Thomas, and the problems which agitate him, and the informal mockery of his assassin's alibis become our companions in the present.

If eyes as well as ears and hearts as well as heads are suddenly quickened by the horrific drama, the relentless humor and the ultimate beauty of this stirring and unforgettable last act of this *Murder in the Cathedral,* it is because it is here for the first time in his script that Mr. Eliot has completely fused his action and his words, and allowed his spectators and his players to share a common language.

In achieving this memorable effect—indeed throughout the entire evening—Mr. Eliot, the undramatic poet, is helped enormously by the constantly dramatic and imaginative manner in which the WPA has projected his play in theatrical terms. No production of recent memory stands more in the debt of its director and its designer than does *Murder in the Cathedral*. In his handling of crowds, in the lovely fluidity of his choral groupings and in the high visual excitement of those moments when his stage swarms with ominous lancers and red-robed assassins, Mr. Welles shows himself to be as resourceful as he is inventive. Mr. Cracraft's evocative arches and ever-serviceable platforms are no less contributive in turning the WPA's production of Mr. Eliot's untheatrical script into what finally proves to be one of the most notable theatrical offerings of the winter. No wonder the Federal Government has found itself with a "hit" upon its hands.

March 30, 1936

WITHOUT MR. O'CASEY'S GATES

IT WAS George Jean Nathan who once described an author whose ambitions were greater than his talents as an eagle trying to fly with the wings of a butterfly. Had Mr. Nathan been writing of the production given last night of Sean O'Casey's much-touted *Within the Gates*, he could not have hit upon a happier description. For here is a play, by one of the more capable and most eloquent of modern dramatists, which aims high and which—as read—has its moments of true magnificence. Yet as presented it failed to project either its beauties or its turbulence across the footlights at the National.

This modern morality play by the author of *Juno and the Paycock* and *The Plough and the Stars* springs from intentions which—at least so far as good intentions go—cannot but win the advance interest of all persons who have been hoping to see the contemporary theatre break away from the dull confines of photographic realism and achieve a poetic substitute for all that is picayune and cramping in its methods. But as one sits through its performance at the National; as Mr. O'Casey's allegory of post-war dis-illusionment becomes more and more choked in its con-demnation of almost everything from Genesis to Winston Churchill; and as one realizes how flat and tiresome such a muddy attempt at symbolism can prove, one begins to feel a little more friendly to the most trivial examples of realism; to think back longingly to hopeless little plays dealing with regulation characters who are at least doing recognizable things; and to regret the harsh words that have been spoken against dialogue which gets no further than saying "It's not the heat, it's the humidity."

Even in the printed text Mr. O'Casey's play is a baffling jumble of moods. Even when it is read it is a confusing affair in which he has failed either to make his purpose clear or to achieve those things which—judging from the confident explanations of his work that he has published since his arrival here—he seems to think he has succeeded in doing. On the printed page, Mr. O'Casey's drama has brilliant though scattered virtues it cannot claim at the National. In the library it remains more involved than is necessary, and more pretentious than is pleasant. Yet there is a lusty, earth-sprung quality to its writing which gives a keen edge to its satire. It rises, too, in some of its poetic out-bursts as well as in much of its richly cadenced prose to an eloquence as compelling in its force as it is occasionally breath-taking in its lyric beauty. That, however, is in the printed text. It is not true of the performance. As it is spoken at the National, the language of *Within the Gates* proves strangely ineffective. Its satire flattens disastrously.

Its humor is dulled beyond recognition. Its eloquence is muffled almost to the point of being nonexistent.

What one sees is a play that takes advantage of choruses, of verse, of songs, of dancing, of prose and some very good actors to paint a group picture of contemporary England in terms of the various types who meet in a park during the four seasons of the year represented in Mr. O'Casey's four acts. In a world of nursery-maids, policewomen, gardeners, soap box orators and chair attendants (each of whom has a more definite meaning to Mr. O'Casey than he confides to his audience), we are asked to follow the ineffectual attempts of "The Bishop" (who symbolizes conventional religion) to save the soul of an unfortunate female, known as "The Young Whore," who has determined to die game and dancing and who has listened to the songs of "The Dreamer."

"The Young Whore," wrote Mr. O'Casey in the *Times* last Sunday, is a "symbol of those young women full of life and a fine energy, gracious and kind, *to whom life fails to respond*(!!) and who are determined to be wicked rather than virtuous out of conformity or fear." "The Dreamer" he described as being among other things a "symbol of noble restlessness and discontent; of the stir in life that brings to birth new things and greater things than those that were before . . . and of the rising intelligence in man that will no longer stand, nor venerate, nor shelter those whom poverty of spirit has emptied of all that is worthwhile in life."

I quote Mr. O'Casey out of gratitude for whatever specific information he has to offer on the subject of *Within the Gates*. It would be greatly to the advantage of his play if he had characterized any of his types as definitely as he described them in the *Times*.

Mr. O'Casey follows the fortunes of his three main symbols in a world that is frankly upside down. He places his entire action before the helmeted statue of a soldier on a war memorial. Rising ominously from time to time above the wranglings of his puppets is the chant of "The Down and Outs," an army composed of "all who are dead to courage, fortitude, and the will to power . . . of those, young or old, rich or poor, who in thought, word and deed give nothing to life and so are outcasts from life even as they live."

It will be easy enough for Mr. O'Casey's most ardent champions to blame the production at the National for everything disappointing in the evening *Within the Gates* has to offer. But in fairness to all concerned, it must be said that a large share of the blame is Mr. O'Casey's own. To be sure Melvyn Douglas's direction is wooden and awkward, save in the final scene. He neither succeeds in creating a stylization appropriate to the text nor in keeping the majority of his players from performing in anything but the most literal manner of the workday theatre. Most of his actors seemed last night to be as perplexed by what they were doing as was the audience which watched them.

Miss Gish plays "The Young Whore" with all the delicate beauty with which she is associated. She brings a new strength—and a new and much deeper voice—to a part that abounds in difficulties. Moffat Johnston indicates only a fraction of the satire that has gone into the writing of "The Bishop." In the large cast it is Bramwell Fletcher who more than anyone else preserves the beauty of Mr. O'Casey's lines and achieves the stylization needed throughout.

With all due respects to Mr. O'Casey one can't help wondering how *Within the Gates* would have been received if either Channing Pollock or John Howard Lawson had written it. Though at times it almost seems as if they had, it is none the less a brave failure in a fine cause. Those who are always happiest and most impressed in the presence of what they cannot understand will undoubtedly put up with its pretentiousness and salute it as the masterpiece it most assuredly is not.

October 23, 1934

CATHLEEN NI HOULIHAN AND *SHADOW AND SUBSTANCE*

NO new drama of recent seasons has contained more arresting dialogue than does this script Paul Vincent Carroll has written about the Catholic Church in Ireland. No new drama has had a prouder spirit, or spoken for a sharper, more literate mind. It is by all odds the best play to have come out of the Irish theatre since Mr. O'Casey wrote *Juno and the Paycock* and *The Plough and the Stars*. You may suspect, as Mr. Nathan has suggested, that when Mr. Carroll uses a pure young servant girl as a means of bringing a super-sophisticated canon back to the first principles of his faith, the instrument of regeneration is not so very far removed in its essence "from the celebrated little Editha of several generations ago who used to come downstairs in her nightgown, encounter a burglar, and convert him to rectitude and the chaste life through her ingenuous and artless prattle." But, Nathan-wise, I think you would find it impossible not to admit that Mr. Carroll has made an old contrivance so definitely his own that its age does not matter.

He does this by the sheer magic of his writing, by the cold play of his wit, by the warmth of his revelation of the people. He does it above everything else by the overtones which vibrate from his simplest phrases; by the constant

sense he gives you that what he is saying says more than
it seems to say, that his most trivial observation is a symbol
fraught with meaning. His play is before you, and interesting in its own rights. It draws a complete, self-contained
portrait of a sardonic canon, educated in Spain and representing the accumulated wisdom of the universal Church,
who finds himself at odds with the peasant-like simplicity
and violence of his curates and his spiritual charges.

Mr. Carroll's drama is no less self-sufficient in telling of
the warfare that exists between this canon and the rebellious
schoolmaster he has appointed, who has dared to publish
under an assumed name a savage attack on the Church.
Merely as narrative *Shadow and Substance* creates, moreover, a definite interest in the tale it tells of the sweet little
caretaker who thinks she talks directly with St. Brigid, and
who loses her life after giving her innocent affection both
to the schoolmaster and the canon. Yet always one sits before the play, fascinated by what it means in terms of that
other, unseen play which is also there. Mr. Carroll does
more than write eloquently. His pen draws a double line.
His text has more than one exposure. It raises it own mirage
of allegory. As is almost always true in the better Irish
plays, you do not have to look further than beneath this
sofa or behind that door to find Cathleen Ni Houlihan
hiding there and begging you to recognize her. The substance of Mr. Carroll's drama casts whatever shadow you
are willing or able to tack on to it.

The never-ceasing search for implied intentions adds to
the fascination and the beauty of what is actually spoken.
The mind, as well as the ears and eyes, is kept busily employed. Sometimes the quest is an elusive one. Often one
wishes the passion lying beneath this Irish allegory were
not quite as smothered as it is by Mr. Carroll's literary ret-
icence. Or that he would not be so obstinate in his refusal

to squeeze a scene dry. Still one leans forward incessantly, listening in rapt silence and with both a curiosity and an intellectual satisfaction uncommon in the theatre.

One does not only listen. One admires, and admires along with the high quality of Mr. Carroll's writing the no less high quality of Mr. Dowling's production. Sir Cedric Hardwicke gives as the austere canon the freest performance for which he has so far been responsible in America. His characterization is a masterpiece of acting which burns its way into the memory. His canon preserves to the full the frigid values of the wit Mr. Carroll has given to his aloof, inhuman prince of the Church. It is proudly arrogant and authoritative throughout, but it smolders with a pent-up passion.

Julie Haydon's playing of the caretaker possesses a luminous quality which must banish any memories of little Editha even from Mr. Nathan's retentive mind. It has a radiance seldom encountered on the stage. It is pure without ever dwindling into sentimentality. Its beauty is that of a lovely lyric. It burns with a childlike, unalloyed faith, and shines with an all-conquering simplicity.

January 27, 1938

4. *America Speaks*

BEFORE AND AFTER 1929

IN the years which followed the war, when the so-called New Movement in the theatre was really new in this country, Art, with a capital "A," was very much in the air; Art, of course, as opposed to Commerce, of which there still was plenty. Everywhere there was mutiny on the bounty of Broadway.

A whole generation of young designers and directors, of young electricians and architects, of young dancers and theorists, and even a few young playwrights and actors, appeared, who had for some time been dreaming their individual dreams of a "new" theatre. Now, at long last, they were eager and ready to band together, to open playhouses of their own, to turn their dreams into realities, to break with commercial Broadway, to drive the money-changers out of the temple and replace them with altruistic backers, and to bring a new beauty and a new significance to the gambler's paradise of Times Square, where the dollar rather than Dionysus was the worshiped god.

Some of us can still vividly remember the excitement of those years when classrooms rang with discussions of the latest books of Kenneth Macgowan, or Sheldon Cheney, or Hiram Motherwell (he was known as Moderwell then). Gordon Craig and Appia were the high priests of scenic innovation. The settings of Lee Simonson, Robert Edmond Jones, and Norman Bel Geddes were constant sources of wonder. Each issue of *Theatre Arts* (which started as a quarterly) was filled with distinguished examples of European and American décors, or with plans for community centers, or cross-sections of famous continental playhouses, or eloquent pleas for a kind of writing and production hazily identified as Expressionism. Realism was an object of undergraduate scorn in those days. We could hardly see the play for the scenery. The "long run" was frowned on as an abomination. Repertory was the common ideal. Little theatres were threatening to replace goldenrod as the national flower. Otto Kahn was reverenced as the Mæcenas of the burgeoning American theatre. Mr. O'Neill was writing the first of those plays of his to be heard 'round the world. And the Theatre Guild, the Provincetown, the Neighborhood Playhouse, the Greenwich Village Theatre, the Stagers, the Actors Theatre, and Miss Le Gallienne's Civic Repertory were all of them making in their different ways what we in New York knew to be history.

There was no question about it. The American theatre had grown up. In a phrase of Mr. Woollcott's it had achieved puberty with a bang. It had its rivals even then, and new competitors were soon to appear, mightier than the old ones. The old ones, however, were formidable enough. They had already raided its provinces and reduced its sovereignty. The far-flung empire which might once have been its inheritance had shrunk largely to the confines of Manhattan. When one spoke of the professional theatre in America what one meant more and more was the professional theatre in the city of New York.

Yet it was a vastly exciting place, this theatre east of the Hudson, in the first vigor of its newly discovered powers. It was full of hope. It was full of energy. It rang with aesthetic controversies. And its standards were high. That it boasted its full number of *précieuses ridicules* no one can deny. But they, too, served a purpose. Their starry-eyed dedication to the "Art" of the theatre, and the sense they gave of having to slip on a Greek tunic every time they mentioned the word "Drama," were not without their value on a Broadway willing to appeal mainly to the "boobletariat" and unaccustomed to thinking about much except its box offices. Fortunately, the *précieuses* were not the only ones attracted to this changing theatre of the twenties. Fine strong talents of every kind were drawn to it, instinctive professionals no less than congenital amateurs, and little by little the Broadway which had not understood these newcomers, and upon which they had been making war, surrendered to them.

Now that the twenties have slipped into the thirties, our theatre still stands in the debt of those men and women who entered it in the post-war years. Ours is a very different theatre from what it would have been if they had not altered its course. If the "art" theatres have disappeared, it is because they have long since outlived their usefulness. Their ideals may seem to have been vanquished. Some of them have been. But many of the standards they set have merely been appropriated. To this day they are discernible in Broadway's better offerings, where they furnish another illustration of the conquest of the conqueror by the conquered.

The American theatre did not grow up alone in those well-endowed twenties at which the humorless now smile because these years were divorced from the harsher realities we must at present face. Our audiences grew up with it. They were asked to bring their minds to the theatre. They were introduced to a whole library of distinguished foreign plays which the old-time managers had kept from them, deeming them well over their heads. They saw memorable productions. They became accustomed to settings of a new and evocative simplicity. One by one they heard from those dramatists upon whom, from Mr. O'Neill down, we still depend for the majority of our better plays.

Neither our audiences nor our theatre have forgotten what they learned in those fruitful years. To be sure, Broadway has changed. Its earlier newcomers are no longer new. Some of them have disappeared, and others seem spent and middle-aged. But many of them have more than fulfilled their promise. And interesting new talents have appeared. Faced with the problem of interesting and amusing an altered world, our theatre has not lost its vigor, its excitement or its interest. It is less self-conscious than it was, and, fortunately, much less arty. But it is decidedly alive. My hope is that some sense of the qualities and diversities of its many activities may be suggested in analysis of the work of the playwrights whose successes and failures are recorded in the following pages.

MR. O'NEILL'S *MOURNING BECOMES ELECTRA*

FOR EXCITING PROOF that the theatre is still very much alive, that it still has grandeur and ecstasy to offer to its patrons, that fine acting has not disappeared from behind the footlights' glare, that productions which thrill with memorability are still being made, that scenic design and stage direction can belong among the fine arts, and that the Theatre Guild, in spite of any causes for discouragement it may have given in the past, is still the most accomplished as well as the most intrepid producing organization in America, you have only to journey to the Guild Theatre these nights and days, and sit before Eugene O'Neill's new trilogy, *Mourning Becomes Electra*. It is a play which towers above the scrubby output of our present-day theatre as the Empire State Building soars above the skyline of Manhattan. Most of its fourteen acts, and particularly its earlier and middle sections, are possessed of a strength and majesty equal to its scale. It boasts, too, the kind of radiant austerity which was part of the glory that was Greece.

It is one of the most distinguished, if not the most distinguished, achievements of Mr. O'Neill's career. It is—as the dull word has it—uneven, but so—as the no less dull retort phrases it—are the Himalayas. It has blemishes which are obvious, especially as it reaches its third section. But it remains to the end a *magnum opus* beside which *Strange Interlude* and most of the earlier, simpler plays sink into unimportance. For it is an experiment in sheer, shuddering, straightforward story-telling which widens the theatre's limited horizons at the same time it is exalting and horrifying its patrons.

It retells, as everyone knows, a story of revenge; a saga of the way in which fate calls upon Electra and her brother Orestes to avenge the murder of their father, Agamemnon, by slaying their wicked mother, Clytemnestra, and her no less wicked lover, Ægisthus. It is a myth all three of the great tragic dramatists of Greece have told in their own way, taking their own liberties with its details, distributing the emphasis according to their own sensing of its moral and dramatic values, and managing to make it decidedly their own in each of their independent versions. Mr. O'Neill, needless to say, has taken even greater liberties with this classic myth than any of his ancient predecessors dared to do. By taking them, he has made the story very much his own, without robbing its terrible sequence of catastrophes of either their force or their essential outlines.

The play finds Mr. O'Neill forgetting the pseudo-scientific jargon of Mother Dynamo and the mystic laugh of Lazarus, dispensing with such special technical devices as masks and asides, and writing without any hindrances of form as an emotionalist. As an emotionalist, who knows how to dramatize the curdling rancors of hate, the surgings of thwarted passion, and the taut demands of murder, he has no equal in the contemporary theatre. As his title makes very clear, Mr. O'Neill's concern is with one of the grandest, most spine-twisting tales of murder the theatre's history knows. It is, in short, the Electra story he is retelling in more or less modern terms, substituting the white pillars of a country house in Civil War New England for the Doric columns of ancient Argos.

Mr. O'Neill's play is a testing of his strength with that fable of the luckless house of Atreus which Æschylus first treated in the *Oresteia,* which Sophocles and Euripides both dealt with in their respective *Electras,* and which such a modern as the late Hugo von Hofmannsthal vulgarized into a Reinhardtian guignol of lights and leers and snakelike gestures. Unlike Sophocles and Euripides, who contented themselves with the writing of a single play about the "recognition" of the long-separated Electra and Orestes, and the murder of Clytemnestra and Ægisthus, Mr. O'Neill has turned to Æschylus for the model of *Mourning Becomes Electra.* Like this earliest of the Greek tragic writers, Mr. O'Neill has chosen to give the story in full, to prepare for its coming, to catch it at the height of its action, and to follow his avengers (he follows both Electra and Orestes) past the awful deed fate has demanded of them to the time when the Erinnyes (or Furies) are pursuing them. Accordingly, just as Æschylus divided his *Oresteia* into the *Agamemnon, The Choephoroe,* or *Libation Bearers,* and *The Eumenides,* so Mr. O'Neill has divided his *Mourning Be-*

comes Electra into three parts bearing such Bulwer-Lytton titles as *Homecoming, The Hunted* and *The Haunted*. Contrary to the example of Æschylus, and much more according to the practice of Sophocles and Euripides, Mr. O'Neill gives his trilogy to Electra. It is she who dominates its action and fuses it, even as Orestes fused the Æschylean original into one long play—with pauses—rather than three separate dramas.

Mr. O'Neill's Agamemnon (Lee Baker) is Ezra Mannon, a hard, unbending New Englander, who has been off to the Mexican War in his youth, who has studied law, been a skipper, achieved great success in business and served as Mayor of the small town in which his family is outstanding. His Clytemnestra (Alla Nazimova) is Christine, a foreigner who has long been out of love with her husband and who has now come to hate him. Their children, Lavinia (Alice Brady) and Orin (Earle Larimore), are, of course, the Electra and the Orestes of Mr. O'Neill's piece. While old Ezra Mannon had been away from home, winning the praise of General Grant for the military abilities he has shown as a brigadier general in the Civil War, his wife has had an affair with a Captain Adam Brant (Thomas Chalmers), the Ægisthus of *Mourning Becomes Electra* who in this case is the illegitimate son of a wayward Mannon who has brought shame on his family.

Lavinia, who has also been in love with Captain Brant, follows her mother to New York, learns of her infidelity to her father, and resolves to break up the affair. She confronts her mother, makes her promise to see no more of Brant, and prepares to welcome her father and brother home from the war. Meanwhile Christine has already confided in Brant that their one way to happiness lies in the death of Ezra, who stands between them. She is prepared to murder him, and murder him she does by taking advantage of the heart trouble from which he suffers. Not only does she bring on one of his attacks by naming her lover to him but she offers him as a medicine the poison Brant has sent her. Lavinia comes into her father's room just before he dies, hears him accuse her mother, sees the powder she has administered, and resolves to take justice into her own hands in avenging his death.

Both Lavinia and her mother fight for the love of Orin, but he, like the spineless Orestes of Sophocles and Euripides, soon falls under the domination of Lavinia. She proves her point to him by leading him to the clipper ship Brant commands and there shows him their mother in Brant's arms. Thereupon Orin kills Brant when his mother has left him; she commits suicide when she learns of her lover's death (thus sparing us the mother-murder of the Greeks); the ghosts of the dead who refuse to die haunt Orin and Lavinia; Orin shoots himself; and Lavinia forswears the happiness her impending marriage might have brought her, has the shutters nailed down on the Mannon house and locks herself inside it to atone during the rest of her life for the sins of her family.

As Mr. O'Neill rehandles this venerable story it preserves its awesome fascination. It emerges, as it has always emerged, as one of the most gripping melodramatic plots in the world. It also comes through its present restatement as a tragic melodrama of heroic proportions. The poetic beauty the Greeks gave it is lacking in Mr. O'Neill's prose modernization. But the dilemma remains, and so does much of the agony and exaltation that belong to it. Mr. O'Neill's treatment of it is vigorous with the kind of vigor our theatre rarely sees. It is stark, unadorned and strong. It has dignity and majesty. Nearly the whole of it is possessed of such an all-commanding interest that one is totally unconscious of the hours its performance freely consumes.

That it is longer than it need be seems fairly obvious, as does the fact that, like so many of O'Neill's plays, it stands in need of editing. It is at its best in its first two sections, and most particularly in its fine middle portion. But its last part seems overlong and lacks the interest of its predecessors. It marks the same falling off from what has preceded it as the *Eumenides* does from the *Choephoroe*. Deprived of plotting which sweeps forward to a climax, and dealing with the conscience-stricken course of its avengers, it goes a tamer, more uncertain way. Nor is it helped by the incest motive Mr. O'Neill has added to it. It rises to the very last act of all, however, to a final curtain that is Greek in its whole feeling and flavor.

The production the Guild has given *Mourning Becomes Electra* is one of the most successful feats in the Guild's long career. It has been superlatively well directed by Philip Moeller, with a fine eye for pictorial values and a shrewd sense of pace. Robert Edmond Jones has done his best work in recent years in his settings for the trilogy. They have the sort of vibrant beauty at which he, more than any of our designers, excels. They are simple in detail, rich in atmosphere, and strong in line. They are the ideal backgrounds for a tragedy touched with greatness. The white columns Mr. Jones has given the Mannons' country home, and the steps below them on which Lavinia and Christine sit, are constant and exciting reminders of the fact that the house of Mannon is vitally connected with the house of Atreus.

Mme. Nazimova's Christine is superbly sinister, possessed of an insidious and electric malevolence, and brilliant with an incandescent fire. As Lavinia Miss Brady gives the kind of performance her admirers have long been waiting to see her give. It is controlled. It has the force of the true Electra. And it is sustained throughout as long and severe an actor's test as any player has been called upon to meet.

The moments when she stands dressed in black before the black depths of Mr. Jones's doorways are moments no one can forget who has felt their thrill. Mr. Larimore's Orin is a vivid picture of frenzy and weakness.

There were flaws here and there in last night's performance, details which were not quite right, and a few scenes which were slightly muffed. But the lack of flaws was far more remarkable than their presence. *Mourning Becomes Electra* is an achievement which restores the theatre to its high estate. It is an adventure in playgoing no wise lover of the theatre will be so foolish as to deny himself.

October 27, 1931

S. N. BEHRMAN AS A COMIC DRAMATIST

MR. BEHRMAN is in many respects the most civilized of our dramatists. His characters share not only his wit with him but also his mind. They are sophisticated in the best, most literate sense of the word. Although they manage to represent different points of view and to emerge as individuals in their own rights, they none the less contrive to speak for Mr. Behrman, too.

As a comic writer of unquestioned brilliance Mr. Behrman chooses to depict the sorrows and perplexities of a changing world in households in which the will to reason rather than the need for action is uppermost. Week-ends rather than battlefields are the scenes of such conflicts as are dearest to his heart. His people take to expensively stuffed sofas as eagerly as the heroes of romance used to take to charging steeds. Yet static as their bodies may be, in the reposeful moments in which we see them between swims or after games of tennis, these characters of his ride off in all directions with their minds.

They have a Socratic respect for talk. Their conversation is an open window to their egos, their wit and their divergent interests; a window which, while it may look in on a beautifully furnished interior, bristling with every comfort luxury can afford, looks out on a landscape that instead of being happily ordered is a garden choked with weeds. They take a proper delight in the felicities of badinage and are expert at them. Still they are never idle jokesters. They may "gag" in the fleetest tradition of American repartee. But what they really gag on is the gnawing problems of their own time, their own maladjustment, their own dim or belligerent awareness of the swiftly altering standards of life, and their touching endeavors to orient themselves in a confusing universe.

Although Mr. Behrman is a stylist whose choice of words belongs to a vanished period of candlelight and polished marquetry, his mind is not closed to the grim dilemmas presented by Marx. As a comic dramatist he cares almost as little for plot as Congreve did when he came to write *The Way of the World*. From the time he wrote *The Second Man* and dramatized *Serena Blandish*, through such of his scripts as *Meteor*, *Brief Moment* and *Rain From Heaven*, right up until *End of Summer*, his major concern has been how his characters are affected by the world rather than how the world is affected by them. In this sense his plays have been as passive as they are reflective. Occasionally they have suffered from being so, just as *Rain From Heaven* did by withdrawing too far from the specific instance which, by its author's own confession in his preface, provided him with his subject matter.

Interested as Mr. Behrman is in ideas, he is no rabid

propagandist. He is too rational, too intelligent, too wise to limit his vision to what his eyes would be permitted to see if he covered them with the blinders of any single social panacea. He is aware (as who is not?) that mighty forces are at work today which are destined to make the world of tomorrow different from the world of yesterday. His *End of Summer* finds him recording some of the first impacts of those changes in the kind of special world of privilege which has always been the realm of high comedy. His very title shows he is keen-witted and warm-hearted enough to know that all changes, however beneficent they may prove, do not come without their toll in suffering, and hence have their elements of pathos.

It is this sense of change, with all it implies, which really provides *End of Summer* with what little action it contains. Mr. Behrman's central figure is Leonie, a kindly, flighty but irresistible woman of great wealth who has been brought up in a protected social order to judge people solely by such pleasant standards as their niceness or their charm. She is the summer flowering of a family oil has made far richer than it needs to be or than it can survive being. Not only Leonie but also her social-minded and far more adult daughter are the victims of their great wealth. Leonie, in particular, has been separated by it from reality and lived a radiant, if a futile, life in a playroom of her fortune's creation. Little by little the stern present intrudes upon her standards and her world in terms of the talk and action of her very different house guests. And little by little Leonie becomes aware of the changing values of the present, and more and more of a delightful, if poignant, anachronism. Even her charities doom her, for she is finally reduced to backing a radical magazine which, if it succeeds, will work to outlaw her and her kind.

Some people have been bothered because Mr. Behrman

takes no final stand in *End of Summer*. Others have objected to the play's lack of plot. But to my way of thinking Mr. Behrman's Sir Roger de Coverley attitude is alive with dramatic strength, and his dialogue is so brilliant and perceptive that it far more than compensates for the comedy's defiant dearth of action. His symposium is scintillant in his best manner. Yes, and more than that. It is as thoughtful as it is witty, and its very irresolution is part of its validity as well as of its charm.

March 6, 1936

WINDOW-SHOPPING THROUGH LIFE WITH ZOË AKINS

MISS AKINS has never been one to burden her scripts with thoughts "too deep for tears." She is the most incorrigible romanticist in our theatre. Mature woman though she is, she still approaches life with all the wide-eyed astonishment one associates with a young girl at her first dance. The intellectual content of her dramas has always lain somewhere between *The Five Little Peppers* and *India's Love Lyrics*. One suspects that Miss Akins herself must be part Cinderella, part Daisy Ashford. Prince Charmings abound in most of her plays. So do pumpkins and mice which, when seen through her eyes, turn immediately into heavily gilded coaches and prancing white chargers. You could swear that all of her characters were shod with glass slippers.

Miss Akins loves the rich things of life. She likes fine, perfumed phrases, sentences that are smeared with poetry, talk that is as thick as are the carpets at a movie palace. She likes to drape her women in ermine and sables; to encircle the throats of her heroines with necklaces which will finance them when fortune has turned against them and they must part with their pearls one by one. She is happiest when her men belong to the right clubs, when they are faultlessly attired, when they are descended from noble families, when they smoke special brands of cigarettes, and discourse upon the pleasant evenings they spent in the Hapsburgs' box at the opera years and years ago in dear old gay, mad, sad Wien.

She prefers champagne to gin, platinum to gold, shepherdesses to sheep, caviar to roast beef, incense to ozone, *pâté* to prunes, white violets to roses, stilts to bedroom slippers, penthouses to coal mines, and *Romeo and Juliet* to *Hamlet*. She will admit from time to time that poverty exists, but it seems to figure in her scheme of things no more than Manhattan Transfer figures in the worries of a traveler who is headed from New York to San Francisco. It is only an unimportant stop on the way up from rags to riches, or on the way down from riches—never to rags, but to a proud and well-dressed death achieved by jumping off the cliff at Monte Carlo after losing some $50,000, and bidding Lord Eric Hamilton a haughty good night.

Miss Akins has the good fortune to believe implicitly in everything that everybody else would like to believe true. Where skepticism and experience may have soured others to a certain extent, Miss Akins remains all faith, and sweetness, and soft lights. She may have been born in Humansville, Mo., but no one would ever guess that she came from Missouri. She is one of the few adults who, if *Peter Pan* were being revived just now, could be counted upon to jump to her feet—before the children could rise from their seats—to make vocal and visible her belief in fairies. One suspects her of this because life as recorded in her plays has been a long succession of Hans Andersen's most gossamer tales, equipped with champagne glasses, placed in orchidaceous modern settings, and costumed by Bergdorf Goodman and Hattie Carnegie.

It was only natural that the varied career of such an actress as Marie Dressler should have appealed to Miss Akins, especially as it began with success and ended in a blaze of autumnal glory. Miss Akins loves the theatre as much as she loves riches, or exclamation points, or poetry's purpler passages. It has glamour, and that to her is a word which must always be spelled with a big, big "G." She not only loves the glamour of the stage, but in many of her plays has shown a decided ability to add to it in her own hot-house way.

The one truly remarkable thing about *O Evening Star!* was that, when dealing with a subject dear to her quivering heart, Miss Akins did so little to keep it dramatic. No one expected her to make a comment in it on the emptiness of success, the heartlessness of fair-weather friends, or Hollywood as a haven of art. Among the many plays Miss Akins could never have written is *Timon of Athens*. Perhaps it heads the list.

But one did expect her to dramatize the stage story with which she was dealing, to seize upon its ready-made emotional possibilities, and to drain it of its easy tears. As, however, she did nothing with it except to state it in terms of an undeveloped scenario, and as she failed to brand it with the unmistakable marks of her own authorship, it is not surprising that *O Evening Star!* twinkled so briefly at the Empire. It disclosed a Miss Akins who had been caught napping, even at the quite considerable job of being Miss Akins, the Dream-Child.

January 13, 1936

MAXWELL ANDERSON

WINTERSET

MAXWELL ANDERSON is a dramatist to be respected even if he is not always one who can be enjoyed or understood. He has courage, a mind of his own and—rarest of all —he has ears which he likes to bathe in sound. The petty cadences of daily speech and the dull uses to which even the best of words are put by most playwrights do not mark the limits of his interests. He is poet, not a dictaphone. As such he has a proper love for language and dares to take his chances with it even in a theatre where little or no respect for its singing beauties is shown.

He was at his most ambitious and, if I may say so, his least successful at the Martin Beck last night, when Mr. McClintic gave a visually stunning but for the most part sadly muffled production to *Winterset,* that new play of Mr. Anderson's which finds him attempting for the first time to array a contemporary theme in the poetic diction he employed successfully in *Elizabeth, the Queen* and *Mary of Scotland.*

It is not the modernity of his subject which bothers Mr. Anderson and his audiences in *Winterset.* It is his muddled treatment of a story often as cheaply plotted as it is confused in its thinking. Then, too, trouble lurks in the distressing fact that Mr. Anderson's melodramatic action and his frequently beautiful poetic outbursts do not live a single life. They are not—as the headlines in small-town newspapers used to say when announcing an elopement—"two hearts that beat as one." Married they may be, but it is Reno rather than posterity which is considerably nearer for them than just around the corner. Each of them—the action and the poetry—requires its own individual thinking. Each of them insists upon going its own way and upon making separate demands on the attention.

By so doing, by failing to achieve that happy fusion which is necessary to all dramatic poetry, by dividing what is to be followed for its story-telling interest from what is to be listened to for the sheer joy of its music, they make it difficult to respond to whatever emotional force may be lurking in either the sound or the sense. At least, they make this response difficult at the Martin Beck, partly because of the poor diction of many of Mr. McClintic's actors but mainly, I feel confident, because of those qualities in Mr. Anderson's script which condemn it to being the kind of literary effort which always reads better than it plays.

In *Winterset* Mr. Anderson has not only turned his back on the tragedies of the Tudors but given vent in poetic form to some of that resentment which the Sacco-Vanzetti case left smoldering in his heart and which he stated in prose some years back with Harold Hickerson's aid in *Gods of the Lightning*. Under the high tower of one of New York's bridges, with its magical span in full view, Mr. Anderson has assembled a group of derelicts. His mob is a cross-section of the waterfront; Communists, sailors, beggars, and lovesick chippies who live at odds with the police and resent the simple pleasures they are denied by the Mayor's ban on hurdy-gurdies. His main characters are part of that mob. They belong to the army of the Down-and-Outers who served as a chorus in *Within the Gates* and who peopled the whole of *Night's Lodging*.

Fifteen years have passed since the father of the tortured boy, who is Mr. Anderson's hero, has been "burned" for a crime he did not commit. During all these years the boy has sought to clear his father's memory. He has now come to New York in search of evidence. There he finds under the bridge—owing only to Mr. Anderson's reliance on poetic license—the now insane judge who presided at his father's trial, the gangster who really staged the holdup, and a Jewish boy who, since he was present on the fatal night and knows the identity of the real murderer, lives in constant fear of the gangster. The dead man's son falls in love with the Jewish boy's sister; upbraids the addled judge for his handling of the case; learns of his father's innocence from one of the gangster's enemies, and because of this knowledge is shot down, with his sweetheart, by the gangster's henchmen in a death scene which is so overlong that it likewise kills whatever interest in the play the first act may have aroused.

Although Mr. Anderson's verse is sonorous, alive with modern idioms, often beautiful, and welcome as an experiment, it proves strangely inactive in the theatre. It is more contemplative than dramatic, and more difficult to follow than is either good for the story or suitable to it. It has its purple moments of sheer pretentiousness when it guards the meaning of its lines as carefully as if they were so many state secrets. Mr. Anderson also dresses up some very indifferent generalities in some extremely gaudy plumage. But somehow one does not lose one's respect for his high intentions.

In his visualization of the bridge, Mr. Mielziner has provided *Winterset* with one of the finest backgrounds our contemporary theatre has seen. It is a setting of great majesty and beauty, full of strength, and alive with a poetry of its own. It is as simple, direct and impressive as one wishes the play were.

September 26, 1935

WINTERSET REVISITED

EVER since it opened, and was severely dealt with in these columns, Maxwell Anderson's *Winterset* has been more or less on my mind and conscience. Although not yet driven into the streets, as was the remorseful judge in Mr. Anderson's play, I have found myself disturbed by the finality with which I condemned a play that, whether or not it succeeds entirely in doing what it set out to do, is most certainly the kind of play our theatre is fortunate to have written and produced.

A second seeing has made me realize I was wrong about many things. The faults of the first-night performance kept me from surrendering to the excitement the production now engenders in those who see it. This excitement—which is the result partly of the music of Mr. Anderson's lines, partly of the shuddering tension of his melodramatic plotting, partly of the resentment against injustice which the two of these create, partly of Jo Mielziner's magnificent settings, and partly of the proud way in which most of Mr. McClintic's actors now speak their lines—is no common excitement. It is born of that warming sense, radiated by the play, that at the Martin Beck the theatre is doing something worth the doing; that its aims are still high; that its reach can still be heroic; that the mere melody of language, which has some regard for sound and imagery and rhythm, continues to stir emotions in a way no prose, however eloquent, can hope to do; and that playwriting can still function as the distillation of proud man's spirit.

A second seeing has not changed my mind entirely about Mr. Anderson's verse. I feel now, as I did after the first night, that, though it has moments of real beauty, it also includes moments of windy pretentiousness. I still feel it has its many pedestrian stretches; that the attention its music demands and the interest its plot creates do not always coincide; that its "Shakespearean" comments are neither as frequent nor as probing as they might be, and that it does not by any means offer a final or always happy solution to the metrical problems presented by a modern theme. I still feel Mr. Anderson's play is confused and fuzzy; that something or other is wrong with either its language or its action which keeps it from doing completely what it sets out to do. Once again I left the theatre wishing the writing and the thinking were surer, stronger, and more pointed than they are.

But these reservations and these doubts no longer blind me, as they once did, to the positive and compelling virtues of *Winterset*. I happily confess I can no longer deny—or resist—the strange and fascinating spell Mr. Anderson's drama is able to cast over those who sit before it, in spite of its obvious shortcomings. Whether or not it does what it sets out to do remains a matter of individual response. As far as I am concerned, it still fails when its last act comes, and still leaves me unsatisfied. But I have now come to see that, in the case of *Winterset*, what Mr. Anderson has tried to do matters much more than what he may or may not have succeeded in doing. His is the kind of play, although by no means the actual play, upon which the hope and glory of the future theatre rest.

October 26, 1935

HIGH TOR

TO say Mr. Anderson has written a play about a boy who owns and loves a mountain up the Hudson, inhabited

at night by the wraithlike figures of a shipload of the Dutch
who were lost when Hendrick Hudson sailed up the river
that bears his name, and then to point out that this same
boy and his sweetheart and some youngsters who have held
up a bank and the two crooked real-estate operators who
are trying to buy the mountain are all visited one night by
the shades of these ancient Dutchmen, is to make one of the
most imaginative plays to have come out of the theatre
sound like so much nursery tosh about the "little folks" taking possession of the woods under the cover of darkness. It is
to describe a rainbow by listing the colors which blend to
make it what it is. It is to try to explain in day-time speech
the night-time qualities of a dream. It is to miss the strength
as well as the fascination, and the comedy no less than the
fact-facing bitterness, which combine to make *High Tor*
the exceptional work it is.

Mr. Anderson's play is delightful as a fantasy quite independent of its meaning. Its meaning completes it and
colors it, even as the lighted candles on a cake explain its
purpose without affecting its taste. What he has to say is
the very last thing one expects to have him say in a script
dealing so poignantly with the past and so harshly with the
present, which starts off by seeming to be a drama of escape.
His conclusion is a sternly realistic one. Although he believes man builds only to erect ruins, he urges us to remember that for no mountain (take it as a symbol for what you
will) should a man's life be sacrificed, regardless of how
rich that mountain may be in associations with the past.
Whether he wants to do so or not, man must recognize the
present. Men today, with all of their unpleasantness, their
miraculous machines, their noise and cheapness and false
sense of their own importance, are as wraithlike as are the
Dutch ghosts who haunt *High Tor*. But the present belongs
to the present. It can not, must not, be ignored in favor

of the past. It must be faced, even if it is not admired.

Do not be misled into believing that such solemn sermonizing in any way suggests or captures the vital and engaging quality of Mr. Anderson's play. The point of *High Tor* may be solemn, but it is neither solemnly nor sententiously arrived at. What Mr. Anderson has done is to put to beguiling use the rich imaginative materials lying at our doorsteps. Washington Irving may have prepared you for the little Dutchmen playing at bowls in the highlands along the Hudson and raising thunderstorms by their games. But it has taken Mr. Anderson to intertwine America's folklore with its present so that each has a persuasive bearing upon the other.

When he dealt with social injustice in *Winterset*, Mr. Anderson had a larger theme than he now has. When he turned to history for *Elizabeth, the Queen* and *Mary of Scotland*, he managed to meet with the melody of his verse the glamorous needs of themes abounding in ready-made glamour. But Mr. Anderson, it seems to me, has never created with more originality than he has in *High Tor*.

Although he remains a poetic dramatist, he has fortunately misplaced his Shakespeare for the time being. Occasionally Mr. Anderson writes verse in *High Tor* but it is verse which has both power and persuasion. For the most part he proves himself a poet not so much in the poetry he writes as in the mood he creates and sustains. Where Shakespeare's influence shows most clearly in this decidedly American fantasy is in the skill with which Mr. Anderson has blended and developed several stories, each of which has a mood of its own, and demands a special treatment.

At moments Mr. Anderson comes perilously near to overworking such a simple comic device as having his two real-estate operators suspended in mid-air by a steam shovel. When he has a shadowy Dutchman eat a sandwich for the first time and refer to it as a "Sand Witch" you may think an old joke is being carried further than its age permits. The fine thing about *High Tor*, however, is its very simplicity, and the fact that it never betrays its theme.

The result is no silly whimsy. The play is strong where most fantasies are weak. Its thinking is sound, its humor indigenous and contagious, and its poetry satisfying. It manages to make its unrealities real, uproarious, tender and exciting. If you can imagine what is eerie in *Mary Rose*, crossed with what is delectable in *Peter Pan* (a *Peter Pan* for grownups, mind you) and then made a vital part of our own American traditions and problems, you may have some hazy notion of the quality and appeal of Mr. Anderson's play.

January 11, 1937

THE STAR-WAGON

"YOU don't expect me to know what to say about a play when I don't know who the author is, do you?" asked one of the critics in the epilogue to *Fanny's First Play*. The point he was making was that if he were reviewing a play by Pinero and one by Jones he naturally would have different things to say about each one of them, if only he knew their authors' names. At the Empire last night Mr. McClintic was kinder to his critics and his audience. He made no secret of the fact that Maxwell Anderson was the author of *The Star-Wagon*. It was Mr. Anderson who made this a secret —and kept it. His name was on the program, but he was missing in his play.

Had Mr. McClintic seen fit to pull a Shavian trick and

hide his dramatist's identity, I doubt if any of the wise-acres would have pointed a damning finger at Mr. Anderson. "Here," they would have said, "is a strange play that is hard to place. It's about a man who invents a machine which carries him back in time; lets him see how unhappy he would have been if he had married 'the other girl' (the rich one who would have contaminated him with prosperity); and hence makes him realize how much happier he is as a poor inventor in his Caspar Milquetoast present."

Like the preacher at the funeral who insisted that the deceased resembled George Eliot in everything—except her genius, these same wiseacres would have continued, *"The Star-Wagon* suggests Dunsany's *If* in the time problem it discusses. But *If* was a better play. It bears a certain resemblance to *One Sunday Afternoon.* But James Hagan would have made it more sentimental, would not have cheated so, and would never have allowed it to become confused. Its literary merits are on par with those of *Merrily We Roll Along.* But *Merrily We Roll Along* was at least a shrewd stunt in showmanship. We give up. The author must be a new man with a vigorous and pleasing sense of humor, who is old at playgoing. Yet surely the very same Channing Pollock who wrote *The House Beautiful* must have been called in to write the last act."

Mr. Anderson might have thrown them off by momentarily abandoning the poetic form one has come to associate with him. But the reasons for not guessing him as the author would have run far deeper than this. Mr. Anderson, the poet, is not the only Mr. Anderson who is missing in *The Star-Wagon.* The realistic Mr. Anderson who wrote *Saturday's Children* with warm humanity is also missing, except in the delightful interlude of the choir rehearsal and in the highly amusing picnic scene. So is the Mr. Anderson who proved such a sage satirist in *Both Your Houses.* So is the Mr. Anderson whose fantasy was captivating in *High Tor*.

Mr. Anderson is, of course, entitled to change his style at will. Such changes can be as healthy as they are productive. But what is disturbing, regardless of the style he uses, is to find, as one does here, that his thinking has temporarily lost its vigor and his dramaturgy its skill.

Since Mr. McClintic has given away the identity of the author of *The Star-Wagon*, it is easy to know what to say about Mr. Anderson's contribution to the evening. Unfortunately, however, it is his faults rather than his virtues which demand attention. Worse still, some new shortcomings have put in their appearance. Although the choir rehearsal is, as noted, delightful, and the picnic scene is amusing, and there are pleasant touches scattered here and there throughout the entire script, *The Star-Wagon* suffers from that pretentiousness which has characterized many of Mr. Anderson's writings. It says a very simple thing in a very elaborate and wearing way. Like most of his later dramas, it stands in desperate need of cutting. It takes an unconscionable time getting started. It is inexplicably feeble in the "wealthy" might-have-been scene which is supposed to explain the play's final point. Then, contrary to Mr. Anderson's wont, it has its moments of sheer hocus-pocus which find a charwoman being oracular under a spotlight. And it reaches a final scene that is downright diabetic in its sweetness.

What it takes Mr. Anderson eight scenes to say is that we are happier with *what is* than we would be with what *might have been;* that time is an illusion; and that life is an interlude of light, through which we pass on our way from darkness into darkness and about which we may some day know something. Although Mr. Anderson does indicate what his inventor has escaped by marrying the woman he did, he naturally has difficulty in trying to show that his other characters can all call themselves blessed because of the choices they made back in 1902. His thesis in defense of the present may be reassuring. But it is as untenable as his proof of it is confused. His characters, often likable and really original in the case of the inventor's friend who soliloquizes irreverently, become the victims in his play neither of their pasts nor their presents but of his playwriting.

Far more satisfying than the idea behind Mr. Anderson's script is the nostalgic glimpse into the age of bloomered bicyclists, stiff straw hats, Gibson coiffures, strict chaperons, and the first horseless buggies which his "Time Machine" makes possible. Mr. Mielziner has supplied all of these period details amusingly in Mr. McClintic's excellent production. Naturally enough, *The Star-Wagon* is vehicular. Indeed it is only in its acting that it reaches its destination. Lillian Gish gives the best, most fully rounded performance of her stage career as the inventor's wife who must change from the scold she now is, to the laughing girl she once was, and become the tender and reconciled wife of the final scene. Never has her aggressive innocence been displayed to better advantage.

As the harassed inventor, Burgess Meredith once again shows himself to be the most interesting younger actor in our theatre. Although he loses his authority when we see him as he might have been if he had become a prosperous manufacturer, he gives through the rest of the evening a memorable performance. He is versatile and compelling. He is warm and intelligent. His voice is a fine instrument. And there is no player today, including Mr. Evans and Mr. Gielgud, who can out-read him. Mildred Natwick, ever an admirable performer, is highly entertaining as a sharptongued and posey duenna. Kent Smith is a capable tycoon.

And as the inventor's soliloquizing friend, Russel Collins is superbly irrepressible.

The only trouble is the play is NOT the thing. It is neither what it ought to have been nor what we hoped Mr. Anderson would have made it.

September 30, 1937

MR. BARRY'S *HOTEL UNIVERSE*

THE occasionally fine, often moving, frequently boring, and generally confusing discussion which is the subject of *Hotel Universe* makes as clear as anything else could that Mr. Barry has a will and a way of his own. It makes equally clear that he has the courage to satisfy himself without stooping to any of those compromises in subject matter or in treatment which are usually made in the hope of satisfying audiences. Certainly he has never shown a greater willingness to go his way, regardless of who may care to follow him, than in this most pretentious of his plays. In *Hotel Universe*, Mr. Barry has not only been intrepid enough to ask playgoers to remain in their seats for a full two hours without granting them a single moment's recess. He has also been bold enough to ask them to sit before a play as unlike the common run of plays as it is dissimilar to those highly individual and charming comedies Mr. Barry has written in the past.

One difference, and a striking one, between Mr. Barry's former comedies and his present cosmic discussion springs from the fact that, where all of Mr. Barry's comedies in the past were reducible to a main idea which could be expressed in a single sentence, there is no sentence—indeed no paragraph—which could hold the ever-wandering ideas of *Hotel*

Universe. Nor can any first-night review hope to do the play justice. It can only make a confused record of the script's confusion, while admitting the integrity of its aim and the frequent highness of its reach.

Instead of arguing any single case, as he was content to do when he stated the case of marriage versus art in *You and I,* or marriage versus divorce in *Paris Bound,* or marriage versus money in *Holiday,* or life versus fiction in *In a Garden,* or progressives versus reactionaries in *White Wings,* Mr. Barry has pondered in *Hotel Universe* upon the world's imponderable questions.

Stirred, as everyone must be at one time or another, by the "Everlasting Ayes" and "Nays" to which all are heir both in and out of college, he has sought, with the all-too-considerable aid of Freud, to plumb the mysteries of life, and see behind its appearances into the complicated fabric of the human consciousness.

To do this he has chosen the terrace of a house in southern France which faces on the Mediterranean. On to this terrace, this "fantastic terrace" which reminds people of other places and of their former selves, he has sent Ann Field (Katherine Alexander), the girl who owns the house with her half-mad father (Morris Carnovsky), and her five guests. They are the Ameses, Tom (Franchot Tone) who is a Catholic, and his beautiful but unimaginative wife (Phyllis Povah), whose normal happy life in her children and her home makes her afraid of and puzzled by the strange things which are taking place; Lily Malone (Ruth Gordon), a little actress who is crazy to defy her public and play Cordelia; the completely physical Alice Kendall (Ruthelma Stevens), who is in love with Norman Rose, a Jew (Earle Larimore), and Pat Farley (Glenn Anders), who is in love with a girl who is dead and is loved by Ann Field.

Each of these in his or her own way are samples of the "lucky ones," those same lucky ones out of whom Mr. Barry has built so many well-dressed comedies in the past. Now, however, it is disillusionment and unhappiness which they face, because of the strange spell this strange place has cast over them. They are thinking, as Mr. Barry has one of them tell us, of the estates of man, of his mortal estate, his imaginative being and the world that lies beyond the grave. As Mr. Barry also tells us, "the breezes blow from one to another" of these estates. In addition to the threefold world in which they live, his characters are troubled with the enigma of time and the consideration of their own worth.

It is nearly nine o'clock when they begin talking. But as the time goes by Pat has instructed a servant to appear to inform them of each half hour as it passes, for all of these guests must take a train at eleven. They are sitting on the moonlit terrace discussing the death of an acquaintance. Four out of the six of them admit they, too, would be willing to die.

Little by little they begin to think back to their childhoods, turning to the past as so many of Mr. Barry's characters have done before. Finally the three men start playing "under the piano" or "under the apple tree," changing into boys who are playing at Father Damien, and fighting over "Jew," "Catholic" and "heretic" in what is the best scene in the play and one of the best scenes Mr. Barry has written.

From then on *Hotel Universe*, which holds its own remarkably well for its first hour, suddenly begins to decline if for no other reason than that Mr. Barry is faced with the dilemma of having to solve his questions as well as put them. From then on, too, the thinness and the empty pretentiousness of his material begin to show through the necromancy of his dialogue. For tortured as he may be, and sensitive and gifted as he undeniably is, Mr. Barry has not yet acquired the wisdom or the philosophic stature with which to answer the Sphinx's riddle.

He brings the weird and clairvoyant Mr. Field on to his terrace, and thereupon his play begins to slip through his hands—even away from his habitual taste—into obvious and hackneyed scenes which at times are amazingly insensitive and silly. His young people, or at least most of them, begin to see in old Mr. Field the priest, the rabbi, or the drunken father who has influenced them in their youth. But the worst of Mr. Barry's more uncertain scenes is the inexcusable one in which he has Alice Kendall slip off her evening gown in the unsubtle attempt to symbolize her desire for Norman Rose.

When old Mr. Field dies, Mr. Barry's young people shake off their pasts, discarding both their cloying inhibitions and their childhood memories, all of which leads to Mr. Barry's conclusion that whenever there is an end, then there is a beginning, a conclusion which it must be confessed does not come as a sufficient solution to two solid hours of seeking out the mysteries of life.

Bromidic and sophomoric as are some of the preachier stretches of the second half of this unusual and strangely uneven play, *Hotel Universe* is admirably acted by the Guild's acting company and its guest players. Miss Alexander as Miss Field, Miss Gordon as the actress, Phyllis Povah as the wife, Earle Larimore as the Jew, Franchot Tone as the Catholic, and Glenn Anders as the egotist, give admirable individual performances, contributing to an ensemble extraordinary for its fluidity and general excellence. Morris Carnovsky, as old Stephen Field, undoubtedly does all that can be done with a part intrinsically false.

But in spite of the excellence of the acting, Mr. Moeller's capable direction and Mr. Simonson's excellent atmospheric setting, yes, and in spite of the general interest and the earlier and better portions of the play, *Hotel Universe* comes as a disappointment. Not that it is not a brave experiment and a finely sincere effort, for it is. But that it shows that, like Mr. O'Neill, Mr. Barry is happiest when he is not thinking too deeply.

April 15, 1930

ALLEGORY AND MR. SHERWOOD

THE PETRIFIED FOREST

ONE of the many pleasant features of Robert Sherwood's *The Petrified Forest*, is that—in the best Pauline manner—it has been made to mean all things to all men. It is perfectly possible to enjoy it as the fantastic and very exciting and amusing melodrama it is, and to take, at its own story-telling worth, the tale it so adroitly unfolds about a literary panhandler who in the course of his wanderings falls in love with the waitress in the lunchroom of an Arizona gasoline station and is suddenly involved with a famous killer and his gang.

Or it is just as possible to share one's admiration for the melodrama—as a melodrama—with the very real admiration one at all times feels for the uncommonly skillful manner in which it has been directed by Arthur Hopkins and in which it is acted by such capable players as Humphrey Bogart, Charles Dow Clark, Peggy Conklin and above all (as goes without saying) Leslie Howard.

Yet to those who want to look deeper there is more to find in *The Petrified Forest* than either an enjoyable melodrama or an excellent performance—even if the search for it is sometimes a challenging job. Unless I miss my guess, Mr. Sherwood has put his heart into the writing of a tantalizing allegory which, underneath its romantic and ingratiating trimmings, is as grimly stoical as one could imagine, and which is shot through with interesting implications.

The petrified forest of his tale is no mere natural curiosity in far-off Arizona. It is the whole of our American civilization which Mr. Sherwood believes to be fossilized. Some talk of Communism in the form of a mild argument is the first thing we hear in his desert lunchroom. Then his more prominent characters stray one by one into his drama. Little by little we begin to get some hints at what it is Mr. Sherwood is saying obliquely and in highly acceptable theatrical terms.

I may be entirely wrong, but I suspect he is telling us that the pioneer (as represented by the waitress's grandfather) who has no new country to explore and who can only look back wistfully to the days of Billy the Kid is an obsolete figure deserving to die; that the football player (who works at the filling station and is also in love with the waitress) is an example of fatuous but physically courageous "third generation" youth whose only glorious hours were his college years; that the play's American Legionnaires are men who have ceased to be the men they once were in the particular emergency which created them; and that the hard-boiled killer and the disillusioned panhandler (or, if you will, the writer who has failed to do what he set out to do) are the last "rugged individualists" left in our established order as Mr. Sherwood has painted it. The waitress, who is a frustrated artist and who may yet become a great painter, is the hope of the future. For her sake the panhandler gladly persuades the killer to shoot him (without her knowing of his request) so that she can escape from her bondage in the stagnant present and so that the dream which has died in him may become an actuality in her.

I may misread Mr. Sherwood's meaning. His symbolism (which is written so that each spectator can make it his own) may prove somewhat mystifying on occasion. But his play is an engrossing one. It is as entertaining as it is stimulating, as exciting as it is provocative. In its quiet, indirect way it is the most ambitious of Mr. Sherwood's dramas. It has genuine felicity of thought as well as of phrasing. Throughout it protects its fantasy by a sense of humor which is as irresistible in its high spirits as it is neat in its statement. I have already hinted at the skill not only with which Mr. Hopkins has directed the production but with which it is acted at the Broadhurst. But I cannot resist adding that as good as Blanche Sweet (of movie fame) is as the rebellious wife of a rich man, and commendable as are the performances of both Charles Dow Clark and Peggy Conklin as the garrulous grandfather and the sensitive though profane waitress, Mr. Bogart and Mr. Howard are even better as the killer and the panhandler. Mr. Bogart, who since *Cradle Snatchers* has suffered a good deal from the drawbacks of type-casting, cuts loose from the suave young worldings he has played with varying success, to act the killer in an excellent and quietly dominating "tough guy" way.

Mr. Howard is to be seen at his most charming, casual and effective best as the literary panhandler. He brings a rich imagination to his playing. He manages to combine something of the indescribable pathos of Charlie Chaplin with the attractiveness of a matinee idol. He continues to be the completely ingratiating master he has always been of pointed and humorous understatement.

January 8, 1935

IDIOT'S DELIGHT

IN *IDIOT'S DELIGHT*, Mr. Sherwood shows that, solemn as his major theme may be, he cannot resist laughing when the world's funeral is interrupted by the gay tinkling of a musical chair. The background of this latest of his entertaining allegories is the grim outbreak of the next European war; time, any day now; and the special observation turret from which he surveys it is a hotel in the Italian Alps near the Swiss and Austrian frontiers.

His foreground includes a group of stranded travelers who, for the most part, are more typical as spokesmen for their respective nations than are the high-hatted representatives who assemble in Geneva. Enlivening this foreground is an American song-and-dance man who, with the six scantily dressed maidens in his troupe, is ready to oblige his fellow tourists with the liveliest enticements of a third-rate floor show. Spanning the middle distance which separates this gaudy carnival from the black apocalypse behind it, and attempting to fuse the two of them into an integrated whole, is the diverting story of the past knowledge the American hoofer thinks he has had of a mysterious Russian lady who has also signed the hotel register.

It is out of these sharply diverse materials Mr. Sherwood has built one of the most haphazard but engrossing of his dramatic pictures. That he has taken on a job which would have challenged the best efforts of Snug, the joiner, goes without saying. If an artist had attempted to create unity of mood in a single canvas by placing the gay details of one of Reginald Marsh's impressions of a burlesque show before a background by Goya depicting the horrors of war, he could not have set himself a more difficult problem.

That Mr. Sherwood manages to do as well as he does (which is very well indeed) in getting an arduous task done is the result of his ability to mix aphrodisiac with allegory, flesh with spirit, sunshine with sermons, comedy with tragedy, and good showmanship with interesting thinking.

Idiot's Delight may not rank among the best-carpentered of his plays. In his building of it you may find he has not entirely boarded the long hall which connects his ballroom with his library, his bar with his chapel. Yet regardless of what structural defects the blueprint boys may find in his building, or of the mild fogs which some of the weathermen may claim surround his edifice, Mr. Sherwood is a dramatist who can be counted upon to be an accomplished and generous host. He knows how to make his paying guests feel at home and to give them a good time. He is a stimulating talker who is accomplished at preventing a conversation from becoming too solemn by enlivening it with a timely jest. His heart may be heavy but his tongue continues to be glib.

Whether one grasps the full meaning of all of Mr. Sherwood's symbols or not, or feels he has not said all that might have been said on the subject of war and the hysteria which causes peacetime internationalists to revert overnight to the blindest prejudices of nationalism, *Idiot's Delight* can be counted upon to provide an amusing, often stimulating, evening.

In providing this amusement, Mr. Sherwood is aided by one of the Theatre Guild's suavest productions, by a company which includes such accomplished performers as Richard Whorf, Sydney Greenstreet, Francis Compton and Edward Raquello, and by the captivating presence of Alfred Lunt and Lynn Fontanne at their superb best. As actors who know their business and are masters of it, these two are a peerless team. As the song-and-dance man and the mysterious Russian lady in *Idiot's Delight*, who is more Russian than the Romanovs, they supply enough art and entertainment in their own rights to make anyone happy.

March 28, 1936

AMERICAN "FOLK" PLAYS AND *GREEN GROW THE LILACS*

AT THE Guild these nights, where Lynn Riggs's *Green Grow the Lilacs* is playing, can be heard the most flavorsome, full-chested speech at present being spoken from any of our local stages. It is rich, vigorous cowboy speech, sprung from the soil of the Oklahoma territory and given the cadences of poetry by Mr. Riggs. It is filled with strange idioms and unknown words which ring picturesquely in our Eastern ears. So joyous and rambunctious does it prove as dialogue that it emerges as the chief glory of Mr. Riggs's play.

If the idioms and rhythms of *Green Grow the Lilacs* are more interesting than its story-telling and characterization, the reason is, of course, that Mr. Riggs's is a folk play. And folk plays, since the time of the Irish Dramatic Movement at the beginning of the century, have been plays in which words have counted for much, if not, as they have in some cases, for all. By intention they are dramas which turn their backs on towns and take to the open country. City air is not in the lungs, and they do not have city worries on their minds. Their aim is to desert the ways of sophistication and the "joyless and pallid words" of Ibsen and Zola. They revel in "the rich joy" which, as Synge once phrased it, is "found only in what is superb and wild in reality."

For a time, particularly when Synge was exploring the Irish countryside and dropping into the little cabins he found in Geesala, or Carraroe, or Dingle Bay, it seemed as if the Irish had a monopoly both on folk dramas as a form and on the "peasantry" which makes their writing possible. Since then, however, America has discovered it contains within itself the untouched materials of a folk drama of its own. It has realized the vastness of its spread has created regional types (our equivalent for "peasants") as different from one another as they are quaint in the eyes of city folk. It has learned that these types speak in idioms "fiery, and magnificent," and that they come from coastal plains, mountain communities, or Indian territories "where the springtime of the local life" has not been forgotten.

Accordingly, it is to New England, Kentucky, Wisconsin, the Carolinas, Louisiana, and the West that our ever increasing "folk" dramatists have turned. They have set new characters on our stages and ventured down new byways, often with an authentic firsthand knowledge of the materials they were handling. Their ideals have remained much the same as were those of Lady Gregory and Synge and the other Irish dramatists who first prided themselves on putting the city behind them.

With Synge they have felt that "in a good play every speech should be as fully flavored as a nut or apple, and such speeches cannot be written by anyone who works among people who have shut their lips on poetry." With Synge they have believed that "in countries where the imagination of the people, and the language they use, is rich and living, it is possible for a writer to be rich and copious in his words, and at the same time to give the reality, which is the root of all poetry, in a comprehensive and natural form."

Since they appear to have heard the oft-repeated story of how Synge, when he was writing *The Shadow of the Glen*, pressed his ear to a chink in the floor of the old Wicklow house in order to catch the phrases the servant girls were using in the kitchen below, they have doubtless lent their ears to many chinks and knotholes up and down the country. Because, just as Synge held art to be collaborative and was anxious to give credit to the fishermen of Kerry and Mayo for the richness of his language, so many of our folk dramatists—among them Mr. Riggs—have publicly stated their indebtedness to the people of whom they were writing, giving them the credit for the poetry of their dialogue.

Admirable as the intention of our folk dramatists has been, and interesting as are some of their plays, good playwriting and good folk-playwriting have rarely flourished side by side. Mr. Riggs's *Green Grow the Lilacs* is a case in point. In it he has written speech after speech which is a pleasure to read and a joy to listen to. His people are "hearty" folk. His story bristles with dramatic opportunities. Yet the only scene which is stretched to the full, probed as a dramatist and not a poet might probe it, is the fine and deeply stirring one between the cowboy and the hired man in the smoke-house which ends the first act. Elsewhere Mr. Riggs's playwriting takes a secondary place beside his dialogue. It is, moreover, interesting to see in the published script of *Green Grow the Lilacs*, that Mr. Riggs gives no indication of having planned his play as it is now bettered in performance. His scenes follow one another singly, without that sense of simultaneous action by means of which Mr. Biberman as director and Mr. Sovey as designer have supplied so much of the drama it possesses at the Guild. In the printed text you do not see Jeeter stalk out of the smoke-house and pause at the window, while Curly and Aunt Ella are talking in the living room, nor follow the whole action around the farmhouse at one time. Neither do you find any indication of the cowboy songs which at the Guild supply—for a time at least—so much extraneous atmosphere between the story-telling scenes.

Mr. Riggs has heard his cowboys, and recorded their speech admirably as folk speech. He has flavored his play with the pungent, welcome flavor of the land in which it is set. But he has not seen it as we see it in performance, or as O'Neill saw and sketched the set for *Desire* before it was produced. Except in the smoke-house scenes, other hands have dramatized it for Mr. Riggs. Although he shows decided promise as a playwright, he is still more poet than dramatist. His play is still a folk play, and no more than a "folk play," which is only one way of saying it is not yet a full-grown script in its own dramatic rights. The Irish knew better.

Mr. Riggs should turn to Yeats and his prefatory chapters in *Plays and Controversies*. There he would read among other things a sentence which might help him. It runs, "Let us learn construction from the masterpieces, and dialogue from ourselves."

February 14, 1931

A SETTING AS A PLAY: MR. KINGSLEY'S *MEN IN WHITE*

AS A five-finger exercise in the tricks of production the dedicated members of the Group Theatre could not have found a better play upon which to try their skill than Sidney Kingsley's *Men in White*, which has been greeted with such salvos of critical praise at the Broadhurst. It is a piffling script, mildewed in its hokum, childishly sketchy

in its characterization, and so commonplace in its every
written word that it in no way justifies its own unpleasantness.

In the most elementary terms it indicates the dilemma
all doctors must face in choosing between "Life" as less altruistic mortals are fond of living it, and "Service" as the
followers of Aesculapius must be prepared to give it. Its
feeble approach to such a worthy subject can best be
grasped by remembering it has the temerity (or shall we
say the mediocrity) to build its biggest scene upon a varia-
tion of that good old motion-picture crisis which uses an-
esthetics and an operating table as a means of informing
one woman that the man to whom she is engaged has been
living with another.

But—and this is an all-important but—Mr. Kingsley's
text does provide the talented members of the Group with
a scenario of which they can, and do, make much in production. The very fact that it is laid behind the scenes of a
hospital; that it is concerned with the awesome details of
surgery; that it teems with patients, nurses and doctors;
that it deals with pain and death and the mysterious science
of healing; and that its costumes are the grim uniforms of
medicine, means it offers the members of the Group many
ready-made chances for the macabre, of which they take
quick and intelligent advantage. They document their script
admirably. They make it smell convincingly of ether and
iodoform, blood and bandages. They trick it visually in
terms of the ominous black-and-white contrasts of Mr.
Gorelik's settings. They people it with some good actors
and others whose deficiencies turn into virtues because they
are dressed as internes. In general, they succeed in transforming the Broadhurst into a well-run hospital, even if
they can't quite manage to create the illusion that Mr.
Kingsley's play is a good one.

Men in White is the best production the members of the Group have yet made. It demonstrates, as none of their previous offerings have done, the value of the ideals upon which their organization is based. It is expert. It is diligent. It has outward dignity. It is directed with consummate skill and with a fine use of pauses by Lee Strasberg, and is so well integrated as a group effort that its poorer performances are lost sight of because of the strength and directness of Mr. Kirkland's and Mr. Bromberg's playing. It makes much of little. But at its best it is no more than just one more journalistic effort on the part of our theatres to report a novel setting with a scrupulous attention to details, and to make that setting, so reported, do the major portion of an evening's work. As for the much-admired scene in the operating room, which is the "big scene" of the evening, it seems to me to be a rather tawdry triumph for the Group. It offers its catchpenny excitement to ambulance-chasers, and is admittedly a highly effective example of reproductive staging. But merely turning a stage into an operating room, or transferring the melodramatic features of an operating room to a stage, appears to me to be a fairly shoddy way of succeeding as an "art theatre."

Aesthetically such a minute reproduction is of no more consequence than is the Belgian Village at the World's Fair, the Queen's Doll House, box hedges that are trimmed to look like peacocks, or flowers made of ice cream. It awakens, and may even satisfy, our naïve curiosity. Yet no matter how accurate the reproduction may be in the playhouse, the finished result, as Arthur Hopkins once observed when Mr. Belasco had converted his stage into a Childs' Restaurant, is *"only remarkable because it is not real."*

October 7, 1933

DODSWORTH DRAMATIZED

BEING a dramatization, *Dodsworth* is bound at times to bear the same relationship to the original that the snapshot in your album does to the Grand Canal of which it was taken. When all is said and done, the theatre is one medium of expression, the novel another. The two are no closer than East and West. In the process of being turned into a play any novel is forced to go on a strenuous diet. For one thing, it loses its leisure. For another, it is denied its native habitat. It cannot but be robbed of its descriptive passages and its author's comments. In the case of a play made from one of Mr. Lewis's tales this means a good deal, inasmuch as his astonishing eye for factual detail, his close documentation of scene and character, and the satiric use to which he puts his Sears-Roebuck observation are among the most pronounced and delightful features of his work.

It seems unnecessary, therefore, to point out that, although Mr. Howard's dramatization of *Dodsworth* makes for a steadily interesting evening in the theatre, it has become a Jack Spratt of its former self. It is, I suppose, only natural that, as it has been refashioned for the stage, it should occasionally seem to Mr. Lewis's readers like *Hamlet* with—I won't say Hamlet—but the Court left out.

One of the principal characters of this novel about a great automobile magnate from Zenith, who retires from business to go abroad with his vain popinjay of a wife, was the Europe Sinclair Lewis let us see through the different eyes of Sam and Fran Dodsworth. That Europe—which Mr. Lewis noted with precision and wit as it affected the lonely manufacturer and his pretentious and emotionally unstable wife when they wandered over it from England to

France and from Italy to Germany—is, needless to say, too large a character for any dramatist to put upon the stage. But much as one may miss it and the characterizing values it boasts, the story of *Dodsworth* (which is the dramatist's meat), and the universal implications it holds, are strong enough to carry a play, particularly when that play moves forward with the cinematic swiftness of Mr. Howard's text and is as vitally projected in terms of acting as it is by Miss Bainter and Mr. Huston.

Mr. Howard has done a difficult job well. For theatrical purposes he has caught the shadow of the novel as effectively on the stage of the Shubert as ever the shadow of Peter Pan was imprisoned in the dresser-drawer of the Darling's nursery. He has included the main points of the narrative; advanced them in swift and telling emotional form; and compressed and heightened them effectively for dramatic purposes.

He may have overlooked Dodsworth's diminished ego when he finds himself away from his work, an unknown person in a foreign land. He may have muffed several other points. Yet as a carver Mr. Howard has shown much skill in slicing off the fourteen scenes which make his play. As a cook he has shown no less skill in preparing them. If, as written, his script has its moments (particularly in the earlier scenes in England) of resembling a rather hurried scenario instead of a fully developed play, the fault is not his. Such empty moments merely mean he has at times succumbed to the insuperable difficulties of the dramatizer. What is surprising about his dramatization of *Dodsworth* is that it is as complete as it is; that it holds the attention as unswervingly as it does; and that it provides the agreeable, often quite moving evening in the theatre it succeeds in offering.

Along with the rest of us, Mr. Howard has Mr. Gordon's

casting and Mr. Sinclair's direction to thank for this. Most particularly, however, it is Miss Bainter and Mr. Huston who are deserving of gratitude. Miss Bainter is an actress who has the rare virtue of never repeating herself. If in appearance, figure, dress and personality she is far more attractive than Mr. Lewis ever persuaded you Fran was, she never loses sight of the contradictory qualities Mr. Lewis took pains to write into his heroine. Her characterization is obviously—and rightly—derived from Mr. Lewis's novel rather than from Mr. Howard's dramatization. Even when Mr. Howard has given her very little to do, or vague hints at best, Miss Bainter is busily and keenly engaged in creating the Fran Mr. Lewis wrote.

Mr. Huston is a complete and magnificent realization of Dodsworth. There is something fundamentally and inescapably American about Mr. Huston; something of Old Hickory and Honest Abe Lincoln which gives nobility and strength and a final rightness to his Dodsworth. His characterization is so quietly stated, so shrewdly indicated and so deeply satisfying that overnight it takes its place along with Mr. Cohan's editor in *Ah, Wilderness!*, and Mr. Hull's farmer in *Tobacco Road* as one of the outstanding performances of the year. Thanks also are due to Mme. Ouspenskaya for her unforgettable bit as the proudly impassive old baroness, and to Nan Sunderland, who, before she flounders feebly in her final emotional scenes, is charming as the divorcee Sam Dodsworth marries after he and Fran are separated.

I wish many of Mr. Mielziner's settings were lighter in line and feeling than they are, and deplore particularly the unaccountable heaviness of his garden scene in Montreux. I wish, too, he had read Mr. Lewis's book a little more carefully. If he had he would never have made the living room in Zenith the ridiculous exaggeration it is. But I do admire

him for the amazing efficiency with which he has facilitated
the movement of the whole production.

February 26, 1934

THE SENSIBLE INSANITIES OF *YOU CAN'T TAKE IT WITH YOU*

IN A world in which the sanity usually associated with
sunshine is sadly overvalued, *You Can't Take It With You*
is something to be prized. It is moonstruck, almost from beginning to end. It is blessed with all the happiest lunacies
Moss Hart and George S. Kaufman have been able to contribute to it. The Sycamore family is the most gloriously
mad group of contented eccentrics the modern theatre has
yet had the good fortune to shadow. Its various members
comprise a whole nest of Mad Hatters. They are daffy
mortals, as lovable as they are laughable. Their whims are
endless. So, too, for that matter, is the fun they provide,
except when Cupid is foolish enough to force his way into
the family circle.

The Sycamores, bless them, live uptown in New York.
They are, however, not nearly so far removed from Wall
Street as they are from the rent-day worries to which most
of us are heir. Grandfather Vanderhof (Henry Travers) has
for some years now refused, on very sensible grounds, to pay
his income tax. More than that, though he still has some
money, he has long ago retired from business in order to
seek happiness in attending commencements, visiting zoos,
and collecting snakes and stamps. All the members of his demented household have hobbies of their own and practice
the gospel of relaxation which he preaches. His daughter,
Mrs. Sycamore (Josephine Hull), has abandoned painting,

to which she temporarily returns, for playwriting because eight years ago a typewriter was delivered by mistake to the Sycamore bedlam. Her husband is as vague as she is. His hobby is fashioning boats and skyscrapers with a mechano set, and making violently eruptive firecrackers in the basement with the iceman (Frank Conlon) who came to the house years ago and somehow neglected to go home.

Mrs. Sycamore has two daughters. One of them (Paula Trueman) is a candy-cooking maiden who thinks of herself as a ballerina and is always taking dancing lessons from a fiery Russian. She is married to a crack-brained fellow who divides his time between playing the xylophone and printing, for the fun of it, cheery little messages which urge people to blow up the Supreme Court and dynamite the Capitol. The duckling in Mrs. Sycamore's happy barnyard is her younger daughter (Margot Stevenson), a perfectly sane girl, who has fallen in love with her rich boss's son, Tony Kirby. How the wealthy Kirbys are introduced to, and then won over by, the deranged Sycamores, is the plot of *You Can't Take It With You.* And a good, side-splitting plot it turns out to be as Mr. Hart and Mr. Kaufman make use of it, except in the few embarrassing interludes of sanity and sentiment.

Add to this basic situation two uncommonly droll Negro servants, a drunken actress, a Russian Grand Duchess, a setting by Donald Oenslager which is a triumph of humorous detail, snakes which raise their hungry heads at just the wrong moments, cats crawling around on a cluttered desk, firecrackers that explode, darts that must be thrown, an Internal Revenue Collector and three sulking G-Men who invade the Sycamore home—and you may have some vague conception of how gorgeously goofy is the new play at the Booth.

That the Sycamores are odd is unmistakable from the rise of the first curtain. That they are hilariously funny is no less clear from the outset. But one of the chief reasons for their being convulsing is that the actors who play them never let anyone know that they consider themselves either odd or funny. By being mad in the most straightfaced, natural manner, they not only create at once the topsy-turvy spirit essential to the well-being of the play, but maintain it thereafter. Their manifest goofyness becomes the more enjoyable because they so obviously assume it to be normal and commonplace. One smile, one burst of overplaying, one self-appreciative bit of exaggeration which betrayed that they thought themselves exceptional or humorous would detract from the very attributes which now make each and all of the deranged Sycamores so ridiculous and so ingratiating.

The quiet lunacy of the family is established by Henry Travers, who, as Grandfather Vanderhof, is as lovably gentle as he is unworldly. His performance has about it the sweetness of Androcles and the wisdom of *Alice in Wonderland*. The character he creates is as genial as he is "different." Old though he is, he is happy because he has been able to remain a child of impulse in a sternly coercive world. He is more than strange. His strangeness is the measure of his wisdom and the point of his philosophy. His is a serenity and a goodness which make it possible for him, when saying "grace," to speak directly to his Creator with a reverent simplicity such as has not been equaled hereabouts since *The Green Pastures* and such as should be the property of all bishops and archbishops in a Panglossian universe.

As Mrs. Sycamore, Josephine Hull is immensely droll. Her head may be light, but her heart is filled with the same kindness which floods Grandfather Vanderhof's. She, too, sets about the business of being flighty and foolish with a blessed unconsciousness of how laughable she succeeds in being. So, also, does Frank Wilcox as her amiable husband. And so, for that matter, do the rest of the agreeably demented Sycamores.

It is only when workaday reason invades the Sycamore home; when dull normalcy makes its appearance; when an orthodox Cupid bursts into this inspired bedlam, that *You Can't Take It With You* suffers. The Sycamores, both as written and as played, are too fortunate in their nonsense ever to be disturbed by something as illogical as ordinary common sense.

December 15 and 19, 1936

THE FAIR SEX AND *THE WOMEN*

IT WAS Walter Winchell who recently described a dressy woman at a first night by saying, "There goes a skunk in sables." Had he had in mind most of the fashionable females whose purrings and clawings combine to make Clare Boothe's *The Women* the entertaining side show it is, Mr. Winchell would have been compelled to alter his phrase only by pluralizing it. It is doubtful if a nastier group of women has ever been assembled on one stage than Miss Boothe has brought together in her comedy at the Ethel Barrymore. They may wrap themselves in sables, but, with two or three exceptions, they are skunks, every one of them. That, oddly enough, is just where the fun comes in.

Perhaps "skunks" is not entirely accurate. At least the perfume of these ladies is of the best. Maybe it would be better to catalogue them as tabbies encountered in a night-

mare; at any rate, as prize females from the choicest ken-
nels of Park Avenue.

One thing is certain. When Miss Boothe wrote her play
she was not seeking the presidency of the American Feder-
ation of Women's Clubs. Although most women, and unquestionably a great many men, will find her comedy as
titillating as it is interesting, Miss Boothe says things in it
which doubtless will cause Southern colonels of the old
school to choke over their mint juleps, even as they will
induce ladies in the "uplift" groups to buzz with pleasant
protest. This is at once the chief virtue and greatest defect
of her script. What Miss Boothe over-says, and over-says
audaciously and amusingly, is what provides her text with
its unquestionable merits as entertainment at the same time
that it renders it specious as a drama. Here is a machine-
made comedy which boasts more wisecracks than a good
plum pudding does plums. Yet the fact that it is a hollow
play, essentially false in its point of view and jammed full
of easy, if not cheaply cynical "comebacks," does not in-
terfere in any serious way with the fascination it holds as a
stunt in story-telling.

It is not so much a "slice of life" as it is a comic strip—
the kind of bitterly laughable cartoon a Benedick might
have dreamed of drawing but which only a Beatrice would
have had sufficient data to pen. Although it is written from
the outside of truth, it is set down with a special, often
hilariously frank, inside information on the sex it vilifies.
What Miss Boothe has done is to tell the story of a nice
married woman who, owing to the gossip of her women
friends, loses her husband to a cheap gold-digger and then
finally recovers him. Miss Boothe's method, however, is as
original as her dialogue is unorthodox in its choice of subjects.

The self-imposed feat which she performs with considerable ingenuity is to exile all men from her text. Her comedy is as completely feminine as *Journey's End* was masculine. It is a paradise, entirely filled with Eves and serpents and apples, in which no Adam dares to put in his appearance. But, though it is as innocent of men as the Hotel Martha Washington is supposed to be, or as *L'Aiglon* was of the physical presence of the first Napoleon, believe me, it is far from innocent.

As it weaves its way in and out of a bridge game, a hairdresser's establishment, a fitting room, a reducing class, a pantry, a bedroom in a lying-in hospital, a Reno hotel, the gold-digger's bathroom with the gold-digger clothed in soap suds in her tub, its heroine's boudoir, and ultimately the ladies' powder room in a night club, it manages to touch on a good many subjects not ordinarily touched upon behind the footlights. These topics range from obstetrical whispers to rest-room confidences, and are at all times enlivened by "She-She" jokes on "He-She" subjects which for the most part are as entertainingly phrased as they are unconventionally conventional. Yet, regardless of how superficial or funny-paperish, or false and tricky *The Women* may be as a comment on life, there can be no denying that as a stunt in showmanship it makes for an arresting and rewarding evening.

It is a play which has the advantage of one of Max Gordon's most satisfying and smoothly professional productions. It has been felicitously staged by Robert Sinclair. Its many changes of scene are handled with genuine skill by Jo Mielziner. And it is uncommonly well-acted by a large and expert cast. If Miss Boothe had been aiming at truth or valid comedy instead of at what is only effective theatre, she would have made her heroine worthy of her antagonists by supplying her with sense as well as decency. But, no matter how she might have written the part, neither

Miss Boothe nor anyone else could ask for a better performance of it than Margalo Gillmore gives. It is a tender, wise and mellow characterization which finds Miss Gillmore at her gifted best. As Miss Gillmore's mother Jessie Busley is breezily compassionate. And as her young daughter Charita Bauer is touchingly direct.

When it comes to the harpies, in which the text abounds, and all of whom are capably acted, Ilka Chase stands out because of her brilliant playing of a sharp-tongued troublemaker who suffers from acidosis of the *esprit*. Some special mention must be made, too, of Phyllis Povah as a careless matron who is always doing her bit by posterity; of Jane Seymour as a venomous lady novelist; of Margaret Douglass as an ever-marrying harridan whose password is "l'amour"; and of Betty Lawford as the merciless gold-digger. All of them contribute much to the pleasures of this heartless but highly enjoyable comedy which is full of kennel fodder.

December 28, 1936

MR. STEINBECK'S *OF MICE AND MEN*

AS ANY reader of Mr. Steinbeck's novel knows, *Of Mice and Men* was fated to be either extraordinarily good when transferred to the stage or extraordinarily bad. It had to be one thing or the other. There could be no halfway measure about it. It was bound to be a case of all or nothing. The chances were it would be the latter. May we hasten to report that as Mr. Kaufman has directed it, as Mr. Oenslager has set it, and as it is acted at the Music Box by a cast which is as happily chosen as it is capable, it takes its place proudly in the front ranks of the season's offerings? More than that, *Of Mice and Men* is one of the finest, most pungent, and most poignant realistic productions to invigorate our stage in many seasons.

In book form Mr. Steinbeck's story was obviously dramatic. Mr. Steinbeck has confessed in print that he built the dialogue and planned the episodes of his horrendous, yet strangely tender, tale on what amounts to the ground plans of a playwright. His dramatization proves how right is his contention. He had comparatively little to do to turn *Of Mice and Men* into a play. He had mainly to tear away the brick and plaster af his novel-writing and leave bare the girders and the cement of his narrative. It was here that some of us were blind. Although we had sensed the drama and the architectural structure of Mr. Steinbeck's book, we dreaded to see it on the stage. We kept asking ourselves, How will they do this? How will they do that? How will the mood and atmosphere of the novel, which are so beautifully maintained in Mr. Steinbeck's prose, be preserved when the theatre attempts to take possession of this gay, tragic story of the friendship of two tramps who get a job as hands binding barley on a California ranch?

Who will play George and the poor, brutish, halfwit Lennie so that their relationship retains the elusive tragic power Mr. Steinbeck has given it? How can Lennie's daydreams of a rabbit farm be kept from being merely laughable when we must listen to them? How can those episodes keep their full terror in which he must be seen stroking the soft fur of a mouse or a puppy whose neck he has just broken unintentionally with his giant hands? How will it be possible to capture on the stage the heavy heartbreak of that moment when old Candy's veteran dog is taken away to be shot? Won't the secondary characters lose their completeness? What will happen in the theatre to that last scene in which as a final act of friendship George must save Lennie from the mob that seeks him as the murderer of Curley's fair-haired wife by shooting him through the back of the head while he talks to him of rabbits and the farm? Can canvas and paint ever capture the out-of-doors and the bunkhouse reality so essential to the novel? Is George S. Kaufman, the super-sophisticate and First Satirist of our Theatre, the director to do justice to these of all materials?

We must admit we entertained many such misgivings when we entered the Music Box last night. But they were groundless, every one of them. The play Mr. Steinbeck has made by whittling away his descriptions is an uncommonly good one. Its plotting has a design to it which is as sinister as it is symmetrical. Like the book, it wrings beauty from ugliness; beauty of a weird, vibrant, and uncanny kind. Nor is its perfection of form the only source of power *Of Mice and Men* can claim on the stage. Its dialogue has a Chekovian richness to it. It is salty, flavorsome, earth-sprung, and authentic speech. If its outspokenness is rare, its effectiveness is no less exceptional. Only occasionally, as in the scene in the barn between Lennie and Curley's wife, does the tangential dialogue appear mannered. Elsewhere it is as fresh as it is tender, as strong as it is high-spirited, as natural as it is right. It is the kind of fully-flavored, vivid, realistic speech which our arty makers of folk plays have tried again and again to create in vain. Mr. Steinbeck's characters seem to be speaking for themselves. Yet by means of their pungent phrases, they, their aspirations, and their simple, frustrated lives stand revealed as proofs of Mr. Steinbeck's unusual artistry.

As a dramatist Mr. Steinbeck enjoys the good fortune of finding that what he did superlatively well as a novelist has been done for him no less superlatively by the theatre. His novel gains a new amplitude on the stage. It emerges behind its footlights as the most poignant statement of human loneliness our contemporary theatre has produced. Mr. Kaufman's direction is a joy to follow. Never has he shown himself to be more expert or more sensitive. In the difficult terms of a different medium he manages to realize all the subtleties of the book. His timing is perfect. His pausing of the episode in which Candy's old dog is shot is as audacious as it is praiseworthy. Without any hocus-pocus about Stanislavsky and "the inner line," Broadway's Mr. Kaufman achieves a production which should be the envy of our more self-conscious art theatres. In doing this he is aided by Donald Oenslager's admirable settings. They are among the finest realistic backgrounds Mr. Oenslager has so far designed in his distinguished career. Literal as they seem to be, they look beneath the surface and contribute richly to the emotional needs and meaning of the various episodes. They make tangible the elusive, yet all-important, mood and atmosphere of Mr. Steinbeck's novel.

Mr. Kaufman's casting is felicitous in almost every case. His production gains in significance and interest by being starless. His actors work together to create an ensemble in which nothing is allowed to detract from the driving power of the play as a whole. Broderick Crawford, who is Helen Broderick's son, gives a performance of exceptional skill as the Gargantuan, child-like Lennie. In every unsparing detail he suggests the blind devotion, the feeble-mindedness, the depravity, and the brute strength of Mr. Steinbeck's amazing character. Wallace Ford is no less successful in meeting the even more difficult assignment presented by George. John F. Hamilton's Candy is another fine characterization. So is the Slim of Will Geer and the Crooks of Leigh Whipper. Although all the actors at the Music Box are good, I for one wish Curley had been entrusted to a more arrogant type of bantam than Sam Byrd suggests, and that, effective as she is, Claire Luce were not so obviously Broadway's idea of what Curley's overgenerous wife should be.

Such reservations, if indeed they are reservations, are very minor ones in the case of so fine a production of so interesting a play. *Of Mice and Men* is one of the season's events. An event for adults, not for children of all ages. After all, adults do deserve some consideration in the theatre. What is more, they get it at the Music Box.

November 24, 1937

THORNTON WILDER'S *OUR TOWN*

NO scenery is required for this play. Perhaps a few dusty flats may be seen leaning against the brick wall at the back of the stage. . . . The Stage Manager not only moves forward and withdraws the few properties that are required, but he reads from a typescript the lines of all the minor characters. He reads them clearly, but with little attempt at characterization, scarcely troubling himself to alter his voice, even when he responds in the person of a child or a woman. As the curtain rises the Stage Manager is leaning lazily against the proscenium pillar at the audience's left. He is smoking.

The chances are that if, during the course of one of those parlor games which offer to hostesses and guests alike an ideal retreat from bridge and conversation, some playgoers were asked to identify the play for which these stage directors were intended, they would not guess *Julius Caesar* at the Mercury. Yet they might be sufficiently foolhardy, in this season of sceneryless scripts, to pick upon Mr. Blitz-

stein's *The Cradle Will Rock* or Mr. Wilder's *Our Town*.
If they choose *Our Town*, because the demand for a Stage
Manager, leaning against the proscenium and smoking a
pipe, brought the genial Frank Craven to their minds, they
would at least be "getting warm," as the gamesters have it.
Still they would be very far from being "hot." Although
Mr. Wilder is the author of these stage directions, *Our
Town* is not the play for which they were intended. They
were written for a charming one-act of his called *The Happy
Journey To Trenton And Camden* which was copyrighted
in 1931 and which can be found not only in a volume of his
short plays called *The Long Christmas Dinner* but also in
Professor Woollcott's first *Reader*.

I go back to Mr. Wilder's earlier usage of this frankly
presentational form only because some theatregoers have
been tempted to talk and write about *Our Town* as if it were
a production which found Mr. Wilder and Mr. Harris trying to climb upon the Mercury's band wagon. It is important to note that when Mr. Wilder sent the script of
The Happy Journey to Washington seven years ago, all he
was attempting to copyright was the use to which he put
this particular form in this particular script, and not the
form itself. What really matters in all art is this very thing.
Forms and subjects are comparatively few. Yet they can
be made as various as are the talents of the many artists
who have repossessed them.

Playgoers with short memories have found Benrimo's
popularization of the conventions of the Chinese stage in
The Yellow Jacket a convenient means of pigeonholing the
outward form of *Our Town*. They might just as readily have
recalled Quince, drawing up a bill of properties for *Pyra-
mus and Thisbe*, "such as our play wants." Or the Chorus
in *Henry V* asking the audience to let their "imaginary
forces work." Or Mei Lan-Fang. Or Ruth Draper and Cor-

nelia Otis Skinner. Or the Lutterworth Christmas Play.
Or the *Quem Quaeritis* trope. The form Mr. Wilder has used
is as old as the theatre's ageless game of "let's pretend" and
as new as the last time it has been employed effectively. The
co-operation it asks an audience to contribute is at heart
the very same co-operation which the most realistic and
heavily documented productions invite playgoers to grant.
The major difference is one of degree. Both types of production depend in the last analysis upon their audiences to
supply that final belief which is the mandate under which
all theatrical illusion operates. The form Mr. Wilder uses
is franker, that is all. It does not attempt to hide the fact
it is make-believe. Instead it asks its audiences to do some
of the work, to enter openly and gladly into the imaginative
conspiracy known as the successful staging of a play.

What such a drama as Mr. Wilder's does, of course, is to
strip theatrical illusion down to its essentials. Mr. Wilder
has the best of good reasons for so doing. What he has done
in *Our Town* is to strip life down to its essentials, too. There
is nothing of the "stunt" about the old-new form he has
employed. His form is the inevitable one his content demands. Indeed so inevitable is it, and hence so right, that
I, for one, must confess I lost all awareness of it merely as
a form a few minutes after Mr. Craven had begun to set
the stage by putting a few chairs in place. There have been
those who have been bothered because the pantomime was
not consistent, because real umbrellas were carried and no
visible lawn-mower was pushed, because naturalistic offstage sounds serve as echoes to the actions indicated on
stage. I was not one of the bothered. I found myself surrendering, especially during the first two acts, to the spell
of the beautiful and infinitely tender play Mr. Wilder has
written.

John Anderson has likened *Our Town* to India's rope-trick. He has pointed out it is the kind of play at which you either see the boy and the rope, or at which you don't. Although I refuse to admit there is anything of the fakir's touch in *Our Town*, I think I understand what Mr. Anderson means. Mr. Wilder's is, from the audience point of view, an exceptionally personal play. More than most plays, since by its sweet simplicity it seeks to get in contact with the inmost nerves of our living, it is the kind of drama which depends upon what we bring to it.

Mr. Wilder's play is concerned with the universal importance of those unimportant details which figure in the lives of men and women everywhere. His Grover's Corners is a New Hampshire town inhabited by decent New England people. The very averageness of these quiet, patient people is the point at which our lives and all living become a part of their experience. Yet Mr. Wilder's play involves more than a New England township. It burrows into the essence of the growing-up, the marrying, the living, and the dying of all of us who sit before it and are included by it. The task to which Mr. Wilder has set himself is one which Hardy had in mind in a far less human, more grandiose way, when he had the Chorus in *The Dynasts* say:

> *We'll close up Time, as a bird its van,*
> *We'll traverse Space, as Spirits can,*
> *Link pulses severed by leagues and years,*
> *Bring cradles into touch with biers.*

Mr. Wilder succeeds admirably in doing this. He shows us the simple pattern behind all simple living. He permits us to share in what are the inevitable anguishes and joys, the hopes and cruel separations to which men have been heir since the smoke puffed up the chimneys in Greece.

To my surprise I have encountered the complaint that

Mr. Wilder's Grover's Corners is not like Middletown, U.S.A. It lacks brothels, race riots, huge factories, front-page scandals, social workers, union problems, lynchings, agitators, and strikes. The ears of its citizens are more familiar with the song of the robin than they are with the sirens of hurrying police cars. Its young people are stimulated to courtship by moonlight rather than by moonshine. They drink soda water instead of gin. Their rendezvous are held in drug stores rather than in night clubs. Their parents are hard-working people. They are quiet, self-respecting, God-fearing Yankees who get up early to do their day's work and meet their responsibilities and their losses without whining. The church organist may tipple, and thereby cause some gossip. But he is a neighbor, and the only good neighbor policy they care about begins at home.

They do not murder or steal, borrow or beg, blackmail or oppress. Furthermore they face the rushing years without complaints as comparatively happy mortals. Therefore to certain realists they seem unreal. "No historian," one critic has written "has ever claimed that a town like Mr. Wilder's was ever so idyllic as to be free from intolerance and injustice." Mr. Wilder does not make this claim himself. His small-town editor admits Grover's Corners is "little better behaved than most towns." Neither is Mr. Wilder working as the ordinary historian works. His interests are totally different interests.

He is not concerned with social trends, with economic conditions, with pivotal events, or glittering personalities. He sings not of arms and the man, but of those small events which loom so large in the daily lives of each of us, and which are usually unsung. His interest is the unexceptional, the average, the personal. His preoccupation is what lies beneath the surface and the routine of our lives, and is common to all our hearts and all our experience. It is not so much of the streets of a New England Town he writes as of the clean white spire which rises above them.

There are hundreds of fat books written each year on complicated subjects by authors who are not writers at all. But the ageless achievement of the true writers has always been to bring a new illumination to the simplest facts of life. That illumination has ever been a precious talent given only to a few. It is because Mr. Wilder brings this illumination to his picture of Grover's Corners that I admire *Our Town*. New Hampshire is the State which can claim Mr. Wilder's village, but his vision of it has been large enough to include all of us, no matter where we may come from, among its inhabitants. Personally, I should as soon think of condemning the Twenty-third Psalm because it lacks the factual observation of Sinclair Lewis and the social point of view of Granville Hicks as I would of accusing *Our Town* of being too unrealistically observed.

Anyone who hears only the milk bottles clink when early morning has come once again to Grover's Corners has not heard what Mr. Wilder wants them to hear. These milk bottles are merely the spokesmen of time, symbols for the bigness of little things. In terms of the Gibbses and the Webbs, Mr. Wilder gives the pattern of repetition of each small day's planning, each small life's fruition and decline. He makes us feel the swift passage of the years, our blindness in meeting their race, the sense that our lives go rushing past so quickly that we have scarcely time in which to hold our breaths.

Only once does he fail us seriously. This is in his scene in the bleak graveyard on the hill. Although he seeks there to create the image of the dead who have lost their interest in life, he has not been able to capture the true greatness of vision which finds them at last unfettered from the minutiae of existence. Both his phrasing and his thinking are inadequate here. He chills the living by removing his dead even from compassion.

Nonetheless Mr. Wilder's is a remarkable play; one of the sagest, warmest, and most deeply human scripts to have come out of our theatre. It is a fine play, and Mr. Harris, and such of his fine actors as Evelyn Varden, John Craven, Martha Scott, and, above all, Frank Craven (who plays the Stage Manager with the warmth of sunset), have given it a fine production. It is the kind of play which suspends us in time, making us weep for our own vanished youth at the same time we are sobbing for the short-lived pleasures and sufferings which we know await our children. Geographically *Our Town* can be found at an imaginary place known as "Grover's Corners, Sultan County, New Hampshire, United States of America, Continent of North America, Western Hemisphere, the Earth, the Solar System, the Universe, the Mind of God." At the Morosco you will find Mr. Wilder's play is laid in no imaginary place. It becomes a reality in the human heart.

March 14, 1938

5. "Sing Me a Song with Social Significance"

THESE FULL LEAN YEARS

ALTHOUGH none of us realized it at the time, the two most important events known to the American theatre in our day did not take place on Broadway. They were not openings in the usual stiff-shirt sense. They were closings of an extraordinary kind. The scene of one of them was Wall Street, October 29, 1929, when the Stock Market crashed with so Gargantuan a thud that its echoes still thunder in our ears. The other occurred some four and a half years later in those marble halls where we had dreamt security dwelt, and was identified, with an optimism uniquely American, as "The Bank Holiday."

Closings these events may have been. Yet with all that they symbolized and all that was to come after them, they set free America's conscience and pried open the American mind to new vistas of thought, no less surely than they left locked and bolted forever the doors leading to our old ways of life and our old habits of thinking.

The boom days were gone; their assumptions discredited. Question marks were written large after the most venerable and hitherto unassailable of our national axioms. A search —selfish, uncontrolled, and mad—for overnight profits had proved worse than disturbing. It had proved unprofitable.

America, rich and poor, tightened its belt and opened its mind. The breadlines, which fed the stomachs of the poor, nourished doubts in the consciences of rich and poor alike. Starvation in the midst of plenty was food for thought.

Young America, like the rest of the world, was sick; sick from old abuses, sick with the disillusionment of a war fought seemingly in vain, sick from a peace treaty which had made the world safe for dictators, sick from a host of diseases which had suddenly become manifest in its own social and economic system. Discontent was in the air. Locusts covered the countryside. Injustices, long tolerated or overlooked, were dragged into the light. The "haves" became increasingly aware of the "have nots," as strike followed strike in the front-page news and then entered one distant home after another in terms of passed dividends. Labor was on the move. Unrest was all around us. Agitators of every kind were plentiful; so were the causes for agitation. Fanatical groups screamed their dogmas shrilly. Termites seemed to be eating into the foundations of our national structure. The "Good Society" did not appear to be so good. But the public good became everyone's concern. So did politics and economics. The underprivileged suddenly enjoyed the privilege of having the nation's attention. Beliefs for which only small and "radical" minorities would have protested—and then in vain—a few years back, became the commonplaces of our national life, as our legislation, our taxation, and our government agencies indicated. The Forgotten Man was remembered, even if the Remembered Man was forgotten.

A new voice was coming from Washington, and its Groton-Harvard accent fell on new ears. The many who refused to be included among the President's fireside "friends," could not, as his countrymen, escape the problems with which he had newly dealt. Above everything debatable in this policy or that short-lived panacea, above everything reprehensible or alarming in such-and-such a sample of political chicanery, above the hatreds and disagreements of party strife, above everything confusing in the confusion of shifting means and constant contradiction, that voice, and the administration for which it spoke, and the conditions which had swept it into office, made one thing clear. They had given America a liberal education such as all the schools in the land had hitherto failed to give it. Whether it liked it or not, whether it admired the President or detested his policies, had nothing to do with the fact that the American conscience had been jolted into activity. In the days of prosperity, it had refused to look for work. In the days following the depression, it could no longer be counted among the unemployed.

Long before the Government had placed the theatre on relief, the theatre in this country had given relief to playwrights who in the post-depression years were burning with indignation and anxious to have their say on economic and political subjects. They may have been men appalled by what had happened to justice, as was I. J. Golden when, in *Precedent*, he made eloquent use of the testimony in Tom Mooney's fight for freedom; or as John Wexley was when, in *They Shall Not Die*, he worked the ugly facts of the Scottsboro case into a stirring melodrama. They may have exposed municipal corruption with the bitter mockery Albert Maltz and George Sklar brought to *Merry-Go-Round*, or condemned the Nazi's persecution of the Jews as did such scripts as *Kultur* and *Birthright*. They may have written such a play about strikers as Mr. Wexley wrote in *Steel*. They may have dashed off one bruising melodrama after another showing the horrors of lynching in the Deep South. They may have run through a whole catalogue of national abuses as did Elmer Rice in *We, The People*.

They may have banded themselves into such a militant Leftist group as the Theatre Union represented when it acquired Miss Le Gallienne's abandoned Civic Repertory down on Fourteenth Street and devoted itself quite frankly to operating as a playhouse of the barricades. They may have brought to the stage, as Mr. Odets has brought, a talent equaled only by their resentment of "The System." Many of these propagandist scripts may have been childishly unfair. More of them may have been crude. Most of them have been feeble. But all of them have given a new vitality to our theatre. Their significance cannot be overstressed. They have not only widened the limited horizons of our stage. They have burst upon it, bringing to it new subjects, new performers, new aims, new interests, new techniques, and, above all, new audiences.

That propagandist scripts were known to America before the depression, everyone realizes. Each season had produced them, for propaganda in the theatre is as old as the Greeks and as new as today's cause which can win a champion. That we had seen dramas filled with fresh impulses and written from a fresh point no one can forget who sat before John Howard Lawson's *Processional*, Mr. Rice's *The Adding Machine*, or Toller's *Man and The Masses* at the Guild, and John Dos Passos' *The Moon is a Gong*. Or who saw (perhaps for the first time) a Sunday morning fashion parade on Fifth Avenue through the eyes of Mr. O'Neill's stoker in *The Hairy Ape*. There was even a playhouse down in Greenwich Village where, as endowed by Otto Kahn of all people, those dramatists who used to be referred to laughingly as "The Revolting Playwrights" produced their bitter indictments of Capitalism and Big Business. Few people took them seriously.

Since the crash and "The Bank Holiday," however, and right down to the Federal Theatre's *Living Newspapers*, or such productions as *The Cradle Will Rock* at the Mercury and *Pins and Needles* at the Labor Stage, there has been a marked difference not only in our propagandist writing but in our theatre. The "Yellow Book" days of the twenties now seem very remote. The ivory towers have crumbled. The protest is no longer of a purely aesthetic kind. Karl Marx, not Gordon Craig or Adolf Appia, is the storm center of the new insurgents. Ideology has replaced aesthetics. The American scene seems somehow to have become more important than American scenery.

Troubled times, hunger, and old abuses do not make for moderation. It is men with grievances who become agitators. Their hope is to make their own agitation contagious. They are not apt to understate, or to weigh both sides. To the unfairnesses they attack, they are willing to add their own unfairness. From their point of view this seems more than justifiable. If they hit hard it is because their beliefs are militant. That they have not often talked as liberals is not surprising. If one excepts Shakespeare's Brutus as subdued by Orson Welles, the liberal has had a hard time holding his own of recent seasons as a stage character. With his eagerness to weigh the evidence and to grant the opposition its right to state its case, he has had difficulty making himself heard. Speaking with affection for what he hopes the new America will preserve of the old, his voice has been drowned out by the strident cries of those dogmatists who have had anger in their hearts and Red Russia in their minds. Dogmas are noisier than doubts; intolerance can yell down tolerance any day.

But there is more to these propagandist scripts than this. Judged as plays most of them may have been mediocre or inept. Judged as propagandist scripts they may be said to have failed if their authors have persuaded only those who already shared their convictions before they took their seats. For the test of a play of propaganda is not the yes-men who come to it conquered, but the no-men who leave it forced to say "yes." It takes a superior play to accomplish this, which is quite another thing from a previously shared conviction. Yet good, bad, or worse than indifferent as these propagandists scripts may have been, they have proven as socially significant as they may yet prove theatrically important.

All these many years we have been hearing about the theatre's being the most democratic of the arts, forgetting that the only democrats it included were those who could afford to go either to its box offices or to Tyson's. To them, and to them only, has it had any possible appeal, and for them, and for them only, has it attempted to speak. It has stated their viewpoint, echoed or affronted their prejudices, reflected their living, considered their pleasures, and confined itself to catering to their interests. Its admission fees have soared and its old galleries disappeared. Little by little it has closed its doors on all but purse-proud democrats.

If the Federal Theatre had done nothing else, it should have made clear to commercial managers that there are thousands upon thousands of people anxious to come back to the theatre as audiences, if only the ticket rates are within their means. The Federal Theatre has not been alone in teaching this lesson. It has done so along with numerous other groups who have devoted themselves to speaking for the millions of men and women forgotten on Broadway. That these men and women are entitled to consideration, no one can deny. The pursuit of happiness follows life and liberty on their bill of rights.

Of recent years a new department of our theatre has appeared, addressing itself to this new, huge, long-overlooked audience. That it has done so is one of the most encouraging developments to have taken place on our stage during the past decade. The groups who have effected this change have exiled themselves deliberately from Broadway's standards and interests. Their first objective has not been entertainment. They have turned their backs on escape. They have sought to have the theatre function as a place of reminder rather than a palace of forgetfulness. They have been sponsored by or concerned with those very same proud members of a craft who served Tom Dekker as his heroes in *The Shoemakers' Holiday,* even if these craftsmen often appear to have lost their gentleness. They have devoted themselves to the interests and the worries, the grudges and the simplicities, the grievances and the hopes of this new public.

As producers and dramatists some of them may have been as untrained as their audiences were unaccustomed to playgoing. They have had scant knowledge of the "Art" of the theatre, and cared even less for it. They may have made the fatal mistake of offering their American spectators little or no humor. Their subscribers may have soon wearied of the ever-repeated devices of their earlier, crasser melodramas. Still, these labor groups have invaded the theatre with such vigor that the so-called "carriage trade" must at times wonder if it does not really belong back in the days of the horse and buggy. Whether these proletarian theatres have produced good plays or bad, one thing is certain. They have not left our consciences alone. They were provocative when they were angry. They became important when they learned to laugh.

When Hazlitt reprinted his dramatic reviews in book form, he insisted in his preface that his opinion of Edmund Kean had not changed since first he saw him. "Why should it?" he asked. "I had the same eyes to see with, the same ears to hear with, and the same understanding to judge with." Unfortunately for readers of this book, as they well know, and for myself, as I know equally well, I am not William Hazlitt. Rereading the reviews which follow, I am not persuaded I would have seen the plays they cover through the same eyes, or heard them with the same ears, or judged them with the same understanding. With my statement of their merits or demerits purely as plays I would in all probability agree. Yet I trust—in fact, I know—that many of the prejudices through which I saw them have been dislodged. So, too, have the easy assumptions which they and these troubled years have challenged—and slowly routed. For doing this, for extending my horizons by having widened the theatre's, and for having opened my eyes and quickened my conscience, I feel grateful to the hatred and the violence, and the bad art of even the sorriest and most sullen specimens in the lot, with the overstated opinions of which I still disagree, and abhor.

GENTLEMEN OF THE GENTLE CRAFT

THE SHOEMAKERS' HOLIDAY

THE Walt Whitman who once complained that Shakespeare's "comedies are altogether non-acceptable to America and Democracy" because they "have the unmistakable hue of plays . . . made for the divertisement only of the elite of the castle, and from its point of view," could find nothing to object to in *The Shoemakers' Holiday*. Dekker's "pleasant comedy about the gentle craft" is a play to warm Whitman's huge democratic heart. In the most Lincolnian sense it is a drama of the people, by the people, and for the people.

Its artisans are happy men, fortunate in their master,

proud of their profession. "Are not these my brave men, brave shoemakers, all gentlemen of the gentle craft?" cries Simon Eyre, the genial cobbler, to his wife when she is quarreling with him and his journeymen. "Prince am I none, yet am I nobly born, as being the sole son of a shoemaker. Away, rubbish! Vanish, melt; melt like kitchen-stuff."

That is the spirit of Dekker's play, and a contagious spirit it proves to be. His is a mad, roistering comedy, fed on red meat, soaked in ale, and filled with the sunshine of a simpler age. Mirth—lusty, earth-sprung, vigorous mirth—is its author's sole objective. And abundant mirth he provides by the inexhaustible energy of his phrasing, by the capering skill with which he draws low comedy figures, and the sheer, dancing lightness of his own heart.

Three hundred and thirty-eight years have passed since *The Shoemakers' Holiday* was first acted before "The Queenes Most Excellent Majestie." As a rule that is far more time than is needed to tarnish a joke. But in the Mercury's production, Dekker's comedy survives the centuries with amazing brightness.

It remains a lusty, joyous creation. It bursts with the vitality of the age it mirrors. It is warm with the cheer of the plain-spoken citizens who are its heroes. Their pride in their craft as shoemakers illumines the genial excesses of its dialogue. The "Merrie England," which some have endeavored to say was not so merry under Bess as tradition claims, has never seemed as carefree or as merry as it does in this vivid picture of the life of Elizabeth's artisans. As drawn by Dekker and projected at the Mercury, these light-hearted, ale-loving, uninhibited workmen are the most uproarious of companions. For all its baffling complexities of plot and subplot, the play in which they caper continues to be what its author would have saluted, and we gladly welcome, as "fine, tickling sport."

Probably no one needs to be reminded that, in its jubilant way, *The Shoemakers' Holiday* is one of the first democratic comedies. Its *dramatis personæ* includes a King, to be sure, who is a very likable and convenient fellow. Yet even he has a hard time elbowing his way into the story. When he does at last bob up in the midst of this proud, rowdy, cheerful, sweaty crew of ancient Londoners, he functions not as an awesome sovereign but as an amiable *deus ex machina*. Dekker turns to him not because as a man he cringes before the throne but because as a dramatist he needs someone to extricate him from the difficulties into which his plot has got him.

The common people are the subject of Dekker's comedy. They hold their heads high, even if their minds are not always elevated. They sing and drink, joke and fondle, and take their troubles lightly. In Simon Eyre they enjoy a good master, and one of the most lovable comic characters in English dramatic literature. Yet they are free men with independent spirits who are willing to stage a sit-down strike at a moment's notice in the interest of an abused fellow craftsman. Theirs is a philosophy of joy. With Eyre they seem convinced, "A pound of care pays not a dram of debt. Hum, let's be merry whiles we are young; old age, sack and sugar, will steal upon us, ere we be aware."

How the Earl of Lincoln's near kinsman disguises himself as a shoemaker to win the hand of a commoner's daughter is one of Dekker's plots. Another has to do with a young journeyman who almost loses his wife and a leg when he is sent off to the wars. There are other stories, such as Eyre's rise to the role of Lord Mayor, which get going with difficulty, and which are somewhat difficult to orient. But what makes *The Shoemakers' Holiday* the *"merry-conceited comedy"* its author claims it to be, is its magnificently hardy realization of the life and manners of old London's simple citizenry.

The problem which Orson Welles and his admirable actors at the Mercury have faced is the ever-pressing problem which a director and his players must always face when they seek to keep an ancient comedy comic. Mr. Welles and his players may spoof it a bit so as to send it on its way across the footlights to modern audiences. But the point is they keep it going for the most part at a merry clip. What they set before their public is probably more Elizabethan in blood pressure than in spirit. Yet it is the gayest and most unblushing excursion into Elizabethan low comedy which contemporary playgoers have been privileged to enjoy.

If you are interested in the drama's past; if you would know what *Pins and Needles* stems from; if you would discover what the groundlings were like for whom Shakespeare wrote his *Caesar;* and have a very good time into the bargain, the Mercury's production of this comedy about the lowborn gentlemen who functioned as proud members of "the gentle craft" is something you will be too self-indulgent to miss.

January 3 and 7, 1938

MR. RICE'S *WE, THE PEOPLE*

ELMER RICE, let it be quickly stated, does not like the Capitalistic system. As a dramatist whose powers of observation have been justly applauded, he has noticed what even the most unobservant of men have recently been forced to observe. The hillside is no longer dew-pearl'd and all is not right with the world. Having arrived at such a startling conclusion and being keenly aware of the suffering which everywhere exists in these years of the locust, Mr. Rice has decided to use the theatre as a means of picturing conditions as he sees them. So far, so good. Certainly the aches and evils of the present day should offer a dramatist capable of dealing with them, the stuffs out of which a stirring play could be made.

Mr. Rice's theme in *We, the People* is a large one which no one can escape. Outside of the theatre, it is everyone's concern. Its raw materials, in their essence, are bound to bruise our sympathies and command our attention. Yet in themselves they are not enough. What is done to these materials matters more than what they offer to a dramatist. Even in these days of economic misery and social change, bigness of theme does not in itself make for a big play, or even a self-respecting one.

If a playwright, who takes it upon himself to indict a whole system of living, is to make his point persuasively, he cannot forget that before everything else he is a playwright. He cannot, as Mr. Rice has been tempted to do, outline innumerable "neediest cases" and feel his task is done. His first duty is to his audience. He must move and interest it in terms of the medium in which he has chosen to have his say. He must adapt his preachment (if preachment he has) to the stage, forget the rhetoric of the soapbox, and remember the needs of the theatre. He must have a heart as well as a head; a head as well as a heart. To be persuasive, and hence win the confidence of his listeners, he must at least make a pretense of being fair. He owes this not only to his audience, but also to whatever side of the social argument he may personally favor.

One of the major faults with *We, the People* is that Mr.

Rice has loaded his dice so obviously that he forces the most willing of liberals to turn into the most ardent of reactionaries, in the interest of fair play. All of his capitalists are such deep-dyed villains and each and every one of his honest toilers is such an innocent and noble victim of upper-class wickedness that at times it is difficult to tell whether Mr. Rice is writing like Dion Boucicault or as one of the erstwhile "New Playwrights." Perhaps the truth is he is writing in the most childishly flamboyant tradition of both.

With one eye closed tight and the other seeing red, Mr. Rice looks at present-day America. For nineteen out of his twenty scattered scenes he presents case after case of social injustice in the manner unworthy of a Sixth Avenue Galsworthy. Not only does he shake his fists angrily at "dat ole davvil, Capitalism," but he also does his own cause much harm by insisting upon hitting below the belt

Mr. Rice has attempted to give unity to the numerous abuses he records by relying upon the depression, even as Vicki Baum relied upon the hotel in *Grand Hotel* and as Mr. Kaufman and Miss Ferber used the dinner party in *Dinner at Eight*. The result is a drama which finds Mr. Rice turning propagandist to such an extent that he has forgotten to function as a playwright. Although his play is an indictment, it is not fired with contagious indignation. It leaves an audience strangely cold when one considers that its obvious aim is to inflame. Stippled with misfortunes as it is, it seems as impersonal as the front page of a newspaper.

Mr. Rice lets loose his grapeshot in one undeveloped scene after another, but only a few stray bullets hit the bull's eye. His catalogue of woes is as long as it is one-sided. He mentions country boys killed by capitalistic greed in Haiti. He shows us a shell-shocked drunkard whose condition is the result of having been a soldier in the last war (a capitalistic war, of course). He points out the racial prejudices which mitigate against the Jew and the Negro in this country. He cites the case of a hard-working schoolteacher who is forced to live in sin with her white-collar fiance because neither one of them is paid enough to get married. He follows the declining fortunes of her one-time patriotic parents. He holds up the police as agents of suppression. He introduces us to a dank group of capitalists who use the transatlantic telephone to buy Titians and who have yachts and extravagant daughters. He tells us they control not only our industries but the nomination of our Presidents. He gives us an insight into the "enlightened liberalism" of the asinine candidate they have selected. He paints this same candidate as the head of a State university so that the evils of education and its threats to free speech can also be attacked. In general he damns everything he can think of in America as it is today.

At the end of this melancholy evening, Mr. Rice suddenly tries to make us believe he has really been writing a play about a luckless poor boy named Allen Davis, who is the little schoolteacher's brother and who by this time has become another victim of our economic system. The boy in question has been forced by the depression to leave college. He has looked for work and found none; stolen coal from a trainyard in order to keep his family warm; been sent to a reformatory for this offense; and has now been sentenced to death, after having been unjustly accused of killing a policeman who has arrested him while he was talking against the Government.

Mr. Rice's last scene, which is his most effective, is his only completely honest one, if for no other reason than that in it he abandons the play he has failed to write and openly takes to a platform to argue his case to his audience at a mass meeting. Mr. Rice's plea is for the right of everyone to a living; his enemy, unequal wealth; his vague hope, a socially and economically reorganized America. With the Declaration of Independence as his text and authority, he advocates a new government, under which all men will be born free and equal, and enjoy the rights of "life, liberty and the pursuit of happiness." He does not say what it will be, or how it is to correct contemporary wrongs. He merely tears down and puts nothing in the place of what he has destroyed. Taking a tip from Mr. Coward, Mr. Rice concludes his harangue with a prayer for a more decent America; a prayer, incidentally, which Saturday night won much applause from an expensively dressed but bewildered audience at the Empire.

There can be no denying that there are effective moments scattered here and there in this doleful tirade (which Mr. Rice probably considers an American *Cavalcade*). The pity is that Mr. Rice, the playwright, has failed so signally to come to the assistance of Mr. Rice, the traveled propagandist. Hence neither as playwright nor as propagandist has he realized the truly anguishing possibilities of his theme.

January 23, 1933

MR. ANDERSON'S *BOTH YOUR HOUSES*

BY HAVING kept his temper in the writing of *Both Your Houses*, Maxwell Anderson has got the better not only of his subject and his audience but also of his fellow-dramatists who of recent years have attempted to turn the stage into a forum for the discussion of public questions. With the calm detachment usually reserved for the penning of drawing-room comedies, he has held up to the patrons of the Theatre Guild as merciless and disheartening a picture of governmental corruption as anyone could imagine. It is a shocking, bitter indictment, calculated to raise doubts in the hearts of even the staunchest supporters of the democratic ideal.

It implies, with no little good humor and with an awful quietness, that honesty is almost impossible in our Government as it at present functions. It presents our lawmakers as a group of respected racketeers who, with no mind to the needs of the Treasury nor the interests of the country at large, devote their energies to petty bickerings, contemptible bargainings and graft of a most blatant kind.

How long, wonders Mr. Anderson, speaking through the young idealist who is his hero and who meets defeat when he endeavors to block the passage of an unusually crooked appropriations bill, how long can the country continue under such a system? Has not the time come for house-cleaning, if not for changes of a more radical sort? Apathetic as the taxpayers are, they will some day wake up. And when they do, Mr. Anderson hints, the Washington merry-go-round will be rudely upset.

What is unusual about Mr. Anderson's play is not that he has elected to expose abuses which concern the public good. Plenty of our more social-minded dramatists have done that very thing. They have turned propagandists with a vengeance. They have shown the horrors of unemployment as the Siftons did in *1931*. They have pointed angry fingers at organized rackets as Owen Davis did in *Just to Remind You*. They have dealt with the evils of city government as the Messrs. Maltz and Sklar did in *Merry-Go-Round*. They have championed popular martyrs as Mr. Anderson and Harold Hickerson did in *Gods of the Lightning,* and as I. J. Golden did in *Precedent.* They have indicted capitalism with the sophomoric ease that Elmer Rice did in his skillfully staged *We, the People.* But in pleading against social evils and injustices these playwrights have, almost to a man, become so indignant over obvious wrongs that they have forgotten to write plays which made their hate as persuasive as it was intended to be.

It is here that Mr. Anderson's *Both Your Houses* is different. Although it is a propaganda drama, it gains immensely by turning its back on all the traditional hysterics of its kind. Unlike his fellow castigators, Mr. Anderson refuses to see red. He says devastating things and he says them bluntly. But he keeps his sense of humor. He is arguing for no special cause. He is not against this system nor does he favor that one. He is interested only in what can be done to salvage this Government of ours and to make it really representative of the best interests of its people.

His play has no villains in it in the melodramatic sense of the word. His lawmakers may legislate as if they were so many public enemies, but personally they are agreeable and ingratiating people. They are the victims of a system; hardened politicians who believe in expediency and are accustomed to bargaining for votes. They know the game as Mr. Anderson's novice from Nevada does not, and they play it for all that it is worth. Yet they are pleasant enough men and the most crafty and unscrupulous among them is the most winning character in the play.

By giving his grafters a break, by drawing them as human beings rather than as Boucicault bankers or Desperate Desmonds from the comic strips, Mr. Anderson proves his wisdom as a dramatist. He is an almost fiendishly good-natured exterminator. His play may not be an inspired affair. It may have its obvious weaknesses. But it is the most telling indictment of social and political evils our stage has seen in recent years. It is the bitterest, most disillusioning and unsparing, too, if for no other reason than that Mr. Anderson has remembered that in the theatre good propaganda is more than the result of good playwriting—it is an inseparable part of it.

March 11, 1933

THE SCOTTSBORO BOYS AND
THEY SHALL NOT DIE

JOHN WEXLEY, who in *The Last Mile* wrote an agonizing melodrama about the prison riots which were spread across the front pages of our newspapers four years ago, and who followed this up with an ineffectual propagandist script known as *Steel*, has now found a ready-made subject for a stirring indictment of Southern justice in the Scottsboro case.

More than that he has risen to his theme—particularly in the tense moments of his final trial scene. So, too, has the Theatre Guild, which gave *They Shall Not Die* a smooth-running and mechanically excellent production at the Royale last night.

Mr. Wexley's playwriting is not all of one piece. It is a little slow in getting started in its brutal first act, which is laid in a small-town jail, and not only overlong but unconvincing in the romantic stretches of its second act when it is attempting to motivate the change of heart that overtakes one of its star witnesses. But it is warm with the same kind of contagious indignation that redeemed such pasquinades as *Gods of the Lightning, Precedent* and *Merry-Go-Round*. And it does rise to a final trial scene (based, as I understand it, on the actual testimony in the Scottsboro case) which more than compensates for whatever deficiencies may mar the effectiveness of what has gone before.

Mr. Wexley writes with the force of a man who knows the right is on his side. He has no interest in the niceties of dramaturgy. He is more of a journalist than a playwright.

He shows the full cruelty to which the Negroes in his story are exposed after they have been unjustly arrested for rape. He blames an ambitious and bullying deputy sheriff for the "frame-up" which results in the sensational case. He lets us see him when, by threats and bribery, he forces two prostitutes into saying they were raped by the Negroes who were with them on the freight train. Then he follows the case through to its second trial, when the whole country is interested in it, and a prominent New York lawyer has taken over the defense, and one of the prostitutes has admitted her original testimony was false.

As has been hinted, the earlier portions of Mr. Wexley's play do not find him at his best. He is particularly unfortunate in writing the love affair between the traveling salesman and the pathetic little perjurer who finally reverses her previous testimony. But there is no escaping the theme of *They Shall Not Die*. Nor, for that matter, is it possible to resist the fine persuasiveness of its final scene.

Both as written and as acted this final scene is one of the most stirring trials to have been set upon a New York stage in years. It forces the audience to take sides. It compels seemingly impassive playgoers to burst into round after round of applause. It dramatizes admirably the mockery of justice which has occurred in one of the most widely publicized of contemporary cases.

February 22, 1934

STEVEDORE AND THE THEATRE UNION

WITH the Theatre Union angrily established in Miss Le Gallienne's old playhouse down on Fourteenth Street, those New Yorkers who pray for such a thing can now console themselves with the thought that they have a Theatre of the Barricades. No longer do they have to stand up in Union Square to hear the inflammatory harangues which are honey to their ears. Union Square— speechifiers and all—has gone indoors. At their own convenience, these indignant champions of the revolution can, without fear of rain, become as agitated as they please in the comparative comfort of the Civic Repertory's auditorium.

When they assemble to see *Stevedore*, the latest bomb that has been dropped upon their soap-box stage, they cannot help being jarred, because *Stevedore* is an uncommonly dynamic melodrama, acted and produced with much skill. It is as disturbing a social preachment as any of our propagandist playwrights has yet dared to deliver in our theatre. More than being a harrowing picture of the unhappy lot of the black race in the far South, it is a call to arms; a plea for the Negroes to take to the barricades; a demonstration of the strength that could be theirs if only they would unite as a people and join forces with the equally belligerent members of a white man's union.

As a propagandist melodrama its more active scenes are unquestionably stirring, no matter which side of the fence you happen to be on. It abounds in pistol shots, fights, deaths and agonizing shouts of terror that do their full amount of damage to the nerves. Some of its moments on the waterfront at New Orleans, in fat Aunt Binnie's lunch-room, and in the courtyard of the Negro district, when the innocent stevedore, who has been accused of attacking a white woman, is leading his neighbors in a pitched battle against the whites, are nerve-wracking in their tension.

Both as a production and as an incitement it is much more alive than was *Peace on Earth*, that pacifist tract which preceded it at the same proletarian playhouse. One reason for this is Mr. Syrjala has given it the benefit of some swiftly changed and simple backgrounds which serve admirably to heighten its effects. Another is that Mr. Blankfort (with Mr. Gordon's aid) has directed its violent mob scenes with a turbulence which benefits their action. Then it is acted with uncanny skill by a company which includes such accomplished Negro players as Jack Carter, Rex Ingram and Georgette Harvey.

The trouble with such dramatic firebrands as the Messrs. Peters and Sklar is that they can win the mob responses at which they aim (and which they most assuredly get down on Fourteenth Street) by resorting to childishly simple devices. Their jobs are made too easy for them by the very nature of the audiences to which they pander. They can write the most regulation "tough guy" talk for their first "frame-up" scene—and it passes for a literary gem. They have only to give one of their Negroes such a line as "White man, don't you dare to talk to me that way"—and the gallery gods become ecstatic. They have only to mention the word "strike" —and every member of the Party who hears it is persuaded that a great speech has been made. By resorting to the old "here-come-the-marines" trick of having their black people saved in the nick of time by the members of a white union, they can provoke almost enough applause to shake the Civic Repertory to its foundation.

Being agitators, the Messrs. Peters and Sklar do not

bother to think their problem through. Like firebugs, they find their pleasure in the flames they start rather than in the arrival of the hook-and-ladder. In the phrase their white foreman applies to their black hero, they are content to be "trouble-makers." They seem much more interested in putting salt into old wounds than in cauterizing them. They have compassion and indignation but very little else. They can lead their characters to the barricades and get their audiences to cheer them for taking them there. But one is forced to wonder what the next act of their play would be like, if, indeed, *Stevedore* had been courageous enough or grown-up enough to have another act.

April 21, 1934

CLIFFORD ODETS

WAITING FOR LEFTY

YOU MAY disagree violently with Mr. Odets's ultimate solutions. You may regret the simplicity of his Communist panaceas and look askance at his willful stacking of the cards. You may say the results he achieves are easier than he has any right to be proud of. You may quibble about this or that lack which, if you are following his work closely, you are bound to find in it. You may point to scenes which he leaves as raw and as undeveloped as if he were dashing off a hurried first draft at midnight. You may even resent the constant angry jabs at the pit of your social stomach which he does not hesitate to administer during the course of an entire evening.

But you cannot fail to realize, in the presence of such of his one-acts as *Till the Day I Die* and *Waiting for Lefty*, that Mr. Odets is doing more than holding your attention. He is commanding it. As an emotionalist he has a sweeping, vigorous power which is as welcome as it is thundersome when encountered in our theatre.

In the writing of his two short plays which the Group Theatre has presented at the Longacre, Mr. Odets seems to have employed a machine gun rather than a pen. His one-acts, unlike his more reposeful and intensely Chekovian *Awake and Sing!*, are angry dramas, almost fanatical in their single-trackedness, their force and their militancy. They may be uncouth and gangling. They may leave you with a mind full of ready objections. They may appear to suggest what they really never succeed in doing—at least in terms of any abiding validity. Yet they have the rare virtue of so occupying your attention at the moment they are being played, that at that time, they—and they alone—seem to exist.

Mr. Odets has an extraordinary instinct for the theatre. He shows this in his peppery action and also in his clipped, human dialogue. He hits hard, and below the belt if need be. But at least he hits. The wallop he commands is a considerable one. He does not care whether he is employ-ing an old Reinhardt trick—as he is when he uses "plants" in his audience to heighten the effect of his taxi-strike mass meeting in *Waiting for Lefty*—or whether he is borrow-ing the tactics of the Grand Guignol to intensify a scene in *Till the Day I Die* by having his hero's wrist smashed by the butt end of a revolver carried by one of his Nazi villains. The simple fact is that his blows rain hard and effectively. The Party ought to find this virtue enough, even if Mr. Odets, as a playwright of genuine promise, is certain to be dissatisfied with it if he continues to develop as a dramatist.

Of his two long one-acts on the Group Theatre's new bill, it is unquestionably *Waiting for Lefty* which is the better play. It bears re-seeing and remains in its present performance as effective as it first was when it was given at special matinees. *Till the Day I Die* has more tension than any of the anti-Nazi scripts yet produced in our theatre. Some of the seven scenes—in which it traces the hideous torture of a Communist who, after his capture by the Storm Troopers, is so abused that he finally has to commit suicide to square himself with the Party—are unforgettable in their bludgeoning strength. But it remains a play "suggested by a letter from Germany printed in the New Masses," rather than a play written from life.

It is well enough acted by the Group and has the vigor of its hatred. But it does not disclose Mr. Odets at his best, for the simple reason that it fails to find him writing out of his own experience, from any firsthand observation of character by means of which he can strengthen his melodramatic scenario or prevent it from seeming at times like a parody of itself.

One thing is certain, however. Clifford Odets is a playwright of unusual potentialities, and the Group is to be congratulated upon having discovered him.

March 27, 1935

AWAKE AND SING!

ALTHOUGH the Group Theatre has produced several interesting plays in its time, and done some of them very well, it has never presented a more fluent production of so living a script as it did last night, when it brought Clifford Odets's *Awake and Sing!* to the stage of the Belasco. You may remember, Mr. Odets is the young actor-playwright whose one-act revolutionary drama about last year's taxi strike, known as *Waiting for Lefty*, was the turbulent high spot of the experimental matinees which the Group recently gave on two Sunday afternoons. This propagandist script of his did more than introduce Mr. Odets as an agitator of vigor. It indicated his uncommon ability to heighten the idioms of daily speech into dialogue as seemingly true to life as it was theatrically effective. Hence one looked forward to his first long play with an interest the writing of *Awake and Sing!* has more than justified.

Awake and Sing! finds Mr. Odets deserting the soapbox he so frankly mounted in *Waiting for Lefty* to write a well-balanced, meticuously observed, always interesting and ultimately quite moving drama about the problems of a Jewish family living in the Bronx. If, as is obviously the case, Mr. Odets has drunk deep of the Chekovian springs before dealing with the Bergers, the simple fact remains that of all the American playwrights who have attempted to employ Chekov's method, none has used it to such advantage as Mr. Odets has in *Awake and Sing!*

Although his text and title are derived from the verse in *Isaiah* reading, "Awake and sing, ye that dwell in the dust," it is comforting to find Mr. Odets has not written one of those naïve scripts in which the right is always on one side. His Bergers represent many points of view. In fact, the main struggle his drama unfolds is not the battle for the Marxist cause in which the old grandfather believes, but the unheroic fight which the boy and the girl in the Berger family have to put up in order to free themselves from all that is grubby and enslaving in their sacrificing parents' lives, and to go their own ways in the world.

The weakest thing about Mr. Odets's drama is his plotting. It is somewhat over-elaborate in its details and decidedly familiar in its outlines. There are moments in it

—such a moment, for example, as the one in which the Jewish matriarch discovers that her unmarried daughter is to have a baby—which remind you not only of the Spewacks' unfortunate *Spring Song* but also of any number of other plays of Jewish tenement life.

What matters, however, in *Awake and Sing!* is not the story Mr. Odets is telling, but the rich, flavorsome way in which he has told it. If his method is Chekovian in its pauses, its sudden and meaningful usage of what appear to be irrelevances, its autobiographical outbursts, its seeming indirection, its amplitude, its pathos and its shrewd eye for the smallest characterizing details—all one can say in fairness is that, when it is re-used as well as Mr. Odets has re-used it, the Chekovian method continues to be a rich and engrossing one.

What Mr. Odets adds to the technique he has borrowed from his master is an exuberant sense of humor, and an ear for the rhythms of highly colloquial speech which is very much his own. He is no *Potash and Perlmutter* recorder of Jewish family life. His Jewish idiom is no traditional comic banter interrupted arbitrarily with moments of stage pathos. He makes it plain that he knows whereof his characters speak. They command a vital flow of idioms which are as colorful as they are personal and as vigorous as they are effective.

Such a play of Jewish family life as *Awake and Sing!* is happily suited to the non-Baltimorean, non-Park Avenue and non-Hollywood members of the Group Theatre's acting company who, as it now happens, have it to themselves. They play with a smoothness, a sense of the ensemble, and a mature completeness in their individual performances they have not shown before and which speaks eloquently for the ideals to which they are dedicated.

February 20, 1935

GOLDEN BOY

IF EVERY line in *Golden Boy* were as good as every third line is, Clifford Odets's new play would be an unusual one. Certainly it is not news to report that Mr. Odets's dramaturgy can be possessed of uncommon vitality. Or that he has an astonishing ear for dialogue. When he is writing at his best, none of our younger dramatists can equal him in giving the essence of a scene or an individual with almost telegraphic brevity. He is a shrewd observer. He has a fierce humor and a relentless vigor. Among his high talents he can count a gift for revealing everything by the uncanny use he makes of humanizing details. But Mr. Odets, the amazing realist, seems also to be an unconscionable romantic.

By this I do not mean he indulges in the cape-swingings dear to the traditional romantics. It is not with their costumes that his characters sink into heroics. It is in those two lines which separate nearly each of his memorable ones. Then it is that he shows himself to be his own blindest critic. Then it is that his writing sheds its rare distinction. Then it is that his people begin to clothe themselves in so much verbal velveteen and strike attitudes. Then it is that he robs *Golden Boy* of the sustained values one wishes it had.

More often than is comfortable Mr. Odets's new play invades the provinces of the pulp magazines. If its intermittent virtues were not so exceptional, the trashiness of much of its writing would not matter. But in telling the dull saga of a prizefighter who chooses to live by his fists rather than his fiddle, I am afraid Mr. Odets, the un-

disciplined romantic, finally knocks out Mr. Odets, the superb realist. His biography of a pugilist is like all prizering sagas—with this one exception. Mr. Odets has written
it. Its details of a fighter's rise to fame and fortune, and
his attendant temptations, are familiar enough. But Mr.
Odets finds his own motivations. He sees characters with
his own piercing eyes. He lays their secret torments bare
by means of his own extraordinary ear for what is unmasking in their speech. Frequent proofs of his authorship
keep jabbing at your attention when it is wandering, and
even when it begins to wander more and more at the
Belasco.

Mr. Odets is at his best when writing of the simple
Italian family from which his Killer comes. Then his
characterization is pointed and fine, and his drama truthful and engaging. A fighter, however, cannot be a professional and stay at home. It is when he mixes Joe Bonaparte
up with his managers and his trainers that Mr. Odets loses
him and his play. Thereupon melodramatics, *clichés* in
plotting, and violent overwriting begin to get the better
of him. His drama's theme leads him up a blind alley
where it leaves him. This is a pity. Because unsatisfactory
as his new play is, it has fine stuff in it; the kind of lines
and scenes only an exceptional dramatist could write.

Mr. Clurman has directed it to perfection. Mr. Gorelik
has set it in terms of helpful suggestions. And the actors
in the group play it with a freedom and a truth worthy of
its best writing. Still, when all is said and done, and Mr.
Odets's pugilist has killed himself and his sweetheart, at
the end of the twelfth scene, in his high-powered automobile, one cannot help wondering why Mr. Odets, of all
people, should have bothered to write this particular play,
which ends up by seeming pointless. One is forced to regret, too, that, though the Group Theatre has done so well

by its favorite playwright, he has not done nearly so well by himself as one wishes that he had.

November 5, 1937

THE WPA'S *LIVING NEWSPAPERS*

DURING the year which separates the Federal Theatre's production of *Triple A Plowed Under* from its production of *Power*, Arthur Arent and his associates in the WPA have made an enormous advance in their editing of the *Living Newspapers*. From the beginning it was clear that the most vital idea the Federal Theatre had as yet contributed to stagecraft, as we know it in this country, lay in these dramatizations of current events which it was attempting to make.

In Soviet Russia, where propaganda has become a fine art and the fine arts so much propaganda, *Living Newspapers* have long been familiar. But in America not only was the form new but the problems of the editors were far more difficult. Instead of being paid by a government tolerating no opposition, the salaries of these editors came out of the pockets of taxpayers of every political and economic persuasion. The problem was to find an editorial policy, at once vigorous and acceptable, which would also be representative of the government. The ethical question immediately arose as to how far these federally-endowed journals had the right to go in championing the interests of any one party; in campaigning for the Administration in power; in setting class against class, and in arguing, as they did in *Triple A Plowed Under*, for a curtailment of such a branch of the Federal Government itself as the Supreme Court.

The ethical questions raised by the earlier editions of *The Living Newspaper* remain unsettled. No doubt they never will, nor can, be settled to everyone's satisfaction. But the vigor of the arguments to which they lead is, in a way, a proof of how effective is the propagandist agent which the Federal Theatre Project has stumbled upon in these acted newspapers.

That the Federal Theatre has brought these newspapers to a high state of development is a fact no one can deny who has seen *Power*. It is one of the most telling propagandist offerings our stage has produced. It is as skillful as it is forceful, and can boast the exciting virtue of having perfected a novel dramatic form. Where *Triple A Plowed Under* made uncertain use of a new medium full of dynamite, *Power* employs this medium so that it takes full advantage of its explosive force. It is a production which has nothing to do with the aims or the methods of the workaday stage.

Its ardent championing of the TVA and its bitter condemnation of the privately-owned utility companies are executed in the most virtuoso of inventive terms. Here is a performance which is part lecture and part history; which utilizes lantern slides, motion pictures and an amplifier to make its points; which resorts to vignetted playlets as well as to statistics; which is as broadly humorous in its stylized manner as it is indignant throughout; and which, though it has little or nothing to do with the theatre of entertainment as we ordinarily encounter it, is none the less theatrically exciting even in its most irritatingly partisan moments.

For having so mastered a novel form Brett Warren, Arthur Arent, and their co-workers in the WPA deserve much credit. They are innovators in whose debt the theatre stands. They have discovered and developed what in this country is a new type of theatrical presentation and a new use for the stage. Not only as propagandists, but also as dramatic technicians they have done the job they set out to do in a remarkably skillful manner.

April 5, 1937

MR. BLITZSTEIN'S *THE CRADLE WILL ROCK*

MARC BLITZSTEIN'S *The Cradle Will Rock*, as acted and sung at the Mercury, is the most exciting propagandist *tour de force* our stage has seen since Clifford Odets's *Waiting for Lefty* burst like a bombshell upon this town.

Mr. Blitzstein's drama is an opera, done as simply at the Mercury as if it were an oratorio. Once again the stage is without a setting and the make-believe is of the frankest type of theatre theatrical. Once again the effect is so complete, so startling, and so satisfactory that unless its directors are careful to use a backdrop or two when they produce *The Shoemakers' Holiday*, the Mercury is apt to find itself picketed—and picketed in vain—by the Messrs. Oenslager, Mielziner, Simonson and other members from the Scene Designers' Local.

Three rows of chairs, occupied by the singing actors, constitute the scenery. The players wear street clothes and most of them have on little or no make-up. The forestage is left bare for the action, and for Mr. Blitzstein, who sits at an upright piano just a little off center playing his brilliant score, taking several secondary parts, and in general doing more odd jobs than have been done by one man

behind the footlights since Mei Lan-Fang's property man
went back to China.

In its barest plot essentials what Mr. Blitzstein has to
say is what a good many propagandist playwrights have
said before him. He is telling the story of a wicked capitalist who uses the very same dirty methods to fight
unionization with which our stage has been long familiar.
Yet familiar as Mr. Blitzstein's ingredients may be, they
acquire a new and irresistible force as he states them—in
prose, rhyme, and music.

His capitalist is Mr. Mister, an unscrupulous boss who
controls Steeltown. He has a judge, a college president, a
newspaper editor, and a doctor under his thumb. By
bribery and intimidation he has coerced them and some
other "leading citizens" to serve on a Liberty Committee
to fight the unions. Mr. Blitzstein does not hesitate to
liken Mr. Mister's Yes-Men, when they are brought by
mistake into the imagined night court which is the scene
of most of *The Cradle Will Rock* and its Odetsian flashbacks, to the little prostitute who has also been arrested.
The only difference between these Yes-Men and the prostitute, Mr. Blitzstein insists, is that she is an amateur.

In terms of the talk and testimony of the people assembled in this night court Mr. Blitzstein paints a picture of
the whole of Steeltown. He lets us see Mrs. Mister and the
artist-gigolos who dance attendance upon her. He lays
bare the tragedy of a Polish couple Mr. Mister's henchmen have decided to "frame." He tells us what happened
to the poor druggist whose son tried to protect them. He
shows us Mr. Mister's pampered son and daughter, and
permits us to see the full extent of their father's villainies.
Then he introduces us to the inevitable union champion
who is strong enough to resist Mr. Mister, who speaks for

the forces of the storm, and who urges the crowd members of the audience to wake up to a proper realization of their rights.

Mr. Blitzstein's writing is often crude and uneven. He mixes realism and stylization, tragedy and farce, burlesque and passionate propaganda at will—but to good effect. His shopworn theme gains by its originality of treatment, by the bitter savagery of its laughter, by the glib ferocity of its rhyming, by the strength of its author's convictions, and by the constant illumination of Mr. Blitzstein's interesting and ever-helpful music.

Most of all, however, *The Cradle Will Rock* gains because of the honest and affecting performance it is giving at the Mercury. The sincerity of the actors sweeps across the footlights carrying everything before it. There is no room for humbug in this kind of unaided acting. To reach our hearts it must come from the hearts of its creators.

December 6, 1937

PINS AND NEEDLES

THERE is plenty of amusement to be had at *Pins and Needles*, so much, in fact, that it lends a special and very different significance to this intimate revue which the members of the International Ladies' Garment Workers' Union are presenting at Labor Stage. *Pins and Needles* is a gay show, and an intelligent one. It widens the theatre's horizons, as they stand in desperate need of being widened, to include the interests and the problems of those who do not belong to what was once known as the carriage trade. It is class-conscious enough to satisfy the most avid propagandist. Yet it manages to say serious things lightly and to indict with a song and a smile. By so doing it makes its points twice as effectively as it would have done had it followed the sober routine methods of agit-prop drama in this country.

The members of the cast, whose union labels range from "white-goods," "cutters," "pressers," "cloak-makers," "Bonaz embroiderers" to "dressmakers" and "underwear," are frankly and proudly amateurish. Although their looks are far from prepossessing, their spirits are high. The pleasure they take in what they are doing is contagious. They have some admirable skits and songs at their disposal. And they have been directed with uncommon zest and professionalism by Charles Friedman.

They aim at getting along without the spangles and the names, the scenery and the vacuity, and the "moon-and-June," "love-and-dove" rhymes so dear to the average Broadway revue. And without them they do get along very nicely indeed. In the place of opulence they put intelligence. Instead of silliness they provide often uproarious satire. Their production can be likened to a labor version of *The Garrick Gaieties* or *The Grand Street Follies*.

If its dances are decidedly weak in execution, they are at least based upon excellent ideas. Several of the sketches are too long for their own good. But all of them have something to say. And some of them, such as "Sunday in the Park," "We'd Rather Be Right," and the hilarious parody of the Theatre Union's production of *Mother* have a joyous, hence deadly, effectiveness. Harold J. Rome's music and lyrics are exceptionally good, especially in the case of "Sing Me a Song with Social Significance," "Vassar Girl Finds a Job," and "Doing the Reactionary."

The whole production eloquently justifies the claims of its sponsors that the labor theatre in this country has found its sense of humor. This makes *Pins and Needles* as significant as it is entertaining. For *Pins and Needles* is related at once to life and to joy. By turning its propaganda into good entertainment, its message is doubly insured, and doubly telling as propaganda.

December 6, 1937

6. "You are Welcome, Masters, Welcome All"

CRITICS ON ACTING

DRAMATIC critics, the poor fools, will forever go on writing about acting as if they knew something about it. Readers may be fooled by them. They may even fool themselves. But they cannot fool actors. It is not that critics tell deliberate lies about acting. They do the only thing they can do. They tell the truth as they see it. Or, rather, as they feel it and then think it. This is a good deal and may even be interesting. To this they may add theories—sensible enough and sometimes more than that. Yet almost always they write about acting from the point of view of the effect gained, and not from the point of view of the person who gains it.

We critics have adjectives, metaphors, similes, and presumably rational prose at our disposal. We are trained to describe what we see, or, if you prefer, to record what we have seen has done to us. We can relate a performance to the words we are hearing, and all it is these words have told us that performance might have been or should be. And we can hold forth learnedly on period styles of acting that we have no way of finding out about except through our often inaccurate intuition, or from books in which other writers have reduced acting to words. To acting, past or present, the critical approach is almost always bound to be a literary one.

Hence it is that we who are reviewers tend to be more at home in dealing with playwrights than with players. With dramatists we at least share the written word and the expounded idea in common. Our vocabularies are the same, no matter how differently we may use them. But with actors we are forced to snatch them out of their chosen medium and attempt to put them in another. We have no other choice than to translate their performance into literary terms. Our approach to acting is, as it were, bound to be illiterate if for no other reason than that it is fated to be literary. We always write about acting in terms of translation, never in terms of the original. We do not know the original. We do not speak its language and it does not speak ours.

From the actor's point of view one trouble with us as critics is that we see them as spectators rather than as actors. Although such an impasse—for it is indeed an impasse—abounds in difficulties and can make for unfairness, it does boast one redeeming feature. It creates a bond between critics and audiences. It guarantees not only actors but spectators, too, that when we attempt to write about acting, we are at least judging it from a spectator's point of view.

There is something consoling about this. It means the actors who are written about are never at a loss for an audience. They travel through time with a full retinue of spectators. Even after their deaths, players are doomed to go down the years not as they have seen themselves but as others have seen them. The pity, as far as they are concerned, is that they cannot choose their seers.

WILLIAM GILLETTE'S SHERLOCK HOLMES

LODGED at the New Amsterdam these cold, cold nights is *Sherlock Holmes,* the most warmly reassuring melodrama New York has seen in many a bloodstained year. This good old thriller has not yet lost its thrills, even though a full thirty seasons have passed since William Gillette first appeared in it at the Garrick. It provides them still, and plenty of them. You could scarcely ask for anything more villainous than the way in which the lovely Miss Faulkner is persecuted by the wicked Larrabees. Certainly, even in your darkest moments, you could not crave anyone more evil than the great Professor Moriarty, who seems to be smudged with sulphur as he generals the crimes of London from the stone recesses of his underground office, or prowls menacingly into Stepney's gas chamber at midnight.

If Mr. Gillette's old melodrama manages to be reassuring, even comforting, as it edges its way slowly through its path of crime and the constant threats of death which confront its hero, the reason lies, of course, with the gorgeous imperturbability of the Sherlock Holmes Mr. Gillette creates. It lies with him because the Master Detective he plays, without ever raising his voice or making a single violent movement, is as vivid and commanding an example of the powers of understatement as our theatre knows.

One feels from the moment he first courts danger in the drawing room of the Larrabees that this lean man—with his dry, casual voice, his fine, clean-cut head and his authoritative calm—is somehow beyond the reach of evil. These people with whom he is contending may be wicked. They may be ingenious. They may even be the most talented of crooks. But they can never hope to be the equals of the great Sherlock Holmes who is on their trail. After all, they are mere men. And he . . . Well, he is different. He is a superman, joined to the lesser race of men only by the slim ties of his one weakness, his call to Watson for the needle.

Accordingly, though the adventures which follow may be exciting (and they still are at times, especially when Moriarty is pitted against Holmes) the fear they stimulate never springs from any real doubt as to what their final outcome will be. Their major excitement centers always not in what Moriarty and his crew may do to Holmes, but in what he will do to them. This shift in emphasis comes as a relief to audiences unaccustomed to having their emotions treated with such mercy. It comes as a pleasant emotion, too, for by relieving you of your most acute worries, it gives you time to enjoy the full-blown language of another day, even while the plot is thickening. It permits you to fill your ears with such of its reverberating phrases as that memorable one Holmes flings into the face of Larrabee, when he says with an awful quietness: "As for you, sir, you continue your persecution of this lady at your own peril."

This relief from the uncertainty of most melodramatic plots also grants you more leisure in which to revel in Mr. Gillette's playing. It lets you watch him as he takes his time over single sentences, note the masterly way in which he handles his pauses, and observe him as he doubles up on all the negatives of his acting until they are skillfully changed into positives of a compelling kind. Watching

him, you cannot but be impressed by the freshness with
which he attacks his lines each night. Nor can you help
marveling that, in spite of the hundreds of times he has
played the part, Mr. Gillette is still the master of that
hardest of the actor's problems, that problem which he
himself once defined in an excellent essay as "The illusion
of the first time in acting."

December 2, 1929

TALLULAH THE MAGNIFICENT

MISS BANKHEAD is a performer of uncommon potentialities. She is fascinating to watch as well as to listen
to. Her personality is aflame with the combustible stuffs
which are the marks of genius in an actor. In the best sense
of the word, her face is what Mr. Woollcott once referred
to as a veritable "playground for the emotions." It is at
once so haunting, so variable and so expressive that it not
only enables her to reflect whatever the mood may be she
is called upon to register but also to give instantaneous
projection to the meaning and the implication of whatever line she is speaking. She gestures with extraordinary
grace. She has eloquent hands and wrists. She moves with
an ease few actresses can match. And her husky voice,
which in reality is no instrument at all in the accepted
usage of the word, is one of the most flexible sending sets
our theatre knows.

Since she has returned to New York from England and
Hollywood Miss Bankhead has had poor luck in her choice
of plays. Yet in the vehicles in which she has chosen to
appear, she has displayed beyond any shadow of a doubt
how exceptionally wide is her acting range. In *Forsaking*

All Others, she was being gay, pathetic, desperate and tragic all in one evening. As the doomed heroine of *Dark Victory,* she demonstrated the intensity she commands when she turns her attention to stark tragedy. In *Rain* she was hard-boiled with a vengeance, and was rasping out the curses of Sadie Thompson in a fair-to-middling impersonation of Jeanne Eagels. And now, in Miss Heilbron's *Something Gay,* which belies its title at almost every turn, she is proving how adept she is as a comedienne, even when no comic materials worthy of her talents are placed at her disposal.

If Miss Bankhead is the mistress of such versatility and brings such uncommon gifts to the theatre's service, you may well ask why it is I do not content myself with urging her to find a play worthy of her talents instead of begging her to discover at the same time a director who can keep her restless energies in check. My reason is that, as I see it, Miss Bankhead's energy is not only one of her most arresting qualities but also one of her misfortunes as an actress. The pacings, the overconfidence of her playing, the very boldness of her ease upon the stage, which sometimes makes you feel as uncomfortable in her presence as you do when you see a person making himself too much at home in another person's house, may, in the case of such a negligible play as *Something Gay,* be her own way of protesting against the obvious worthlessness of a script.

But Miss Bankhead needs to be protected against this fretful energy of hers. It makes her wasteful of her gifts. It leads her into overdoing. It persuades her to be indiscriminate in her use of emphasis. It keeps her unsteady in her playing. Although her acting is enormously skillful, it is sadly lacking in discipline. This lack of discipline prevents her either from giving a definite design to one of her characterizations or from sustaining it as well as she otherwise might. It also tempts her into playing all of her scenes with an equal drive instead of saving herself for her climaxes. Miss Bankhead likewise needs to be protected from the dolts who worship her completely. They will ruin her if she listens to the idiotic applause with which they greet her each and every mannerism; her playing of every scene; her gallops up a flight of stairs as fervently as if Duse and Bernhardt had come to life in one person.

She is so gorgeously endowed that it will be one of the tragedies of our time if, before it is too late, and owing to faults in her own temperament, or to deficiencies in her playwrights, or to her lack of a Clyde Beatty of a director, she fails to take her place in our theatre as the really important performer she might so easily have become.

May 4, 1935

MR. COHAN IN *AH, WILDERNESS!*

AS THE small-town editor in *Ah, Wilderness!* George M. Cohan gives the kind of performance about which, were his name Gregory Mussorgsky Cohansky and Mr. Cohan a member of the Moscow Art Theatre, Oliver M. Sayler would undoubtedly be writing polysyllabic books. The learned weeklies and highfalutin' monthlies would soon be devoting pages to it in which such fancy words as "rhythm," "pattern," and "antiphonal radiance" would be printed in even fancier type. Having been a simple Yankee Doodle Dandy, a flag-waver and a Song-and-Dance man, and being an actor who is even now appearing in a domestic drama which begins on the Fourth of July, Mr.

Cohan may have to content himself with simpler and more enthusiastic adjectives. But praise he has already won in abundance, and cannot fail to win because of this most brilliant of his characterizations.

As is his wont, Mr. Cohan uses no make-up. A pair of spectacles slipped from time to time before his eyes is his only external aid to characterization. He is himself—his old, jaunty self, a little more stooped than formerly and draped in the short coats of an outmoded fashion. His eyes are full of their old mischief and given to occasional winks which are irresistible. His head still sways from side to side. And he meanders about the stage with that astonishing dancer's ease which has always been his.

He is his regulation self—with a difference. Mr. O'Neill's script has found its way into his heart even as Mr. Cohan aids in making it find its way into the hearts of all who see it. He acts with a new depth; with a mellow poignancy born of the play he is adorning.

He is one of our veteran performers, yet he has none of the older actor's tricks. He is a star (even at the Guild) who does not have to take on the cheap prerogatives of stardom. He dominates the stage and conquers his audience by playing down, by dodging all the easy vocal devices for pathos or for humor by means of which lesser performers of his generation would have faked the part—and ruined it. He shares his first entrance and takes positions which give the stage to others. By his very refusal to steal the show the stage becomes his. He dominates it with a generosity which never gets in the way of the real meaning of Mr. O'Neill's play. His pauses, his understatement and his relaxation are in themselves eloquent lessons in the art of acting.

October 4, 1933

THE LUNTS VERSUS CHEKOV

WHAT an artist thinks he has done, what he meant to do, and what he does are not necessarily Dionnes from the same litter. Theory and practice are not more different than intention and execution can be. As a case in point permit me to call attention to Lynn Fontanne's Irina in the Theatre Guild's current and, on the whole, extremely satisfactory revival of *The Sea Gull*.

No one can question the enthusiasm or the aptitude of the Lunts. They are players who in the best sense of the word are professionals. As everyone has read, and no one has cause to doubt, their every waking hour is devoted to the theatre. If they talk in their sleep, it is most probably dialogue they utter. Life for them must be one long and invigorating performance. If not that, then a series of hilarious rehearsals by day and enjoyable performances by night. They are actors to their fingertips. If ever they have pretended to quarrel it must be only because it gives them a chance to make up.

King Midas was the sole member of his household to possess a precious touch. Mr. Lunt is more fortunate. His queen can boast an identical gift. Everything the two of them lay their hands upon is turned not only into grease-paint but often into gold. Their performances throb with a joyous vitality. Obviously, and enchantingly, their very work is play. Set them down in Mr. Shakespeare's Padua, in Mr. Anderson's London, in the Alpine hotel in *Idiot's Delight*, the tragically vanished Vienna of the Messrs. Molnar, Sil-Vara, or Sherwood, or even in Mr. Coward's semi-tropics—and the results can be high-voltaged sport;

sport of that special and delectable sort which is provided only by actor's theatre when it is at its most adroit and glittering best.

The Lunts can march through a play like welcome invaders, entering a conquered kingdom. Their energies are boundless. Their zest is overpowering. They can sweep magnificently through the right kinds of scripts. Without meaning to, or having anyone object, they can turn them into so many red carpets for their royal progresses. Quite rightly, their high spirits, their technical virtuosity, their skill in displaying each other to advantage, their contagious pleasure in what they are doing, and their unstinting dedication to their jobs, are qualities which have won for them the affectionate admiration of a huge army of devoted playgoers.

Yet the very virtues which the Lunts have brought to certain vigorous plays, and the mere fact that they are stars who have usually run away with the wagons their dramatists have hitched to them, would be enough to make one wonder in advance how they, of all people, could resign themselves to the luminous inertia of one of Chekov's masterpieces, and the ensemble playing for which these tragi-comedies of frustration were ably designed.

The Lunts, with their usual acumen, were well aware of the new demands placed upon them by *The Sea Gull*. Confided Mr. Lunt to Helen Deutsch, when the play was in Boston, "We have been accustomed to articulate roles. We are confronted here with the problem of evoking complete characters from the subtlest suggestion. . . . Never before in all my life have I worked on a role (Trigorin) that imposed upon me such restraint and at the same time offered such scope." Miss Deutsch reports Miss Fontanne was in full agreement with Mr. Lunt when it came to describing the subtlety of Chekov's characterizations.

But it seems to me that in *The Sea Gull* Mr. Lunt has succeeded in achieving, where Miss Fontanne has failed to achieve, the aims which both of them completely understood. Mr. Lunt's Trigorin fits into the picture. It is unobtrusive, quiet, filled with comprehension. Rightly enough its key is that same minor key in which Mr. Lunt once played another bearded and negative figure in a tragedy, the Emperor Maximilian in Werfel's *Juarez and Maximilian*. Mr. Lunt does not speak for himself. He is content to let Trigorin speak for Chekov.

Miss Fontanne's Irina is unfortunately more assertive. Undoubtedly without meaning to do so, she makes one think not of the actress Irina as written by Chekov but of what it is Lynn Fontanne is up to as an actress. Her red wig, which is one of the reddest red wigs ever seen, does not help matters. Rightly or wrongly, it seems to symbolize her approach. It is the first of the many externals which stand in the way of her interpretation and make it stand out like a sore and very inflamed thumb. What it says, or rather appears to say, is that, instead of delving into the depths of Irina's character, Miss Fontanne's first thought has been, "What can I do to make my Irina look different? Let's see. I wore a yellow wig with great effect in *Idiot's Delight*. My hair was dark in *Amphitryon*. I know, a red wig! That's the very thing."

I don't for a minute mean to suggest this is the way in which Miss Fontanne's mind actually worked. I only say her Irina, as seen and projected, does her the injustice of making this appear true. Unquestionably Miss Fontanne had subtler reasons for wearing a red wig. As a conscious craftsman she was seeking for some way in which to individualize the woman she saw. She has confessed that Irina, as she imagined her, was not only vain and selfish but also had a painted face. Said Miss Fontanne to Miss Deutsch,

"It is possible to play Irina as a much sweeter and softer character than the woman I believe her to be. I may be in error, but I do not see her as a sympathetic character, except in so far as all Chekov's characters are sympathetic because one pities them for their pathetically exposed human frailty."

Certainly Irina is a woman filled with frailties as written by Chekov. She has all the faults described by Miss Fontanne. But where Miss Fontanne fails the script is by exposing in her very first scene all it is that Chekov has to say against Irina in each of his four beautifully-wrought acts. She does not reveal Irina delicately or slowly. She trumpets her say against her in a voice almost as raucous and as two-toned as was the one she brought to playing her hoydenish Katherine. Although Miss Fontanne has a very definite character in her mind, what she forces some of us to see is only a less pleasing, more strident version of that on-stage character Miss Fontanne has carefully built up, and which, with all its shimmering mannerisms, its gurgling laughs, its purring exclamations, and pagoda-like entrances, she has carried, in different colored wigs and varying make-up, from script to script with increasing regularity of recent seasons.

If Miss Fontanne is not able to project the Irina she sees in truly Chekovian terms, one trouble is the difficulty she has in subduing her own energies to meet the languorous mood of a Chekovian script. Miss Fontanne would be the last player in the world to want to stand out willfully from the ensemble which the Guild has labored to create. Yet her very vitality sets her apart, striking a sharp discord in Chekov's gentle harmony of resignation, frustration, and despair.

Even when Miss Fontanne stretches herself out on the ground to complain about her boredom in the country, she seems anything but bored. There is nothing passive about her. She refuses to surrender to the twilight mood of Chekov's play. She is an athlete resting between games rather than a pre-war Russian communing with her soul and filled with complaints she is too inert to do more than complain about. At such a moment as this, indeed throughout the evening, it is impossible not to wonder what Nazimova or Miss Cornell would have done to suggest the Irina of the text. It is strange, too, that Miss Fontanne, who is herself an admirable actress, should visualize Irina, another excellent performer, in the showy, obvious terms she has chosen. Visually her Irina is no compliment to the profession in which Miss Fontanne usually shines.

April 2, 1938

OSGOOD PERKINS

MR. PERKINS was no Garrick. He would have been the first to toss back his head and laugh at such a suggestion. His would have been a sardonic laugh; an inner chuckle too large to be quite self-contained. It would have been soundless. Yet as a weapon to demolish pretentiousness in any form it would have proved as potent as did the trumpets which leveled Jericho's walls. It would have been that sad but caustically revealing laugh which—although we saw it rather than heard it—we were forced to join in during even the most straightfaced moments of Mr. Perkins' playing in *The Front Page, Spread Eagle, Tomorrow and Tomorrow, Goodbye Again* and *End of Summer.*

One thing is certain. That laughter would have been as visible in Mr. Perkins' hands as it was in his flaming black eyes and mask-like face. Those spidery hands of his were capable of expressing whatever he felt and thought. They were the thinnest, most eloquent hands any player has been blessed with in our time. They literally seized upon the changing emotions of each character Mr. Perkins was acting. They clutched at them, and exposed them, long before the dramatists' lines had revealed these emotions. Then they held on to them as long as the moods were of any dramatic significance.

There was never anything arty about Mr. Perkins' use of his hands. He did not indulge in those studied flourishes dear to the teachers of pantomime. Although his hands had discovered a vocabulary of their own, they employed it without self-consciousness. They were so charged both with tension and with meaning that it was difficult to take one's eyes off them. In the most unfigurative sense Mr. Perkins was an actor to his fingertips. His dynamic hands, however, only symbolized the qualities of his playing.

Primarily he is likely to be remembered as a comedian; as the player of our day who could most tellingly deliver the dryest, most deflating lines our most irreverent dramatists were able to concoct. As the editor he played to perfection in *The Front Page* he was not merely an uncommonly expert actor delivering uncommonly good wisecracks; he was the perfect wisecrack in himself; the epitome of everything ruthless or disillusioning, and yet likable in the cynical twenties which were the Golden Age of Debunking. There was more to Mr. Perkins than this. Because of it he was able to escape from a long series of hard-boiled roles into *Uncle Vanya* and *End of Summer*. Everything he did was possessed of extraordinary tension; of a nervous alertness which made interest compulsory. Each cross he made had the value of a speech. He used his lean body so that it was full of meaning.

There was also a sense of sadness about him. It was a cosmic melancholy; a disillusionment born of a search for something he could not seem to find but which pity and compassion had sent him questing for. His face was a fusion of the Tragic and the Comic masks. His comedy was never crackbrained for its own sake, or unrelated to life. It belonged to that larger sensing of the comic Balzac had in mind when he wrote of the *Comédie humaine*.

September 22, 1937

"GANGWAY FOR DE LAWD"

RICHARD B. HARRISON was more than an actor. He was a character. One of the finest features of his acting, which was effortless, was the fact, we suspect, that his performance of De Lawd was at all times illumined by the gentle, simple goodness which so obviously distinguished his own character. Although hundreds of other performances by Equity's most talented members have been either blurred by the passing seasons or completely engulfed by them, Mr. Harrison's Lawd still remains as freshly fixed in the minds of those who only saw the production once as it was on that memorable night, more than five years ago, when, with his flowing white hair, his white shirt, his bow tie, his long Prince Albert of black alpaca, his black trousers and congress gaiters, he first answered to Gabriel's now famous cue, "Gangway! Gangway for de Lawd God Jehovah!"

His Lawd truly walked de earth as a natchel man. He was possessed of that rarest of mortal as well as theatrical virtues—a nobility which neither was, nor had to be, assumed. Noble as He was He was never stiff or forbidding.

He was human and touching and humorous. Yes, and benign, too—the sort of kindly creator to whom one could have turned with confidence in one's lonely search for understanding and guidance and comfort.

The goodness of Mr. Harrison's own spirit was the only halo needed to set his Jehovah apart from the angels and the archangels, the cherubs and the mammies, the custard-makers and the pickaninnies who crowded Mr. Connelly's and Mr. Bradford's heavenly fish fry, or to prove his right to control the fortunes of the biblical characters who wandered in and out of the later scenes in the play.

So innately reverent, so alive with everything most wanted in religion was Mr. Harrison's Lawd that a "ten-cent seegar," given to him by a custard-maker, could become in his hands as natural and devout a holy offering as incense. Mr. Harrison's Jehovah was something of a miracle. It added considerably "mo' firmament" to the lives of all of us who were privileged to see it during the five long years he played it. It was more than one of the outstanding acting memories of our time. It was one of the most authentic religious experiences of our day.

Most of us cannot think of the grand old gentleman's passing up de gangway of another Lord without secretly hoping that when our own time comes a Lawd very much like Mr. Harrison's will be presiding over the heavenly fish fry all of us would like some day to attend.

March 15, 1935

HOPE AND HOPE WILLIAMS

"HOPE springs eternal in the Williams breast," said Mr. Garland yesterday when reviewing Miss Williams' performance in *The Passing Present*. Hope Williams *is* invariably Hope Williams, for better or for worse, as Mr. Lockridge puts it. Whether she happens to be appearing in *Paris Bound, Holiday, Rebound, The New Yorkers,* or *The Passing Present*, she remains herself—her unmistakable, unchanging self.

When nothing more is asked of her, and she is provided with the right kind of banter, she can be one of the most amusing persons on our stage. She has looks. She has freshness. She has poise. She has charm. She has a neat flair for comedy, and abundant personality. Moreover, she has a method (or, what is probably far more accurate, a lack of it) which is as much her own as her boyish bob. Without any apparent effort, she can saunter into a play and make the whole of its first act hers. She does not raise her voice. She does not vary her intonations. She does not change her expression in any of the approved theatrical ways. She uses practically no gestures, that is, unless one counts the brotherly pats she is often called upon to administer on the shoulders of those playing opposite her.

She simply slouches into a script as athletically as if her heart were set on winning a football letter, with her arms swinging before her, with her head bent forward, and with a suppressed smile lurking in her clear blue eyes. Yet she manages to establish herself in no time; to project herself, too; and to make an audience delight in the fact that she—Hope Williams—is on the stage.

This ability to win an audience by the mere act of doing nothing is the surest token of Miss Williams' charm. It is the most important of her theatrical assets. Incidentally, it is an endowment many better actresses have cause to envy. It has served Miss Williams well whenever she has been well dealt with by her playwrights. It has its drawbacks. It makes things so easy for Miss Williams—when they are right for her—that she is obviously tempted to rely upon it, and it alone, when, as in the case of her present more or less emotional part in Gretchen Damrosch's play, things are wrong for her.

Miss Williams is a negative actress. In light comedies, set in contemporary drawing-rooms, her habit of underplaying is, as it were, a guarantee of her rightness for the company she keeps. It bespeaks her gentility. It differentiates her from the world of actors who have to make a business of acting, and gives both a new point and verisimilitude to her lines. Her comedy is doubly effective because it is effortless. It is offhand, casual, and spoken without those vocal underscorings most professionals are wont to use. It remains, as Mr. Barry or Mr. Stewart (or Miss Damrosch, if she could write it) would want it to remain, just so much high-spirited badinage.

Inadvertently effective as Miss Williams may have been in single moments heretofore when she has been called upon to be tragic, Miss Williams has never been at her best when asked to show an emotion, or to lose herself in either a scene or a character. At such times her technical inadequacies, her absence of variety, her lack of method, her many limitations as an actress, have become distressingly apparent. For that very reason, and because she has so little to do that does not demand some effort in the doing, she is seen to disadvantage in *The Passing Present*.

Miss Damrosch's play, a pale Manhattan restatement of *The Cherry Orchard*, finds Miss Williams in a part to which she is not ideally suited. That is only one way of saying that it finds her in a part which asks her to act. What Miss Williams does when faced with such a dilemma is to ignore the requirements of a very imperfect script, and go on being Miss Williams. Being Miss Williams, and having such a character as Miss Williams to play, can make for an extremely pleasant performance in the theatre. It may have nothing to do with characterization or acting as those words are ordinarily understood. It may mean having some trouble in keeping the second and third acts as interesting as the first one was. It may stand for a pertness which is inflexible. But it can contribute gayety of a very special, ebullient, and welcome sort to the stage. Asking Miss Williams to act is another and entirely different matter as *The Passing Present* demonstrates to its, to hers, and to our disadvantage.

December 9, 1931

MAE WEST

THE CONSTANT SINNER OF STAGE AND SCREEN

THERE is nothing of the nun about Miss West. The characters she plays are children of the wide open places. The sisterhood they belong to is without shame, and Miss West is invariably presented as the least reticent member of the order. Margie LaMont in *Sex* was a dishonorable woman. Babe Gordon, in *The Constant Sinner* was a dishonorable woman. Diamond Lil was and is a dishonorable woman. So have they all been, all dishonorable women. The perfume of the honky-tonk has followed in their wake.

These unregenerate Thaïses of the Tenderloin Miss West loves to play—and plays so grandly—move in a world that has little or no relation to life. Crimes, which are real enough, are committed all around them. Men are shot, white slavers caught, counterfeiters exposed, dopesters die miserable deaths, and jailbirds escape from behind thick steel bars. But everything which happens has about it the heightened unreality of a waterfront ballad. That, as Mr. Galsworthy used to remark, is where the fun comes in.

One reason for this is, of course, that it is Miss West around whom all the sinful solar systems of her plots revolve. And Miss West is a magnificently incredible person. She conquers a bit too easily. Her predatory triumphs have an immediacy about them which mere mortals are forced not only to question but to envy. One slight roll of her *Police Gazette* figure, four measured tosses of her unholy head, and every man for miles around is supposed to be hers. The effect she has on them is no less instantaneous than was the Medusa's, but, unlike that other figure in mythology, she does not turn her victims into stone.

There is something delightfully anachronistic about Miss West; something that belongs to the frontiersman's idea of fun, to the days of free-lunch counters, and yet that has about it the imperiousness of a vanished race of regal sirens. There is an opulence about Miss West's person the world cannot but admire in these lean times. There is, too, a cloudless certainty about her—and her wiles—which wins respect in these darkly doubting days.

The truth is Miss West is that rarest of all species among contemporary artists. She is a pre-Freudian. A Miocene mammal is scarcely more difficult to find. She is a survival of the most tightly fitted. Her approach to what Mr. Hammond has dubbed the "obstinate urge" is as simple as her dress is ornate. To her sex is sex, and that is all there is to it, or, for that matter, to life. She has no inhibitions. It would be grossly unfair to accuse her of being an introvert. No psychoanalysts are needed to point

the way to release for her. She is her own guide down a
very narrow but winding path. Her books are not her
best friends. To misquote George Ade, she is a bad girl
who needs no help.

She also happens to be a grand performer; an actress
who has perfected a style of her own. On stage or screen
she is not only a whole show, but a side show in herself.
She has a voice like no other voice that has ever been
heard, and a method of delivery that no one else can claim.
Her voice is choked. It has a sneer in it which is obviously
directed at all the hearthside virtues. Yet, just as obviously, it is warm. It is the smoke which escapes from a
slow fire.

She shakes speeches out of her mouth as if they were
dice being rolled with terrifying deliberation from a box.
Her sentences writhe like serpents. She can turn the simplest statement into a scorching insinuation; make an innocent "Hello, boys" sound like a traveling salesman's
idea of *The Decameron*. Vocally, she is a hootchie-kootchie
artist. The course she steers is always down the midway.
Her lack of subtlety is the most subtle thing about her.

Constant sinner that she may like to pretend to be,
Miss West has her redeeming virtues. She has a sense of
humor. Her exploits as a saleswoman of sex benefit by
being exaggerated until they belong to the mock-epic class.
Both as authoress and as actress, she continues the Paul
Bunyan tradition. She seems to recoil with an almost gun-
like precision after each of her more tawdry speeches, and
make her own comment (which is the comment of modernity) upon them, even while she continues to play them
seriously. She has a certain air of going slumming in her
own plays. She makes passion palatable to a puritan public
by making even its intensity ludicrous. She burlesques sex
as uproariously as John Held Jr.'s woodcuts spoof the

nineties. By managing to date it, by putting it in the museum class, by substituting fake fangs for real ones, she has conquered Hollywood, even as she once conquered Broadway.

Contrary to the teachings of the moralists, her vicious heroines may always be triumphant. But they are so unreal that they do not matter. Anyway, there is no virtue in her plays to be rewarded. No wonder, therefore, that Miss West has become America's newest sweetheart. She has probably known for years that America could be had. The reports now are that she "has" it.

March 25, 1933

7. Pity the Poor Critic

"NOBODY KNOWS DE TROUBLE AH'VE SEEN"

LET NO one tell you that dramatic critics spend their days recording the adventures of their souls among masterpieces. Masterpieces are even more uncommon than their souls. The reviewers' lot is not always a happy one when constabulary duty's to be done, to be done. On more evenings than one likes to think of, they must reach for their nightsticks rather than their pens. Do not blame them if they hit hard when the switching hour of midnight comes around. Their indifference would be a far greater cruelty. It is the seven deadly sins of criticism rolled into one. The reviewers have no other choice than to defend the theatre, their readers, and themselves. Only the best has a place in the theatre nowadays. Do you believe in slum clearance? Then you must also believe in destructive criticism. It is one of criticism's most constructive functions.

Nobody likes the reviewers when, sometimes for weeks on end, they are called upon to deliver one whacking blow after another on the heads of playwrights and producers, of directors and actors, whose chief crime is that they are not as good as they thought they were and would like to be. The reviewers do not even like themselves. Mysterious

251

strangers telephone to hurl unprintable abuse at them. They get letters from the performers, or the performers' relatives, accusing them of everything from having eaten a bad dinner to possessing gelatinous minds or being sadists. They get called names just as ugly as the names they call. Occasionally an outraged actress or dramatist strikes one of them in the face, which, all things considered, is no doubt a perfectly natural way for an actress or a playwright to try to turn a flop into a hit.

If most often dramatic criticism strikes its readers as being what Percy Hammond once described as "the venom of contented rattlesnakes," the reason is that the reviewers are forced to see (and unfortunately to review) all of those innumerable little fly-by-night productions which, season after season, continue to find their way to New York stages and from attendance on which playgoers are mercifully excused. How bad they are only the reviewers know. Yet, though they may last only a night or two, these "duds," these "turkeys," these abortive efforts, for which there is neither point nor excuse, compose a large number of each year's openings. When Richard Lockridge said that one of them had "opened like a yawn at such-and-such a playhouse," he issued a blanket injunction against the whole lot of them.

No book could hope to catch the likeness of our theatre in performance which passes over them. Like the wart on Cromwell's face, they must also be included in the picture. But let me quickly add that, after all this big talk, I have not the heart to exhume the worst of them. Let them sleep in peace as did those who sat before them. Having been pronounced dead once, and having been dead long before that, there is no need to execute them all over again. Let the sorrier ones, the ones that had to be introduced with such savage leads as "Pardon me for interrupting you, but a play called ——," or "The sooner this is over with, the better," or "The season can do no worse," stay in their graves which, since they are in them, must be yawning. Permit a mere mention of the fact not only that they were, but that they were abundant, serve as a sufficient indication of one aspect of our theatre from which even now you are spared.

The plays sent to the block in the following pages were masterpieces compared to the dramas I have in mind. They belong to an entirely different kettle of fishiness. I apologize to everyone responsible for them if, for no longer than a split infinitive, I seem to link them with the kind of hopeless offerings of which the theatre can be guilty at its incredible worst.

The productions which follow were not of the fly-by-night variety. They were produced under the most reputable auspices. They were well-acted, well-staged, and earnestly written. One of them, alas, was all-too-brilliantly set. Their sins were merely the sins of well-intentioned mediocrity, of materials wasted in the writing and abused in production, or of sweetness without light. That two of them were seen by a good number of playgoers is perhaps justification enough for offering them as samples of our theatre when, in representative fashion, it has been misguided in its aim or failed to do what it set out to do. At such moments the reviewer, if he cares for the theatre and seeks to protect his readers, is compelled, as Douglas Jerrold once put it, to review a play as the east wind reviews an apple tree.

KNIGHTS IN NEW JERSEY, OR
THE HOUSE BEAUTIFUL

SWEET are the dramatic uses of adversity to Channing Pollock, Esq. He is the bold knight among our dramatists who dares to commit acts of sentimentality from which any other playwright would shrink. He is the champion of simple things, the shield-bearer of the common man, and the ingenuous protector of the eternal verities,. who of recent years has donned his armor of shining platitudes, not once but many times, to ride away on a Children's Crusade. Last night, however, he bobbed up with a play called *The House Beautiful*, which represents the biggest Children's Crusade he has yet embarked upon. And there were many members of a large first-night audience who were willing to greet it with enthusiasm.

This most recent of his dramatic sermons is a modern miracle play in which Esquire Pollock, as is his wont, finds tongues in trees, books in running brooks, sermons in stones, and Sir Galahad in New Jersey, even if he does not see good in everything. It is the kind of play that every professional indorser, regardless of where he buttons his collar, will join Mr. Pollock in ballyhooing up and down the countryside. Presidents of women's clubs will doubtless find it to their liking. Clergymen will flock to see it. It is guaranteed to make commuters from the lesser villages of New Jersey feel ennobled. Admirers of Edgar Guest will dote upon it. Camp Fire Girls will celebrate it by rubbing sticks together. Boy Scouts will stand up and salute it with thumbs and little fingers crossed, whenever its name is mentioned in a public place. It is as Arthurian in its more archaic flashbacks as Mark Twain, as wholesome in its attitude toward the present as Dr. Cadman, and about as inspiring as a trunkful of mottoes.

Yet in spite of its all-too-apparent worthiness, its barrelfuls of mush and treacle, its avalanche of bromides, its appalling prissyness and its even more appalling flashbacks, this chronicle of a commuter's trials is none the less possessed of its moving and amusing moments. In any case it is never entirely dull. Even when its sentimentality is at its worst there is an undeniable fascination in wondering what it is Mr. Pollock will dare to do next.

Like many another preacher before him, the unfrocked Mr. Pollock has felt the need of a text. He finds one, appropriately enough, in the line in *Pilgrim's Progress* which reads, "And behold, there was a very stately palace before him, the name of which was Beautiful, and it stood by the highway side." The home Mr. Pollock chooses to call *The House Beautiful* is not a stately palace, but a simple man's home, blessed with a soul, and built in the little town of West Hills, which we presume to be in New Jersey.

The philosophical Mr. Pollock, who has observed "We can't all be Napoleons," takes an average man—one of those "little men, fighting behind, who win the wars"—and shows him failing by the cheap standards of this world, but succeeding by all the nobler standards of the Round Table. His name is Archie Davis (James Bell) and when we first see him he is but newly married to a very good woman called Jennifer (Mary Philips). He buys a lot in West Hills when there is no town there and the village to come is only a realtor's dream. We watch his house as it springs up around him and his wife, and time is ticked off for twenty-seven years within its homey walls by a clock which sounds as if the crocodile in *Peter Pan* had swallowed it.

Mr. Davis—Sir Archibald, Sir Galahad, Mr. Good Man,

or what you will—is no money-maker. He stands for trees, gardens and nice houses in his town. Yet because of his high ideals he is, of course, harassed by debt. His son marries a worldly neighbor's daughter and never goes to college, as he had hoped. But Mr. Davis goes right on trying. He becomes the Mayor of West Hills in the most amusing scene in the play. He makes several flashback visits to Ye Olden Times. He is allowed to vary his ill-fitting business clothes with knightly armor (whenever Mr. Pollock feels called upon to parallel the present in castle scenes taking place behind a gauze over the mantelpiece). He has the satisfaction of seeing his son champion his own ideals. He dies from the worries of this world, and is finally joined by his dearly beloved wife on a drawbridge which apparently leads to a Maxfield Parrish future.

As Mr. Pollock brings his King Arthur's knights to Main Street, he shows that he, like them, is a Sir Galahad, tilting lances with the evils of the present day. He, too, fights his Black Knights. They include Robber Barons in New Jersey real estate, clothes, bridge, cocktails and *The New Yorker;* lost royalties, the cynical sterility of the present, the radio, Wall Street, and all those worldly and sophisticated things which, as Mr. Pollock sees them, have temporarily endangered the eternal verities. As he fights them, he raises his trusty shield to protect such knightly ideals as Love, Honor and Fidelity. Mr. Pollock goes even further. He applauds the squareshooter, endorses the Soul, sees the holiness in small things, deifies the bedroom set which costs $75, hears chivalrous trumpets in the whistles of commuters' trains, and expresses, through Jennifer, his conviction that "life is beautiful and grand and romantic." He may seem to have his moments of despair, but each of his curtains is optimistic, for they respectively tell us that though nobody may see or hear them, "still trumpets sound throughout the whole world!"; that we can keep the flag flying and the house beautiful if only we are brave; and that when our work is done in New Jersey, Arthurian palaces will be waiting for us.

If *The House Beautiful* were badly performed it would be frankly laughable. But at the Apollo it is given a smooth-running, mechanically expert, and excellent production by Worthington Miner, the visual illusion of which is made possible by Jo Mielziner's ingenious and very satisfactory settings. Fortunately for Mr. Pollock and those who like this kind of Sunday school morality, Mary Philips and James Bell as the trumpet-hearing elder Davises, and the many others in the cast, play the parts which fall their way with such simplicity and skill that they managed to keep the ruder, less Arthurian members of the first-night audience from laughing out loud at some of the more trying moments. For so doing they merit our admiration and Mr. Pollock's knee-bent gratitude.

March 13, 1931

MA FROM THE MOUNTAINS

"MA" WAS missin' last night. Yes, suh, and she's the only thing that wah. If by any chance you don't recall "Ma," permit me to refresh your memory. You've seen her a hundred times. She's the old hag who invariably smokes her pipe in mountain plays. She smokes it as she sits broodin' in her corner in the rockin' chair. For that matter, she smokes it when she's gettin' dinner, cussin' pappy, or readin' the Good Book. The only time she's apt to put it down is when she's reachin' for her shot-gun above the door.

You remember "Ma"? She's the sour-faced old woman whose son went over the mountains and brought home as his bride the free-and-easy, neck-showin' city girl who causes all the trouble 'twixt the men-folks when the moon is shinin' bright. Everybody knows "Ma." She's the one who supplies mountaineer playwrights with so much dialogue. When they have nothing else to say, these dramatists know that it's always the right time for someone to turn to "Ma" as she putters ominously around the kitchen, and ask, "Whatcha doin', Ma?" This can occupy quite a lot of time.

Well, "Ma" was missing at the Little last night. And she was missed. Except for "Ma's" absence, Lulu Vollmer's *The Hill Between* was like any other bad mountain play you have seen and not enjoyed. The minute the curtain went up, and you took one look at the setting, you felt at home. The churn was in its proper place. The mountains looked green and properly confining on the backdrop. The shot-gun was hung over the door.

At this point Mr. Cracraft's work as a designer stopped, and Miss Vollmer's work as a playwright began. Once again you knew almost everything, except the harrowing details, the minute Miss Dorothy Patten as Anna asked good old ginghamed Julie (Sara Haden) how butter was made.

Miss Patten was the outsider. In a mountain play that means a lot. She was going to cause all the trouble. And cause all the trouble she proceeded to do. She had just come for a visit to the mountains as the wife of the young doctor with whom Julie had been in love in his barefoot boyhood days. There was the usual talk about the mountains claimin' their own. As a matter of fact there was even more of this talk than usual. And the mountains seemed exceptionally slow. Then, as Anna, Miss Patten made things worse by doing a foolish thing. She allowed the fiance of her husband's sister to kiss her within eye-shot of the cabin. Needless to say, this occasioned a good many goings on, and whole pages of what struck me, as a susceptible plains-man, as being incredibly bogus mountaineer talk about love, honor, the hill-billy code, and what have you.

Miss Vollmer's *Sun-Up* had its moments. *The Hill Between* cannot even claim its split seconds.

Yes, suh, "Ma" was missed. So was a good time.

March 12, 1938

MR. WEBB IN *AND STARS REMAIN*

AS AN actor Clifton Webb, like Alexander Woollcott, is the answer to an upholsterer's prayer. He belongs to the horizontal school of wisecrackers. Give him a sofa, and some of the brighter lines of the Brothers Epstein, and he can be very funny. He adds a lot to the Theatre Guild's first offering of the season by maintaining such a stead-fastly immobile face whenever he appears in *And Stars Remain* that Fifty-second Street is apt to be known for the next few weeks as Dead Pan Alley.

The main trouble with the Epsteins' comedy of social enlightenment is that, while writing it, they did not send a hurry call to Grand Rapids and get more sofas to put at Mr. Webb's disposal. Their comedy picks up whenever Mr. Webb lies down. At such moments it is really very amusing. But instead of providing more cushions for Mr. Webb, the Brothers Epstein have busied themselves with supplying us with a plot. That proves to be a major mistake. For what they have given Mr. Webb to say as a heavily subsidized Couch-Dweller is infinitely superior to the story they tell about how Liberalism first came to Sutton Place.

Their plot is such a feeble and improbable affair that it seems to need the support of even more cushions than those of which Mr. Webb takes full advantage. It is timely in its overtones. It is well meant. One wants to sympathize with everything it is trying to say. But it is such a waste of good comedy on fuzzily-stated politics and economics, and grows so talky in the process of trying to be both clever and good at the same time, that one looks forward with relief to those moments in which it forgets to spank Die-Hard Republicans and remembers to summon Mr. Webb to his sofa to let him have his languid and entertaining say.

If you can imagine *The Servant in the House* as Noel Coward might have revised it, or *The Fool* as S. N. Behrman might have touched up a few scenes here and there, you may have some notion of the mixture of worthiness and wit, of morality and madness, of seriousness and nonsense which the Brothers Epstein have brewed in their earnest comedy.

These brothers are said to be the first twins ever to have written a play together. This is interesting in its way. Certainly it would have proven so to Barnum. But as one unfriendly fellow remarked last night, it is something of a pity that *And Stars Remain* was not written by quintuplets.

October 13, 1936

THE HOUSE THAT GEDDES BUILT

WHEN the curtain fell on the second act of Norman Bel Geddes's production of *Iron Men* last evening, a man who either thought the play must be over or who may have read somewhere about how to act at a first night, stood up and in all earnestness cried "Author! Author!" Had he called for bison in the mid-Atlantic, watermelons at the North Pole or Nicholas II in Stalin's presence, he could not have wasted his breath more extravagantly.

The program insists there was an author. It goes so far as to give his name, which is Francis Gallagher. But if Mr. Gallagher is not just a pen name for one of Mr. Geddes' girders and if he were really present at the Longacre last evening, I, for one, am willing to bet needles to pins (a) that either he would have been only too glad to forget he was ever responsible for *Iron Men,* or (b) that seeing Mr. Geddes' production would have taken his mind off any play he might have written even if that play had been *Hamlet.*

Mr. Geddes has had himself a circus at the Longacre, a circus in which Mr. Gallagher's script is reduced to so much tanbark. Had he been a small boy playing with a mechano set, he could not have had more fun. Adventurous as he always is, he has not stopped with designing a setting. Oh, no! Not Mr. Geddes! He has one built before our very eyes. And what kind of setting is it? A skyscraper which pushes its naked red girders higher and higher into the air with the aid of a huge derrick and a leading man (William Haade), now turned actor for the first time, who has previously appeared on the steel girders of the Barbizon-Plaza, Pierre's, the Farmers' Loan and Trust Company, the Bank of Manhattan, Essex House, the Rockefeller Church and the Lincoln Hospital while they were in the process of construction.

Underneath Mr. Geddes' skyscraper is a super-realistic barroom, in which every other scene of *Iron Men* occurs, and in which one is allowed to follow Mr. Gallagher's plot without cringing before a suspended girder or waiting to see one land triumphantly in place. Indoors, as well as out of doors, Mr. Gallagher's play does not prove to be any kind of drama. It is all about Andy, a great, boastful fellow, and his Three Riveteers. These riveteers are a very strange lot. They are full of more hero worship for Andy than you could find in ten colleges during the football season. In fact, their hero worship takes the form of such an undisguised crush that, if these laborers did not move around so bravely on Mr. Geddes' perilous setting and utter such big he-mannish words and chew tobacco, they would probably be laughed at even in a girls' school. . . .

Come to think of it, Mr. Geddes may have been right in trying to take everyone's attention off the play and focus it on himself. My own guess is he would have been not only more correct but infinitely wiser and more merciful had he devoted his attention to finding a play that was half as well built as is his unfinished skyscraper, and that was not its equal in emptiness. . . .

October 20, 1936

8. For the Tired Business Man and Woman

THE BATTLE OF NIBLO'S GARDENS

THAT our musical comedies and revues are one of the chief glories of our stage needs no special pleading at this late date. Ever since the respectable sixties when Richard Grant White, a solemn Shakespearean scholar, dropped into Niblo's Gardens, the house of *The Black Crook's* ill-fame, and not only saluted the beautiful and (for those days) scantily-clad Pauline Markham as the woman who had found the lost arms of the Venus de Milo but confessed that he infinitely preferred Lydia Thompson's performance in *Sinbad* to much high tragedy he had seen, especially Edwin Forrest's Hamlet, the aesthetes have taken over the girlie-girlie shows in such increasing numbers that speculators have died of exhaustion trying to locate tickets for plain, lusty, and relaxed theatregoers whose lack of knowledge about the choruses of Aristophanes has been equaled only by their ignorance of the *Commedia dell'Arte*, and whose single search has been for an evening of un-footnoted joy.

Mr. Nathan, with his tributes to George Lederer, his gleeful susceptibility to pretty girls and lively tunes, his much-trumpeted hedonism, and wide catholicity of tastes, his keen-eyed appraisal of the wonders of the old *Ziegfeld Follies*, his wisdom in realizing that the theatre is what it happens to invite you to see on any particular night, and his constant reiteration that it must function as a rathskeller and a harem no less than as a library and an art gallery, long ago did more than yeoman's service in winning for our better musicals the critical recognition they deserve. Furthermore he did so without striking any Greenery-Gallery attitudes or mistaking a lily for a pen. You will look in vain through the writings of such sober Bardolaters as William Winter and J. Ranken Towse to find them saying what Mr. Nathan (who is at once a Bardolater and one of the most exuberant of our red-nosed comics) wrote when he confessed, with more gusto than Richard Grant White could muster, "When I write that I enjoy the comedy of Shakespeare more than the comedy of Harry Watson, Jr., I lie."

Even the drama professors in our colleges now know that the theatre does not begin and end with Dan Totheroh and Lulu Vollmer. Or with the Greeks and William Shakespeare, for that matter. Although it threatened to take on the proportions of a hundred years' war, the battle of Niblo's Gardens has long since been won. It was not so much a victory as a massacre. That it had to be fought in the first place is not surprising. But what now seems incredible is that it could have dragged on as long as it did. It was never an even fight. It was always hopelessly one-sided. From the outset it was clear that the guardsmen of the Kembles and of Cushman, of Boucicault and of Brougham, of Percy MacKaye and of Augustus Thomas had no chance against the hosts of Hilarity, the countless Storm Troopers of Female Beauty, the unshocked battalions of Belly Laughter.

Furthermore, the right was always on the side of the forces of Fun. The Black Crooks did not enter the battle as

agents of darkness. They were champions of bright lights
and mirth, of melody and insouciance, of capering and of
clowning. There was no resisting them. They were swept
on to a victory which, though it may not always have been
moral, was from every technical point of view a triumph.
Lydia Thompson's unspiritual grandsons and granddaugh-
ters routed the dwindling enemy no less surely than the
charming Ada S. Harland herself a member of the Lydia
Thompson chorus, routed Professor Brander Matthews
when for the nonce he forgot about Corneille, Racine, Molière, Sardou, Dumas-fils, and Augier, and asked her to
marry him, and she thereafter became the gem of his ocean
at Columbia.

The amazing thing about the generation of critics who
refused to laugh at any jokes which did not contain at
least four "ergos" or five "forsooths," and who had neither
ears nor eyes for amusements of the ear-and-eye variety,
was neither their lack of humor nor their pretentiousness.
It was their deafness and, even more particularly, their
blindness. They had plenty of sacred but no profane love
for the theatre which demands both.

What they failed to note, while they were busily turning
out two-volume biographies of such sleight-of-mind trick-
sters as Belasco or taking Charles Rann Kennedy's dramas
with a seriousness they would have ordinarily extended
only to the works of Sheridan Knowles, was that, at the
very time they were writing, our theatre boasted its highest
standards of technical excellence and its most uncompro-
mising professionalism in its revues. Mediocre as was most
of our pre-war playwriting, imitative as was our theatre
in many other respects, it was original and often distinguished in its musicals. Even then they had achieved in
their clowns and their dancers, their showgirls and their

settings, their music and their choruses, their speed and their technical skill, the easy pre-eminence they continue to hold over the revues, and, of late years, the musical comedies produced in any other country.

Although almost all critics of Mr. Nathan's and subsequent vintages have followed his lead in stating it, a realization of the true excellence of our musicals appears to have dawned slowly on America. As late as 1924 Gilbert Seldes created something of a sensation among sophisticates by daring to point out that in this country we tolerate a second-rateness in novels, operas, and serious plays which "we would not for a moment abide in the construction of a bridge . . . or the production of a revue."

In a revue, rightly argued the aesthetic Mr. Seldes, "the bunk doesn't carry. . . . There are, if you count the chorus, about a hundred reasons for seeing a revue; there is only one reason for thinking about it, and that is that at one point, and only one point, the revue touches upon art. The revue as a production manifests the same impatience with half-measures, with boggling, with the good enough, and the nearly successful which every great artist feels, or pretends to feel, in regard to his own work. It shows a mania for perfection. . . . Jazz or symphony may sound from the orchestra pit, but underneath is the real tone of the revue, the steady, incorruptible purr of the dynamo."

Since Mr. Seldes hymned the lively arts, a great many changes have taken place both in our musical comedies and revues. Our musical comedies are no longer the mossy banks of sentimentality they once were. Ruretanian hussars and merry, merry villagers have slipped from grace, along with love-and-dove rhymes. The hardy annuals among the revues, *The Passing Shows*, *The Scandals*, *The Vanities*, and *Artists and Models*, have disappeared. Only the great

comedians who graduated from them remain, and many of
them are in Hollywood or on the air. Mr. Ziegfeld has gone.
So have *The Follies* as he produced them, with their Ben
Ali Haggin *tableaux vivants,* their magnificent skill, their
unmistakable opulence, their costly frigidity, their honor
roll of comics.

The scene has changed. There are fewer musicals than
there used to be. At times the dearth of them seems melancholy beyond endurance. When they do come in, they
no longer burst with the array of topnotch comedians they
once did. But their standards of production are as high as
they ever were. And the standards of their writing, their
dancing, their musicianship, and of their settings and costumes have soared. If they are not as slick as were Earl
Carroll's *Vanities,* they are far less empty. If they lack the
silky lushness of *The Follies,* they can claim a new vitality.

The public has long since agreed with Percy Hammond
that a knee is a joint, not an entertainment. It wants more
than spangles and velvets. It is tired of stately show girls
parading up and down steps, sprouting plumes appropriate
to the birds they were supposed to represent. It is wearied
of finales placed in Geneva, as they used to be in the days
when nations still went to Geneva, which disclosed these
same stately maidens strutting about as "The Spirits" of
various countries and wearing the flags of those lands
where no army regulations have ever insisted they be worn.

Beauty now finds itself side by side with speed, and
taste has replaced mere lavishness. The ballet has joined
the hosts of percussion. Our best designers do some of their
best work meeting the difficult demands of our musicals.
Our music increases in intricacy and has taken on a new
richness in its orchestration. There is point as well as
opulence, and sense no less than sound. The outside world

is no longer excluded from the realms of the houris, the clowns, and the tunesmiths. All that is mad in it and us is joyously dragged upon the scene—in tumbrils.

Although the old gaiety has not been lost, a new impudence is manifest, good-natured yet demolishing. Satire, fleet, unsparing, and uproarious, has raised its welcome head. No one is safe; no pretension above exposure. A healthy disrespect is abroad. In our musicals we are in truth a land of liberty. Measure the irreverencies of George M. Cohan's old revues with what the same Mr. Cohan is called upon to do in *I'd Rather Be Right*, and you realize the difference. The smaller revues—*The Garrick Gaieties, The Grand Street Follies, The Little Shows* and Charlot's offerings—blazed the trail. Such productions as *The Band Wagon, Face The Music*, and *Strike Up The Band* carried it much further. When Brooks Atkinson described *Of Thee I Sing* as being "funnier than the government and not half so dangerous," the new attitude on both sides of the footlights found á memorialist. The passing years have robbed Mr. Seldes' statement, made in 1924, of its full accuracy. There are now a great many things to be thought about in our musicals. They no longer permit us to be pleasantly relaxed. They demand us to be jubilantly alert. Our laughter at them is the surest proof that we are thinking. It may be because there is less business than there once was, but our musicals are now produced on the assumption that our business men and women are less tired than they used to be.

There remains one ugly question. It refuses to be ignored. It is serious enough to furrow the brow of any devoted admirer of our musicals. With burlesque curtailed and vaudeville gone, where will the comedians of the future be recruited? The old-timers are still our best clowns, if not our only ones. When their fine ranks are thinned, who will replace them?

MARILYN MILLER

MISS MILLER was Broadway's *première ballerina*. The classically-minded Mr. Levinson may never have mentioned her in his essays on the dance. Mr. van Druten may have omitted her from his convert's hymn to the ballet. She may not have figured in John Martin's scheme of things. But she was the Pavlowa of the Tired Business Man; the Taglioni of the world of musical comedy and of jazz; the Fanny Elssler of a whole generation of college boys in search of diversion.

She was possessed of surprising grace. Her pirouettes found her body "self-poised as if it floated in the air." The young gentlemen fresh from the art classes may have told their roommates, when her pink tarlatans were full spread and she was defying gravitation by her nimble leaps through space, that they admired her because she made them think of a Degas figure, turned American in some miraculous manner and suddenly released from the restraints of the rehearsal room and impatient vigils in the wings. But, as *Sally* and her other successes proved, she was far more native than that. It was a saxophone, not a symphony, which awakened her as a dancer. In spite of the chilly classicism of some of her more ambitious numbers, she was a ballerina who was as blatantly American in her way as Ring Lardner was in his.

With her blonde hair, her doll-like face, her unfading smile, her beautifully articulated body, her far-flung skirts, her plumes, and spangles, and pointed ballet slippers, Miss Miller had much more in common with *Polly of the Circus* than with Degas. She was Polly grown up; Polly graduated

from The Big Tent; Polly triumphing in a new career in
Mr. Ziegfeld's super-opulent revues.

She had learned to sing. She had learned to act, too. And
her impersonations of Lynn Fontanne and Joan Crawford in *As Thousands Cheer*, indicated the genuine, if
tardily revealed, talent which was hers for satiric mimicry.
But it is mainly as a dancer—as the perfect response to the
invitation of everything gay, rippling and contagious in
the lighter music of her day—that some of us will remember her.

Such was her innocence of spirit, or, if you prefer, so
zephyr-like was her sexlessness, that to the end she continued to belong much more to the child-like world of the
circus than to the sophistication of a Ziegfeld show. She
was one of our theatre's sunniest and most shimmering
entertainers, and certainly the blithest ballerina of her
time. She was the Titania of the jazz age; a princess in a
grown-up's fairy tale. Yet she appealed to adults as every
Polly of the Circus appeals to those who are young enough
to believe them.

The glory belonging to a tanbark goddess did not desert
her when she danced. *Première ballerina* of this land of the
single eagle she may have been. But when she danced, one
could have sworn it was on the broad white back of a
circus horse, instead of on the carpeted floor of a stage, that
she became the smiling embodiment of grace.

April 8, 1936

ED WYNN, KING OF IDIOCY

IF acting in general has a stubborn way of refusing to
be translated into words, the contribution of such a mad

comedian as Ed Wynn is particularly difficult to capture on paper. You may set him down as a clown, copy his own billing, and hail him as "The Perfect Fool" he unquestionably is. You may mention his fantasy, wonder at the number of his hats, or record the startled timidity with which he wanders from one insane complication to another. You may note his spider-scared hands, or those mildly stifled chortles of self-appreciation with which he punctuates his humor. You may describe his black spectacles, his arching eyebrows, his fabulous suits, and those still more fabulous shoes of his which look like so many camouflaged troopships leaving their berths in Hoboken. You may print some of his jokes, admire the drollery of his lisp, and gasp in pleasant wonder at the absurdity of his inventions. But the Ed Wynn who is portrayed on paper is still very far removed from the Ed Wynn who personally participates in such an uproariously daffy show as *The Laugh Parade,* and steers it from one guffaw to another.

Although he is something of a child himself and although he reduces audiences to just so many screaming children, Mr. Wynn remains unlike, most children inasmuch as he should be seen as well as heard, and not written about at all. The reasons for this are pressing. He is the only complete master of his own special brand of nonsense. He has no imitators who can succeed at imitating him. What he does begins and ends with him. He is like no other laughwinner; his on-stage self resembles no other being that roams this mad, mad world.

He is more than a person, and has become a character. Like many another funnyman he has a make-up, a personality and a patter of his own. Like all truly good comedians, this character audiences have come to know and love and recognize is bigger than himself. It is part of a story one hopes will never end. It strays from production to production and season to season as Sherlock Holmes kept re-appearing in A. Conan Doyle's detective yarns. Hence it is that Mr. Wynn is as welcome as an old friend, though no one knows what new lunacy he will be up to each time he returns. He keeps people guessing even as he keeps them roaring, for no one can match his imagination for addle-pated monkeyshines.

Many of the things he does are funny only when he does them. Many of the things he says are funny only when he says them. His joking may not leave you a hundred de-tailed pleasures you can carry home with you. Those mem-ories which do survive the evening may seem strangely flat when you attempt to relay them yourself. But while he is at work, Mr. Wynn succeeds—as almost no other major comic in our theatre succeeds—in wiping out all recollec-tions of the everyday world outside the theatre and in mak-ing the laughter of the moment seem more important than life itself. He is the king of nonsense, and the emperor of idiocy.

As one of the most willing subjects in Mr. Wynn's wide, wide realm, permit me at this late date to hasten to assure you *The Laugh Parade* is one of the most side-splitting bits of glorious silliness this town has seen for some time. It finds Mr. Wynn at his best. He is on-stage almost every minute of the time, rushing in and out in all sorts of crazy costumes, doing a "Protean Act" which is as funny as any-thing the theatre has to offer, telling stories that make no sense but that cause much uncontrollable laughter, and in general carrying the production on his own two very capable shoulders.

It might be added Mr. Wynn is as good at watching others as he is at making others delight in watching him. He gives the stage more generously to his confreres than any leading comedian I can think of. He is a perfect feeder in addition to being a perfect fool. The result is that *The Laugh Parade* is a wellnigh perfect Ed Wynn show.

November 21, 1931

LADY PEEL AND BEATRICE LILLIE

BEATRICE LILLIE is a comic law unto herself. Even George Bernard Shaw at his most talkative has been unable to keep her clownish mind from triumphing over the dull matter he has put at her disposal. As Mr. Woollcott observed when she was winning most of the laughs in *Too True to Be Good*, it was a case, not of gilding the lily, but of Lillie-ing the Guild. The happy truth is Miss Lillie "Lillies" any material she touches. This material may be good. It may be bad. What invariably seems more important than the stuff she has to deal with is that it has brought her on the stage. Her being there puts one under a certain obligation to even her less inspired lyricists and librettists, because Miss Lillie is a whole show in herself.

Although before the evening is over she can be counted upon to do many gloriously nonsensical things, Miss Lillie really does not have to do very much to make an audience roar with laughter. The playgoers who journey to see her in *Walk a Little Faster* are conquered in advance, if they happen to have seen her before. If they have memories, they cannot have forgotten her in *Charlot's Revue*, when she first burst upon this town, adding it overnight to her dominions. The picture of her, full of middle-class haughtiness and weighted down with packages and balloons, as she attempted to push her way onto a bus, must set them laughing even now—that is, of course, if ever they saw *This Year of Grace*.

Miss Lillie in an absurd costume parodying the manner of a concert singer; Miss Lillie as Gladstone's pet; Miss Lillie spoofing British jingoism in her ridiculous version of "Britannia Rules the Waves"; Miss Lillie as a Channel swimmer; Miss Lillie exposed as Marlene Dietrich in *The Third Little Show;* Miss Lillie as a—oh! well, what's the use? The catalogue could be continued indefinitely. But there is no sense in doing that. All I am trying to say is that, before they hand their ticket stubs to the ushers at the St. James, most contemporary theatregoers have already been conquered by Miss Lillie. They know what to expect and are prepared for it. The recollection of her manner of reading a sense of outraged propriety into so meaningless a phrase as "Oh, please" is enough to send them smiling down the aisles. They look forward with anticipation to the first time she will give a sudden backward lurch, force her voice to strained (and obviously feigned) tones of horror, describe a mad semicircle with her right hand, and wig-wag with her forefinger as only she can make a forefinger wig-wag. Conquered as they may be now, Miss Lillie's audiences had to be won in the beginning. The truth is that she conquers them today even as she victimized them in the days of *Charlot's Revue.*

Miss Lillie is the neatest, the most unruffled of our clowns. No tanbark from the circus ring ever seems to attach itself to her person. No matter how silly the costume, how windswept the wig, how tattered the hat, or how full-blown the sleeves, she possesses a tailored look and appears to be fresh from the tub. This spotlessness of hers is but one of the many surprises in her bag of tricks. By means of it she breaks defiantly with the tradition of grimy antics, by means of which, from Grimaldi to the Fratellinis, out-and-out clowns have sweated for the rewards of laughter. She wears no uniform, such as Charlie Chaplin does, which serves her as an immediately recognizable on-stage costume. She has no comic trademark such as Jolson's blackface, or Bobby Clark's painted spectacles, or Ed Wynn's great coat, antediluvian shoes and repertory of hats, which permit the precious ones to hail her as a reincarnation of the *Commedia dell'Arte*.

She is herself—regardless of the irrational paraphernalia she may wear. Even when she steps onto a stage without the aid of silly getups, her audience is ready to laugh at anything she does. She is a well-groomed, clean-cut, smartly dressed, attractive woman. Yet there is something about the mischief lurking in her eyes, her slightly distorted gestures and movements, and her wicked seriousness which is an immediate cue for the giggles. Both Miss Lillie's clowning and her comedy come naturally to her. She is as poiseful and as grave as an undertaker. Yet from the moment of her first entrance she makes it plain that, if any mortuary comparison is fair in her lively case, she is the musical chair at a funeral. What she is burying, by means of uproarious ridicule, is every dowdy middle-class pretension.

Miss Lillie is a cartoon come to life. Her neatness and her unholy calm only add to the hilarity which breaks out with each of the turbulent, suddenly energetic things she does. Even when she becomes daffy, she never loses her equanimity entirely. She goes goofy only in sections. Her feet, made ridiculous, as in the case of the current sketch called *Scamp of the Campus,* by being shod in preposterous high shoes, may be indulging in enough footwork to win the envy of a bantam boxer, but her body retains its dignity. Her arms may be swirling outward in all sorts of angular and preposterous gestures, but her face is seriousness itself. Chief among her many talents, Miss Lillie must count her genius for what I can only describe as the transference of guilt. She sheds any responsibility for the innuendoes she conjures. Understanding her is done at one's own risk. It becomes the spectator's responsibility and guilt. No matter how smudged the sentence may be she speaks, when she cocks her immaculate little head to one side with a terrier's jauntiness, Miss Lillie remains as clean as Spotless Town while she is speaking it. As a British subject her motto rightly enough is *honi soit*.

Miss Lillie is never completely undignified. Her composure is always contradicting the arrant madness of some of the things she is doing. It shines through all the crazy lines she may be called upon to speak. She can keep as cool as two rows of cucumbers in the rowdiest of rowdy moments, and make these moments doubly funny by doing so.

As a result her comedy always appears to be effortless. It never seems to have exhausted itself. Something is always left in reserve. This is but a part of the ever quickening intelligence Miss Lillie brings to the words she speaks and her all-expressive pantomime. She knows how to poke fun at the gravity which befits Lady Peel in such a ludicrous manner that delighted audiences must sometimes wonder if her proper title is not Lady Banana Peel.

December 10, 1932

GYPSY ROSE LEE

WHERE Josephine Baker was visible in last year's edition of *The Ziegfeld Follies*, Gypsy Rose Lee is now to be seen in the new edition at the Winter Garden. It is a case, as far as certain elemental facts are concerned, of a production having jumped from the skillet into the fire. Europe, as everyone knows, has long admired Miss Baker. In her lithe body and bold contortions it saw a release of primitive frenzy such as it had not witnessed before and has not witnessed since. In the words of so eminent a dance critic as the late André Levinson, Miss Baker was "an extraordinary creature of simian suppleness," "a sinuous idol that enslaves and incites mankind," "a gushing stream of rhythm," a dancer possessed of "the compelling potency of the finest examples of Negro sculpture," and "the Black Venus of Baudelaire" come to life.

To those who had never seen Miss Baker in the flesh before last year's edition of *The Follies*, M. Levinson appeared to have overstated her case. Her body was as well-proportioned and as agile as advance rumors claimed. But her voice sounded gnome-like in the huge auditorium. Although she had some tom-tom numbers which were animalistic by intention, she moved through them so much more like a graceful countess on a slumming expedition than as the embodiment of "pre-human" bestiality that there was never the slightest need to lower the asbestos curtain.

Gypsy Rose Lee is different, as different from Miss Baker as daylight is from darkness. She has no tom-tom numbers at her disposal. She does not symbolize the Congo gone wild; she is no primitive priestess. She does not dance, except a few mincing steps of the traditional "strip-tease" girl's routine. Even if she wanted to, she could not strut her stuff in Miss Baker's celebrated fashion. No one, I feel confident, has suffered from jungle fever in writing about her as M. Levinson did when he took pen in hand to describe the night clubs' Empress Josephine. Abandon, such as we were led to expect in Miss Baker, is not Miss Lee's affair. Yet what she succeeds in adding to the new *Follies* is essentially the same appeal Miss Baker failed to add to last years' edition.

Miss Lee is a stately maiden who seems at first sight to

belong to that race of goddesses known to Broadway as show girls. Although she has great dignity and the kind of poise Réjane would have admired, she is by no means cold or aloof. She has a warm smile, laughing eyes, a likable personality and a spirit so obviously philanthropic that she insists upon doing her bit for the Community Chest.

If rumor, and the lyrics at present assigned to her, can be relied on, Miss Lee is also an intellectual. She would never be confused with the president of a women's college. Or with an ordinary highbrow. Because she carries her learning as lightly as she does her clothing. The big words and long names she is asked to sing cause her no trouble. She rattles them off with an ease that would do credit to Nicholas Murray Butler at the same time that, without embarrassment or any noticeable causes for embarrassment, she is treating a costume as if it were Salomé's seven veils.

Miss Lee is also a competent enough accomplice in several of the hilarious skits in which she finds herself with Miss Brice and Mr. Clark. But it is at doing nothing that she is at her best. She has a walk such as few actresses can equal, and a beauty ideally suited to her craft.

Pretending to strip, you might be inclined to think, is a simple thing. And teasing, you would probably say, is as old as the first rose bush from which Eve could snatch a flower to put into her mouth before Adam's interested gaze. But when you see the two combined by Miss Lee you realize that they take their place not among the seven deadly sins but among the seven arts Mr. Seldes was right in describing as lively.

September 17, 1936

A QUIETER MR. LAHR

IN *Life Begins at 8:40*, Bert Lahr is a quieter fellow than he used to be in the days when as a bogus toreador in *Hot-Cha!* it was his nerve-wracking duty to face a bull in the arena. But he is no less funny than he used to be. As a matter of fact, his quietness becomes him as much as Mr. O'Neill would have us believe that mourning becomes Electra. Not for a moment do I mean to suggest Mr. Lahr has turned church-mouse. He is very far from that, and plunges even now into such a scene as the hilarious one in the stock broker's office with the same explosive energy which has always been his. But he *is* quiet—for Bert Lahr, which in no way implies he does not manage to make himself heard.

His voice is as husky and rasping as ever. And he still is master of those amazingly comical grunts and groans which sound as if they were the croakings of a giant bullfrog cursed with asthma. But Mr. Lahr is now in control of his energy instead of allowing it to be in full control of him. He has harnessed the Niagara of his high spirits. Refusing to be carried along by what was once the wasteful rush of their powers, he has made them work for him. Where he used to wear himself (and some of his admirers) out before the evening was over by maintaining, throughout an entire performance, the tension of a detonating Du Pont truck, he now keeps his explosions in hand. Amusing as they have always been, they gain immensely by not being so continuous.

More than that, in *Life Begins at 8:40* Mr. Lahr proves conclusively he is not the single-tracked zany he once seemed fated to be. Fortunately for all of us, he has not forgotten how to cross his eyes when, by crossing them, he can gain an effect such as no librettist can gain for him. Or to indulge in those averted glances and those raised eyebrows which he can make so unblushing in their implication. Or, on occasion, to pound on a table with that preposterously bent left arm of his which is one of his standbys, and a gesture he used to employ more indiscriminately than was good for his comedy. Fortunately, too, he can still gargle his words when he wants to, rushing them so forcibly together that such an ejaculation as "You-got-me-boy-you-got-me" sounds like one short word as it spills out of his large lips. He also continues—and with very droll, though not Sunday School, effects—to be fond of suggesting a character who is at once as botanical as he is tough.

But Mr. Lahr is more versatile than he once was, even if the contradictory creature just referred to is the blueprint from which he builds most of his characterizations.

You will find him in *Life Begins at 8:40*, for example, appearing in such various roles as a union man who wants to see a Mae West film in a picketed theatre, a Princeton tomboy as conceived by Mr. Lahr, a great baritone performing at a Women's Club, a Frenchman bent on suicide, and a sorely harassed investor. And in each of these skits this quieter and funnier Mr. Lahr, who is wise enough not to forget that his first duty to his public is to be Bert Lahr, succeeds in adding much to the pleasures of a pleasant evening by being, as we like to have him be, a Lahr unto himself.

September 6, 1934

ETHEL MERMAN AND JIMMY DURANTE

THE real truth is Broadway cannot get along without either Ethel Merman or Jimmy Durante. The two of them

are indispensable to its happiness. It becomes a different
place when they are around. There is comfort in the mere
knowledge they are once more to be seen and (as goes
without saying) heard in a local playhouse. Put them together in one show as Mr. Freedley has done in *Red, Hot
and Blue!* and there is just cause for rejoicing.

What *Red, Hot and Blue!* would be without them is a
question in which we have no interest. That it would be
hopeless we have no doubt. That, apart from their contribution to it, it is a very inferior musical comedy we are bound
to admit. What matters, however, is that they are in it,
and that being in it they manage to make some of its madness enormously entertaining.

Cole Porter has not supplied Miss Merman with any
numbers equal to those in which she has triumphed in the
past. He has failed her shamefully. Yet it is Miss Merman's unique gift to sing every song which comes her way,
so that while she is singing it seems good. Miss Merman
can be as hard-boiled as Mae West. But where Mme. West
is ludicrous Miss Merman is always delightful. She is a
zestful comedienne, gay, likable and expert. As a projector
of jazz she is unrivaled in our theatre. She is so poiseful, so
seemingly spontaneous and yet so unfailingly precise that
just watching her is in itself a pleasure. Listening to her
also holds its rich rewards. Certainly hers is not a voice
which would find a place in any heavenly choir. Bishop
Manning would never find a place for it. This is but one of
its most ingratiating qualities. For Miss Merman is Broadway made vocal; Broadway given a melody of its own, and
having found a perfect way of putting it across.

In all of his mad career, the redoubtable Jimmy has never
been as hilarious as he is in Mr. Freedley's new musical.
Mr. Durante singing about data, boasting he could get
along without Broadway, carrying in every wooden article

known below the timber line or cavorting in *Jumbo* are memories from the past of "Schnozzola the Magnificent" we can never forget. But pleasant as these feats were, they pale beside Mr. Durante's new achievements in *Red, Hot and Blue!*

Once again Mr. Durante is as energetic as fifty exploding boilers. Once again his voice is a growl of which the Metro-Goldwyn-Mayer lion might well be envious. Once again he shakes his head from side to side with such frenzy that the wonder is his famous nose does not break loose from its moorings. Once again his eyes light up with what Stephen Leacock used to describe as "Moonbeams from the Larger Lunacy."

But this time Mr. Durante has the best materials he has ever had. Jimmy as a member of the prison polo team; Jimmy singing "A Little Skipper from Heaven Above"; Jimmy interviewing an interior decorator; and, above all, Jimmy cross-examining himself before a Senate Investigating Committee, are episodes of superb fooling. The truth is that not only have we reason to shout "hallelujah" because of Miss Merman's and Mr. Durante's presence in *Red, Hot and Blue!* but that Mr. Freedley has, too. They *are* the show, the whole show and nothing but the show.

November 4, 1936

OF THEE I SING

AS Fred Astaire might sing it, there is a "new sun up in a new sky." Its name is *Of Thee I Sing*. From the first note of Mr. Gershwin's overture to the regrettable dropping of the final curtain, it succeeds in cramming as much gaiety into an evening of giddy spoofing as any evening has the right to hold. By the very nature of that spoofing, and by virtue of the high order of Mr. Gershwin's music, the gay lyrics with which his brother Ira has accompanied it, and the intelligent lunacy of Mr. Kaufman's and Mr. Ryskind's book, it represents not only a new and welcome departure in the world of entertainment, but also in the field of American musical comedy.

Here at last is a musical show which dodges nearly all the *clichés* of its kind, which has wit and intelligence behind it, which brings Gilbert and Sullivan to mind without being derived from them, and which makes hilarious satiric use of the American scene in general and Washington politics in particular. It is an audacious clowning of the sentimentality of our people and the means of our politics which, with no reverence but with much good humor, pokes fun at our campaign methods, invades both the sacrosanct Senate Chamber and the White House, and chucks the august members of our Supreme Court playfully under their bewhiskered chins.

Occasionally it slips into wisecracks for the sheer sake of wisecracks as only Mr. Kaufman can rattle them off. But, for the most part, it remains true to the special and utterly madcap needs of its mockery. As a travesty on voters and candidates and the holders of high office, it manages to come off, as *Strike Up the Band* did not quite succeed in doing, as a parody of war and Big Business. Washington and the roads which lead there offer, Heaven knows, ready-made materials for burlesque. And Mr. Kaufman and Mr. Ryskind (not to overlook the Messrs. Gershwin and Mr. Mielziner) make more than the most of their opportunities by inviting us to follow the superbly mythical John P. Wintergreen (William Gaxton) to the White House.

Mr. Wintergreen is a candidate without definite convictions or a real platform. Though paraders in the street may carry signs reading "Wintergreen Loves You" and "Even Your Dog Likes Wintergreen," Wintergreen's bosses know he is in a bad way. Then and there they decide upon a novel, vote-catching scheme. Wintergreen will be the candidate of love, the greatest lover of a lovesick land. Accordingly, they hold a beauty contest at Atlantic City, announcing the winner is to be "Miss White House," or, as Mr. Gershwin's lyrics have it:

> *If a girl is sexy,*
> *She may be Mrs. Prexy.*

But love, real love, interferes at the very moment when a sugary Southern lass, Diana Devereaux (Grace Brinkley), has won the contest. For Wintergreen suddenly spies a beautiful secretary (Lois Moran) who is not in the contest, decides to marry her and abandon the victorious "Miss White House."

With such slogans as "Woo With Wintergreen" and by means of a courtship conducted in public, Wintergreen and the little secretary become the President and First Lady of these United States, easily outdistancing such rivals as Mickey Mouse, Mae West, Walter Hampden and Goldman Sachs. The deserted Miss Devereaux, however, has not forgotten her sad, sad plight. Discovering she is:

> *The illegitimate daughter of the illegitimate son*
> *Of the illegitimate nephew of Napo-le-on;*

she gets the French Ambassador (Florenz Ames) to intervene in her behalf. He does so and war with France seems inevitable, unless Wintergreen decides to live up to his pre-election pledge and marry Miss Devereaux. Because of this same deserted beauty Wintergreen is brought before the

Senate, and would be impeached if, at the last moment, the
First Lady did not dance athletically into the Senate Chamber, announcing she is to become a mother. At the merest
mention of motherhood, the Senators and the Justices are
so overcome that they rock imaginary babies in their arms,
and are ready to beg forgiveness of Wintergreen. Yet, in
spite of their friendliness, war with France is still imminent
and remains so until the First Lady has been delivered of
two children, and President Wintergreen has pacified France
by giving Miss Devereaux to the Vice-President.

Throughout all of this brisk nonsense, the Vice-President,
Alexander Throttlebottom (Victor Moore), roams unhap-
pily, first as a candidate whose name nobody knows, then
as an office holder no one remembers. As acted by Mr.
Moore this sly, little man—who passes pickles humbly before the election, who goes back to his business of being a
hermit during the campaign, and who gets into the White
House after he has become Vice-President only as a sight-
seer lost in a crowd of other sightseers—is as richly humorous as he is wistfully pathetic. He emerges, in Mr. Moore's
superlatively excellent performance, as one of the most unforgettable characterizations of recent years.

No cold synopsis of *Of Thee I Sing* can hope to suggest
the full-blown nature of its foolery. Its convulsing lantern
slides which announce the election returns, its patter songs,
its recitatives, its fine score, Mr. Gaxton's capable playing of
Mr. Wintergreen (even when he breaks out into an irrelevant imitation of Jimmy Walker), Miss Moran's loveliness, the expert French Ambassador of Florenz Ames, the
giddy members of the Supreme Court and especially Ralph
Riggs's prancing Chief Justice, Miss Brinkley's super-
luscious Diana Devereaux, George E. Mack's side-splitting
caricature of a Southern Senator and Edward H. Robins'
Western lawmaker, the charming costumes of the choruses,

and Mr. Mielziner's simple and extremely effective settings are all contributors—and by no means the only contributors—to an evening which is not only first-rate entertainment but which comes as a milestone in the history of American musical comedy.

December 23, 1931

THE GRIDIRON CLUB AND
I'D RATHER BE RIGHT

AS all of us hoped it would, *I'd Rather Be Right* elects the nation to the Gridiron Club. The most significant thing about it is that it is at all. It does not hesitate to call high public officials by their right names, and, while doing so, call them laughingly to account. It is gay, witty, topical, and audacious—the kind of irreverent satire which could be written and seen only in these much-abused United States. Playing the gentleman known as Franklin D. Roosevelt is another gentleman, known as George M. Cohan, who is loved even in Maine and Vermont. What Mr. Kaufman's and Mr. Hart's new musical would be like without the aforesaid Mr. Cohan is too unpleasant a question to ask. Besides, it is a silly one. It is as foolish as it would be to worry about what the book would be like without the aforesaid Mr. Roosevelt. This much is certain. With Mr. Cohan it is an almost constant delight. If it has been cruelly overpublicized, if it is not (and nothing could be) as uproarious as it has been said to be, it is nonetheless an uncommonly good show. And a healthy, reassuring one.

Let no one be deceived into thinking *I'd Rather Be Right* is a Tory Feast at which the President is drawn and quartered for the delectation of a Bankers' Convention.

Mr. Roosevelt would undoubtedly enjoy it himself. Nor would he have to take laughing gas to do so. It is an unsparing script. The lyrics are no more merciful. The authors have gone to work with their gloves off. But what they have administered is a series of slaps which for the most part are so good-natured that their ultimate destination seems to be the back.

The President in *I'd Rather Be Right* is from beginning to end a likable man. He may have lost his way. He may be spending a lot of money. He may be thinking of ways to increase taxes. His Cabinet members may not, with two or three exceptions, play important roles. Nonetheless he is a lovable fellow who is trying hard. In particular, he is trying to find some way of balancing the budget so that Peggy and Phil, two young lovers he has met during a walk through Central Park, can get married.

Mr. Kaufman and the Zwei Herzen—Moss and Lorenz —get many unsparing and uproarious things said. They have their laughs at the fireside chats, at the Federal Theatre, at the Wagner act, at Mr. Farley, and Secretaries Perkins and Morgenthau. They even get in some thrusts at Mr. Landon and the Supreme Court (though they have dealt far more freshly and effectively with the justices in the past). However telling, timely, or side-splitting their gibes may be, they have the additional virtue of being amiable. Their very amiability and extravagance are in almost every instance the guarantee of the remarkable good taste of the whole proceedings.

Properly enough, this Gridiron's entertainment is the President's evening, and Mr. Cohan makes the most of it. He is on the stage almost all of the time. He comes near to being the whole show. Theatrically this may be a drawback in a musical comedy, but Republicans assure me it only makes the whole performance more accurate as a picture of the present administration. Mr. Cohan's gentle good humor is unfailingly ingratiating. He does not mimic Mr. Roosevelt. Although he suggests him when he wants to, he functions most generally as a Super Song and Dance Man. He sings the by-now familiar lyrics of "Off the Record" (without mentioning Al Smith), tosses his head from side to side, and cuts some of his famous capers which are delightful enough in their own rights to banish politics into the wings. My one regret is that the President himself could not find time to visit *I'd Rather Be Right* and sit in a box, and smile his famous smile, and laugh uproariously into a newsreel camera wired for sound at every gibe, at every thrust, at every good-natured impertinence in the script. The picture of Mr. Roosevelt in a box laughing at Mr. Roosevelt on the stage would be as fine an advertisement for the virtues of democracy as could anywhere be found. I doubt if the film would get by the authorities in Berlin, Rome, or Moscow. Hitler, Mussolini, and Stalin would not understand it or would fear it because their people might. They would be as terrified by its implications as they would be overjoyed to learn *I'd Rather Be Right* had been tampered with by the Government in any way. Tokio would be wary in showing such a film. In England it would be seen and its hopeful implications understood, even if it might perplex Britain's Lord Chamberlain. But to those of us who saw it, and to citizens in democracies everywhere, it would mean a lot.

Even without such a newsreel, the mere fact *I'd Rather Be Right* can be produced and run its course unchallenged should prove encouraging. It should indicate certain of the blessings which are ours and which we frequently tend to overlook. It should swell our pride in the freedom we enjoy and in the gift for laughter which must be counted among our national assets. The more good-humored liberties Mr. Kaufman's and Mr. Hart's musical satire takes, the more liberty its mere performance bespeaks. Regardless of how pointed its criticism may be, the very lack of mercy it is allowed to show should persuade us that even now all's better along the Potomac than some people like to think.

November 3, 1937

9. The Theatre in Print

MR. SHAW'S COLUMBUS

MORE than a quarter of a century ago, Archibald Henderson, a romantic young Southerner who was then doing research work in mathematics at the University of Chicago, was persuaded by a teacher of expression to see some amateurs perform *You Never Can Tell*, a comedy by a man named Bernard Shaw. Mr. Henderson went to the performance, saw the play, and Mr. Shaw conquered. That night in Chicago, when the curtain rose on *You Never Can Tell* as produced by the Hart Conway School of Acting, was not only an all-important night in Mr. Henderson's career, but it may also be said to have been fairly important in Shaw's.

Mr. Henderson, whose reading as a child consisted mainly of Mayne Reid's Indian tales, Jules Verne's scientific romances, and the novels of Scott, Dickens and Dumas, was "immediately electrified." As he listened to "the insouciant frivolity and gay irresponsibility of Dolly Clandon . . . the progenitress of the modern flapper," he felt, "as though immersed in a bath of cosmic rays which at that time had been discovered, not by the scientists, but by Bernard Shaw alone."

Apparently, Mr. Henderson has felt that way ever since, for as everyone must know—who knows anything at all

about Mr. Henderson—in the intervening years he has
made it his sacred duty to write almost as much about Mr.
Shaw as Mr. Shaw has written about himself. (Mind you, I
say "almost.") He has recorded his table-talk, collected
everything he could about his idol, turned out magazine
article after magazine article and book after book, all of
which have benefited immensely by the unfailing interest
centered in their subject. Now, after a lapse of twenty-one
years, D. Appleton has published an enormous tome, some
800 pages long, called *Bernard Shaw: Playboy and Prophet*,
which finds Mr. Henderson serving Mr. Shaw for the second time as his "official biographer."

The way in which he got the job is not without interest.
He spent the year after having been electrified by *You
Never Can Tell* reading Shaw's writings and bringing together the small amount of material then obtainable in
America about the man. Mr. Henderson thought he had discovered a neglected genius (he still thinks so) and he
wanted to make his discovery known. "With the rashness of
youth," he tells us, he wrote to Mr. Shaw, proposing to
write his life. For weeks there was no answer. Then one
day there arrived one of those well-known postcards which,
with every reason, filled Mr. Henderson's heart with terror.
"Send me your photograph!" it read.

Though he sensed he was not conducting a "matrimonial
bureau," Mr. Henderson realized, "perhaps for the first
time, that I was proposing some sort of literary alliance, of
a more or less serious character." Some pictures were duly
taken, the "least forbidding" one of the lot was chosen and
mailed with many misgivings to Mr. Shaw. And again after
an agonizing delay, another postcard arrived. This time it
bore "this incredible assertion: 'You look like the man who
can do the job.'"

If Mr. Shaw had searched the whole world over, he

could not have chosen a more loyal admirer and industrious collector of Shaviana than Mr. Henderson. He could—and has—found more informed expounders of this and that side of his many-sided genius. He could—and has—found more gifted, far less pompous, much less conceited biographers. But I doubt if anywhere he could have discovered one man more devoted or more careful than Mr. Henderson has been in presenting to the world all the G. B. S.'s who have commanded its attention. If Mr. Henderson's book embarrasses Mr. Shaw and some of his readers at times because of Mr. Henderson's insistence upon bobbing up here and there in the narrative as a figure who takes himself with a painfully un-Shavian seriousness, the fact remains that, as far as the sweeping of dusty files and the arrangement of multitudinous materials are concerned, Mr. Henderson's volume is a monumental and admirable piece of work.

Mr. Shaw's life presents unquestionably the most difficult, all-inclusive assignment in biography the admirer of any contemporary man of letters could undertake. It not only necessitates an intimate knowledge of everything Mr. Shaw has written, the countless careers he has embraced, the many arts—such as painting, music and the drama—which he has served as critic, but it must also take into account Shaw's standing as a dramatist, the numerous forebears, such as Nietzsche, Dickens, George, Shelley, Marx, Ibsen and the rest from whom he has freely borrowed, and the whole social, intellectual, panorama of his time.

It demands having a sense of humor, being an authority on religions, being learned in philosophy, keeping abreast with economics, having a documented insight into the growth of the Fabian Society, being so versatile that your love for Wagner equals your zest for prize-fighting, cherish-

ing in your heart the technical excellence and superb ex-
uberance of journalism at its best, following the complicated history of Shaw's first-nights in playhouses the world
over, possessing an ear for the easiest, most vigorous prose
of our time as well as for mystic passages which have the
singing eloquence of poetry, and—oh, well, what's the sense
of continuing. The catalogue, as even the most elementary
Shavians know, is as long as it is formidable.

Obviously these requirements cry aloud for a Superman
to act as Mr. Shaw's biographer. Just as obviously, and in
spite of his real versatility, Mr. Henderson is not that. But
when once he gets past his "Salute" and his "Introduction"
and before he comes to some of his later chapters of attempted characterization, he does an amazingly good job;
the sort of painstaking job for which Mr. Shaw's admirers
cannot but be grateful. Mr. Henderson's is not an inspired
method. But he does possess the patience of a stamp collector. He is an assiduous gatherer of interesting facts and
documents, an alert reader, and a good "arranger." His
conscientious files yield him page after page of exhilarating
quotations—from Shaw's fine preface to *Immaturity*, from
Shaw's reviews, from his opinions on Shakespeare, from his
innumerable and always entertaining letters, from his little-
known Fabian tracts, from his novels, his war writings, and
his plays. And they are wonderful quotes; enough in themselves to make the book extraordinary reading. In no one
volume, that has its origins in Shaw, has their like been
seen.

The truth is, of course, that Mr. Shaw is the most entertaining writer about Mr. Shaw alive, and his own best biographer. Although Mr. Henderson has been enormously
helpful in sorting and connecting many of these quotes,
though his own prose is often fluent and warm, the wisest
service he has performed lies in permitting Mr. Shaw to

speak for himself so often and at such length. The pity is Mr. Henderson has not elected to keep himself out of the book. His humorless self-importance knows no bounds. He includes pictures of himself. He creeps into footnote after footnote in the most ridiculous and painful manner. He boasts in loud tones of his own services to Shaw. He runs in full the laudatory letter Shaw sent his publishers about his—Mr. Henderson's—first authorized biography. He quotes the wise things he said about Shaw at the Town Hall dinner, and reproduces a facsimile of the blarney dedication Mr. Shaw once wrote about him for a student annual published at the University of North Carolina, where Mr. Henderson now teaches.

His "Salute," which ends with a reproduction of his own handwriting, is the most fatuous piece of modern prose I have recently encountered, unless it happens to be Albert Bigelow Paine's *Life and Lillian Gish*. After likening Shaw to Tolstoy, to Santa Claus, to Shakespeare, to Cervantes, to a "Voltaire perfected," to Henry of Navarre, to Mephistopheles, to Richelieu, to Carlyle, to Ruskin, to Gilbert, Wilde, Swift and Molière, Mr. Henderson has the audacity to speak of Frederick the Great's lasting in history because of his friendship with Voltaire, and write, "Through the association, so fortunate for me, embodied and symbolized in this work, shall last the name—not of your sycophant, your Boswell, your Sancho Panza, but of your Columbus— and friend."

In his heavy-handed, unwitty, embarrassing way, Mr. Henderson has evidently tried to ape his master's fondness for mentioning himself. If his laborious attempts to be Shavian prove nothing else, they do at least prove, to Mr. Henderson's credit as a biographer, that there is one, and only one, George Bernard Shaw. Mr. Henderson's assumed Shavianisms are a sad reminder of the verse that went the rounds of the studio when one of Whistler's admirers tried, once upon a time, to paint in Whistler's manner. It ran:

> *I bought a palette just like his,*
> *His colors and his brush,*
> *The devil of it is, you see,*
> *I did not buy his touch.*

December 7, 1932

MR. HAMILTON TEACHES PLAYWRITING IN ONE EASY LESSON

IT MUST be awful being Clayton Hamilton. Of course his life abounds in compensations. He loves the theatre and has served it loyally according to his lights. He is a member of the National Institute of Arts and Letters. He has been active at the Players. He has taught at Columbia and Barnard, and followed Brander Matthews in the writing of many books about the stage. He has lectured up and down the country with great fluency and charm either in his own rights or on behalf of Mrs. Fiske, Mr. Tyler and Mr. Hampden. He has acquired more theatrical anecdotes than a blue serge suit does lint. He has a pleasing vocabulary and apparently writes with an enviable ease. His interests are many and his style is the style of a happy man. He is fond of people and people appear to be no less fond of him. Without doubt the many celebrities to whom he has been exposed from Bronson Howard down to Eugene O'Neill have enjoyed his company and found him to be (in the phrase of Walt Whitman's which is his favorite) "a friendly and a flowing person."

Even so, it must be awful being Clayton Hamilton. It

must be awful to be besieged by so many admirers, by so many questers after knowledge, by so many eager young dramatists who want you to tell them by return mail how they can become Shakespeare or O'Casey, that in self-defense you are compelled to dash off such a book as Mr. Hamilton's—*So You're Writing a Play!* It must be awful to bother to write a book really intended as a sort of "letter to end all letters" from "potential or prospective playwrights," and then to realize it will do no such thing. It must be awful to sense—as Mr. Hamilton will, if he only stops to think the matter over—that his "general communication" to dramatists is not the kind of opus which will prevent him from being pestered by playwrights who may still want to know how to write a play and who will be left in the dark after they have devoured each one of his 260 pages.

But Mr. Hamilton comes through his pages as such an amiable fellow that he will no doubt cheerfully go on adding personal postscripts to his open letter in the days to come. He emerges from *So You're Writing a Play* as a breezy man of the world. He is full of himself—and his friends. He writes with the enthusiasm of a debutante and the condescension of a flag-pole sitter who is confident he can scale Mount Everest. He does not mind letting us know he has known some of the most famous people of the last forty years, or that they have known him. When he was twenty-one and his first play was being produced on Broadway, he sat in a box with Bronson Howard. (Page 74). For many years he has enjoyed the friendship of William Gillette. At the outset of the present century he was closely associated with Clyde Fitch and Augustus Thomas. During the three subsequent decades he has "known intimately almost every author who has arrived at any appreciable degree of eminence in the American theatre."

That's not all. This club man of the arts gets about. For more than a quarter of a century he was intimate with Sir Arthur Wing Pinero and Henry Arthur Jones. (Goodness me, when he was dining with Sir Edmund Gosse in Regent's Terrace one evening, did not Sir Arthur telephone him at midnight and ask him to come over for a talk, and, what is more, did he not go?) (Page 197.) He has "talked (page 75) with nearly all the other important dramatists of England and Ireland." He has also met "many of the leading dramatists of France." And by asking intelligent questions about technique—"in several languages," of course—he has learned much at firsthand from Pinero, Dunsany, Brieux, Maeterlinck, Pirandello and Benavente. Somehow or other Mr. Hamilton never managed to shake hands with Shakespeare or Goethe or Sophocles or Aristotle or even Ibsen. Nonetheless he writes about them all just as warmly as if he had.

He has traveled a lot. He has visited (page 112) nearly all of the ruined, or partly ruined structures of the theatres of the Graeco-Roman world. There is scarcely one of them in which he has "not spoken from the stage, with collaborators seated at strategic points upon the hillside to note down how much or how little they could actually see or hear." He has served as a *claqueur* at the Comédie (page 122) during his student days in the "Quartier Latin." He knows the drama of all times and places. He can trace the history of the stage from the age of Pericles (page 219) down to Maxwell Anderson (page 227). He can give you a short account of Shakespeare's life (pages 40–42), or invite you into Ibsen's workshop (pages 78–88). He can quote critical theories from Aristotle down to Archer, and is as much at home with the Electra story when it is handled by the Greeks as he is when it is retold by O'Neill. Learned though he is, he is not at all pedantic. No one could seem less erudite than he. Or more humorous, as when he smiles (page 10) at the thought that if he should mention the name of Seneca to George M. Cohan, Mr. Cohan would probably assume he was referring to a hotel standing near a theatre in Rochester.

Mr. Hamilton has his sound critical points to make. He understands full well (page 11) that "criticism is analytic; creation is synthetic." He helpfully adds "the dramatic critic takes plays to pieces; the working dramatist puts plays together." He thinks only young people who care enough about the theatre so that they are willing to stay in it in spite of all discouragements should become playwrights or actors. It is his opinion it is much harder to get started on any artistic undertaking than it is "to carry on after a propitious start has been accomplished." "One of the major sorrows of my life," says he, "was that I was never privileged to talk with Synge *before he died*"!

Mr. Hamilton disagrees with Mr. Archer's dictum that "crisis" is a universal element in drama, and argues very interestingly for "contrast." He thinks there are "only four different types of germinal ideas which, by the natural process of psychologic incubation (page 77), may be developed into plays." He is kind enough to consider these four types "one by one." He tells you that "in the reign of Queen Elizabeth there was no system of popular or compulsory education" (page 231). He urges playwrights to write scenarios before tackling their plays. He would have us realize that way back in 1910, when Sir James Barrie did not want to publish his plays, he (Mr. Hamilton) urged him to do so. He is convinced the dramatist of today can find "no common formula for guidance." His belief is that "the most practical advice that may be offered to a neophyte is to pick out some recently successful dramatist who has done more or less the same sort of thing that he himself aspires to do, and to follow temporarily the patterns which have been worked out by this particular predecessor." Needless to say, as Mr. Hamilton is quickly forced to admit, "Maeterlinck would be a poor teacher for a playwright ambitious to write another *Strife*, and Pinero . . . should not be imitated by a playwright eager to compose another *Peter Pan*."

Mr. Hamilton gets some good things said, even if he does not do much more for the potential playwrights he is supposedly helping than his astonished title implies. What concerns one after finishing *So You're Writing a Play!* is not so much the advice which Mr. Hamilton has to give to young dramatists as the thought of what it is that he will have left to say when he comes to write his autobiography. Perhaps it should be noted that the dedication in this volume reads "To Eugene O'Neill who began his career as one of my apprentices and is now fulfilling it as one of my masters." Perhaps it should also be noted that Mr. Cohan's sole remark after he had seen one of Mr. Hamilton's plays, was, "It's got an awful lot of good cuts in it."

September 11, 1935

THE IMPORTANCE OF BEING NATHAN

MR. GEORGE JEAN NATHAN continues very jubilantly to be Mr. George Jean Nathan in *The Morning After the First Night* (Knopf). And that, as only the younger Marxists need to be told, is quite a thing to be. It means being a symbol of impudence, gayety, and irreverence. It means having an unfailingly alert mind; eyes that are ever strained to seize upon the defects of others; and a heart that beats vigorously, even sentimentally, in the interest of all he considers best for the theatre and in it. It means being a man who manages to erupt into criticism at the same time he is doing reviewing. It means being not only a critic but also a vaudevilleian. It means caring for *Hamlet* every bit as much as Goethe did, and then dressing up like Grimaldi or Grock to write about it.

It means being a Bunthorne in bouncer's clothing. It means having a prose style that delights in sentences almost as long as the famous one in which Hazlitt took an inventory of Coleridge's mind, and yet being able to keep most of these sentences trucking to their conclusions at such a merry pace that brevity ceases to be the soul of wit. It means writing as Macaulay might have written if he had spent most of his life at Tony Pastor's or as George Meredith might have written if his last name had been Kaufman. It means seeing through theatrical hokum with the sharpest eyes which have been brought to the job since Shaw retired from the *Saturday Review,* and stating these perceptions as if he were a new bundle from heaven in the Maison Minsky. It means being exceptious at any cost; being hell-bound to be the one contrary-minded member of the jury; and taking a savage delight in being the solitary bison on the range.

It means having a genius for overstatement which is in the sturdiest tradition of American humor. It means having an unholy dread of seeming solemn about serious things, and an uncanny gift for making solemn things ridiculous. It means being four-tenths Boileau and six-tenths buffoon. It means being a wretched guide but an excellent diagnostician. It means having a superlative talent for making his readers see the whole truth more clearly because of the brilliant half-truth he has mistaken for it. It means showing no mercy for the people of the theatre but having infinite faith in the theatre itself. It means being a tonic which could never be sold at Gray's Drug Store but which ought to be sold at every other drug store in the land.

It means being one of the world's best shadow-boxers and most unreliable of reporters. It means having appointed yourself Chief Justice of the Supreme Court, and then capering up and down behind the bench as if it were a runway. It means being part Columbus, part Fouché, and, from the point of view of those he dislikes, the whole of *The Inferno*. It means having a command of billingsgate such as any fishwife might envy, and an ability to rise to moments of true lyric eloquence. It means being able to write about a subject cursed with *clichés*, and avoid them all.

It means disobeying the regulations of the army, as every critic should and some forget to, and raising your standards after sundown instead of lowering them. It means having a genius for creating more synonyms than Soule was able to collect. It means laying out your life so that you are not only the Étoile of your own existence, but your own Arc de Triomphe too. It means having a librarian's aptitude for cataloguing, and yet being able to impart to a card index a jocosity worthy of *Uncle Billy's Whizz-Bang*. It means prodding playwrights without mercy to do their best, and having little respect for actors even when they do theirs. It means being the self-elected Lord High Executioner of all other critics, indeed of all other playgoers, who have dared to go to the theatre and not reacted in Mr. Nathan's manner. It means being able to swim in the Fountain of Youth without the aid of waterwings.

It means being the most gracious host to new talents and genuine older ones modern dramatic criticism knows, and the cruelest dispatcher of mediocrity who writes, or has written, continuously about the theatre. It means thinking of yourself as St. George, with a good deal of reason, and having other people think of you as the dragon, with even more reason. It means that people always expect you to say the unexpected and that you almost never fail to live up to their expectations. It means having a style which is studded with words from nearly every language except Esperanto. It means having maintained for a quarter of a century and without showing any signs of fatigue an attitude which would have exhausted the usual circus performer had he attempted to hold the same pose for four minutes in a *tableau vivant*. It means having an energy worthy of Mrs. Roosevelt and a spirit worthy of Puck. It means being a dean at the same time you are still a collegian. It means that, unlike the other famous bad boy, you are able to stand on the deck and make other people eat pickles by the peck.

It means being beyond manners, above friendship, and gleefully capable of foul play. It means being a master of vituperation and seldom capable of ecstasy. It means excelling at destruction rather than re-creation. It means fighting, often unfairly but nearly always skillfully, for the fair dream of perfection which never ceases to haunt your mind. It means being chiefly consistent in your inconsistencies, and feeling your meannesses are justified by your ends. It means being part judge, part constable, part vigilante, and chiefly exterminator.

It means, in other words, being able to produce *The Morning After the First Night*, which is not only an immensely readable and entertaining book but the most adroit and delightful performance to have been given in a good many years by the virtuoso Mr. Nathan.

January 17, 1938

PERCY HAMMOND

HE was a shy and sensitive man. Getting to know him
was not easy. But knowing him, even as slightly as I regret
to say I did after seven years of seeing him almost nightly
during the winter months and lunching or dining with
him occasionally and foregathering with him at the often
stormy sessions of the Critics Circle, held its ample rewards.
He took pampering, but he gave a great deal. He was a
delightful talker, when the desire for conversation overcame
him, and could erupt into speech of the saltiest and most
amusing variety. He could be profane, but his was the
kind of profanity one imagines must have lurked upon the
lips of a Roman emperor.

Percy's talk was not expressed in the smooth rhythms of
his prose. Yet in its different way it was no less pungent. It
was nervous, jerky, explosive. It came in sudden spurts,
in torrents of anecdotes, reminiscences or hilariously
phrased disgust. The signs of its coming were evident. His
face would turn from pink to crimson, his blue eyes twin-
kle and his head rear back. These were the welcome signals;
these and the hoarse, yet somehow Falstaffian laugh, which
was his acknowledgment of what had just been said and
his prelude to what he was about to say.

His conversation showed his interests extended to many
things other than the theatre. In each case his opinions were
vigorously expressed. In each case, whether the subject was
national politics, world affairs, or the latest play, what
tapped his giant reservoir of infectious ridicule was sham
which refused to admit it was sham. He was an individual-
ist who had to go his own individual way. By temperament
and equipment he was a gleeful and effective dissenter. He

was not only suspicious of group action, he was disdainful of it and refused to be bound by it.

Whereas there may be hundreds of us to whom first nights will not seem the same with Percy absent, there must be thousands of us to whom the mornings after (yes, and Sundays, too) will have lost much of their delight because his reviews will no longer be found in the upper left-hand corner of the *Herald-Tribune's* drama page. Percy's performances as a critic were unique. No daily writer on the theatre in our time has approached him, much less equaled him, in his ability to turn a stabbing phrase. No other journalist of our day has been able to match (regardless of how effortful the process may have been) the sonorous cadences of his prose, which proved such easy and diverting reading.

To those who take the theatre seriously, to those who are art-conscious in its presence, to those who expected him to serve them as a reliable signpost to the productions they were certain to enjoy, to those who expected pedestrian advice from him, to those who did not know him or who had not read him long enough to understand him, Percy must often have proved exasperating.

Criticism as Percy wrote it was not only about a show, it was a show in itself. It was a game played between him and his reader. Once you were on to the rules of this game, you could not help relishing it because it offered topnotch sport. It was, first of all, a continuation of the word game Burns Mantle tells us Percy used to play years ago in Chicago with Julian Mason and Francis Hackett. Then it was a guessing game, in which the fun came from finding out when Percy was serious and when he was joking, and watching for the last phrase of a sentence or a paragraph that would topple over the whole apple cart of praise he had gorgeously piled up. It was a guessing game at the theatre's expense, played for the delectation of those who, like Percy, distrusted the lily-claspers and looked upon the theatre not as an art but as an entertainment, a passing show to be enjoyed at the moment it was passing.

Two seasons back, when Hiram Motherwell complained in *The Stage* that modern critics of the theatre were not as informed in their comments on acting as Lewes, Lessing, Hazlitt and Archer had been, Percy, with his tongue in his cheek as usual, replied by defining his job as he saw it. "I, myself," said he, "am not a drama critic, and even if I wanted to be, I could not. My humble reviewer's job, as I have understood it for many years, is not didactic, teaching playwrights how to write or actors how to act, but to estimate as accurately as possible, in the interest of playgoers, the results of a performance in a theatre. To be, as Archer said, concerned only with the effect produced, not with the phenomena of its production—to apprise values, not to analyze or assay them."

Critic in the soberer Aristotelian sense he was not. He was important for his wit rather than his perceptions; his malice rather than his enthusiasms; as an executioner, not a champion; as an entertainer rather than a serious contributor. He was gay, if not contemptuous, in the presence of art; one of the wise men, according to Mr. Nathan, who is made as merry by beauty as fools are saddened by it. He was never caught floundering off the deep end in aesthetics. Specific instances, not principles, were his concern.

He knew much more about the theatre than he cared to admit in or out of print. And loved it deeply, I suspect, in spite of pretending to despise it. Accurate he certainly was when he included "the interest of playgoers" among his duties. He never bored them. He may have failed them from time to time as a guide to entertainments, but he was invariably entertaining.

His style was as highly polished as marquetry. He loved words and made others love them, too. His reviews were carefully-wrought mosaics, quarried from Bartlett, Roget and the Concordance, enriched by his own vast vocabulary and assembled in designs of surpassing virtuosity. His cadences were the full-blown cadences of the eighteenth century. What he said was all the funnier because on purpose his rhetoric was often cut too large for what he chose to drape in it. This sense of misfit was one of the delights of his ridicule and one of his surest methods of attack.

His periods were Johnsonian; his sense of the absurd something that Stephen Leacock might have envied. He was a master of anti-climax; of laughs won and points made by allowing the final squeak of a tin horn to top the majestic rumblings of his kettledrum English. He loved to release the mighty measures of *Pomp and Circumstance* to bury a mosquito. He gave the impression of being an orator heard in print. Almost every sentence he ever wrote was something that cried not only to be quoted but also to be read out loud. These sentences of his appealed to the throats as well as the eyes and ears and minds and wits of his countless doting readers.

New York and the American theatre will not be the same without Percy. He may have questioned the art of the theatre, even in the title of his single book. But one thing is certain. When he wrote of the theatre, reviewing became an art; an art which is now, alas, a lost one.

April 29, 1936

SPIRITUAL SCURVY AND
MR. ATKINSON

WHEN, after nearly four years spent in the front-line trenches of dramatic criticism, Bernard Shaw surrendered his position on London's *Saturday Review* to Max Beer-bohm, he uttered a complaint which many another city-starved and theatre-fed reviewer must have felt in his moments of dark discouragement both before and since Mr. Shaw's outburst. "I have been the slave of the theatre," cried the G. B. S. who did not then resemble Satan lost in a snowdrift. "It has tethered me to the mile radius of foul and sooty air which has its center in the Strand, as a goat is tethered in the little circle of cropped and trampled grass that makes the meadow ashamed. Every week"—every week, mind you, in Mr. Shaw's case—"it clamors for its tale of written words; so that I am like a man fighting a windmill: I have hardly time to stagger to my feet from the knock-down blow of one sail, when the next strikes me down. Now I ask, is it reasonable to expect me to spend my life in this way?"

Mr. Shaw proved how unreasonable was an affirmative answer to his question by becoming Mr. Shaw. But most reviewers, who cannot hope to find such a pleasant escape from their dilemma, ask themselves the very same question —and then continue to be just reviewers. Most of us never break away from our tethers. We do not really want to. Nor do we need to. The greenest pastures many of us seem able to imagine are the grassless stretches of Broadway. Life to us is the theatre and the lives of other people as we are permitted to live them vicariously in the playhouses. We do not suffer from spiritual scurvy on the diet

we are fed. Ours are not spirits which either crave in earnest
or could survive with pleasure a change in the fare to which
we have been subjected.

We have become accustomed to asking from the passing
moment only what that moment sets before us, and to ex-
pecting others to fill these moments for us. We scrutinize
the lives and works of others but have no time in which to
look into ourselves. Our philosophy appears to be to have
no philosophy. The deeper mysteries of the universe are not
apt to concern us. Man's ingenuity, not God's magnificence,
is our daily concern and wonder. Electric lights are our sun
and moon and stars. The seasons pass us by on Manhattan,
known to us, not by their natural beauties, but by the different demands they make upon our clothing as we set out
for this playhouse, or that.

We take life and the city as we find them, and both life
and the city are apt to be limited for us to "the mile radius
of foul and sooty air which has its center" in our Strand.
Living the lives we like and which satisfy our needs, we
know neither calm nor contemplation, are confused in
values, mixed in standards, and are content (in spite of our
moments of protest) either to wander no farther than "the
little circle of cropped and trampled grass that makes the
meadow ashamed," or unable to get away from it.

I say all this because there is at least one New York reviewer who is a notable exception to these dispiriting generalities. His name is Brooks Atkinson. My reason for
pointing to him today is that I have just finished reading
with enormous joy, envy and admiration *The Cingalese
Prince,* that log of the trip around the world Mr. Atkinson
took a year ago on a freighter from which his book derives
its name. *The Cingalese Prince* is Mr. Atkinson's answer to
the question Mr. Shaw once asked himself. If it does not
find Mr. Atkinson temporarily deserting dramatic criticism

to become Mr. Shaw, it does possess the high virtue of finding him putting Broadway far behind him and remaining Mr. Atkinson.

To squeeze the large subject matter of his book into the routine confines of this small column, I suppose I should quickly state that some of the pages of his philosopher's travel diary are concerned (and delightfully concerned) with such dramatic subjects as a tent show seen in Houston, a performance at the Kabuki-za Theatre in Japan, an Americanized variety show in Peiping, and a performance of a Javanese historical drama in Singapore's Lunar Hall. But what is of greater interest and value than Mr. Atkinson's contacts with the theatre on his trip around the world are his escapes from it. Like Jaques he has the happy gift of "philosophizing the spectacle." And birds, fish, the terrors of a storm, strange Eastern cities, hot jungles, muddy inland channels, the sea in all its changing moods, the stars, the proud profession of Drake and Magellan, life on a freighter, art in the presence of nature, Man, God, and the Universe are but a few of the subjects to which he brings his poetic eloquence, the high calm of his thinking, and the exquisite beauty of his writing.

"I am not one who lusts after sights," writes Mr. Atkinson. "I love to stroll a little and sit a lot and let the world encompass me." The world does encompass him in *The Cingalese Prince* and he encompasses the world. As he writes of it, with a vivid loveliness, a gentle humor and a nobility of thinking in which Thoreau would have delighted, the world also encompasses the reader and makes him yearn for its glories and ashamed of the smallness of his own horizons.

Escape, Mr. Atkinson insists, is no cowardly activity. "To do battle constantly, to be always alert and armed and always on the battlefield is to compound the felony of civilization." Escape from what is only a part of life to all that life is, is the plea he makes with eloquence. "Is it life," he asks, "to be imprisoned within the sooty cloud that factory chimneys belch? Is it life to be thrust into a three-room shelf in an apartment house? Is it life to sleep fitfully within earshot of the traffic, to gaze out on high brick walls, to buck the subway throngs, to live at your neighbor's expense, and to water down friendship to a wide acquaintance? Friendship in our shrieking civilization is a matter of propinquity rather than kinship. If that is life, it would be better if we were all dead and the coroner had officially testified to what the poet suspects. If that is life the joy that leaps up in me when I am under the open sky is ignorance, and the scream of the factory whistle in the morning is the main theme of a heavenly anthem. If that is life, all my instincts have corrupted me."

It is because he is absolutely uncorrupted by his instincts and is lucky enough to know how to live in Manhattan as well as at the most distant corners of the globe, that Mr. Atkinson, the prose-poet and the philosopher, brings much to the theatre that the theatre in particular stands sadly in need of.

November 12, 1934

Index